BEST "NEW" AFRICAN POETS 2018 ANTHOLOGY/ ANTOLOGIE DES MEILLEURES "NOUVEAUX" POETES AFRICAINS 2018/ ANTOLOGIA DOS MELHORES "NOVOS" POETAS AFRICANOS 2018

Edited and Compiled by:
Tendai Rinos Mwanaka/
Nsah Mala

Mwanaka Media and Publishing Pvt Ltd,
Chitungwiza Zimbabwe

*

Creativity, Wisdom and Beauty

Publisher:
Mmap
Mwanaka Media and Publishing Pvt Ltd
24 Svosve Road, Zengeza 1
Chitungwiza Zimbabwe
mwanaka@yahoo.com
https//mwanakamediaandpublishing.weebly.com

Distributed in and outside N. America by African Books Collective
orders@africanbookscollective.com
www.africanbookscollective.com

ISBN: 978-1-77906-360-1
EAN: 9781779063601

© Tendai Rinos Mwanaka 2018

All rights reserved.
No part of this book may be reproduced or transmitted in any form or by any means, mechanical or electronic, including photocopying and recording, or be stored in any information storage or retrieval system, without written permission from the publisher

DISCLAIMER
All views expressed in this publication are those of the author and do not necessarily reflect the views of *Mmap*.

TABLE OF CONTENTS/TABLE DES MATIERES/TABELA DE CONTEUDOS

About editors..xiv
Contributors' bio notes...xv
Introduction..xlix
Part 1: Collaborations..1-25
To the god of fear: *(Best "New" African Poets Collaboration: Mbuthia, Ntensibe, Mairosi, Bolaji, Odewumi, Gwiriri, Malelah The Poet, Guzha, Mwanaka, Mukwarimba, Maina, Swanson, Haile Saize I, Mhondera, Maridzanyere, Mavolwane, Awusa, Agyei-Baah, Abubakar, Jaison)*...1-11
The Love Song: *(Best "New" African Poets Collaboration: Mbuthia, Ntensibe, Mairosi, Bolaji, Odewumi, Gwiriri, Jaison, Malelah The Poet, Guzha, Mwanaka)*..12-17
Human God: *(Best "New" African Poets Collaboration: Mhondera, Mairosi, p'Khisa, Gwiriri, Jaison, Nieuwoudt, Mwanaka)*.............18-25

Part 2: Consciousness, Spiritual, Individual, Existential......19-115

Artist's Trails: *Tendai Rinos Mwanaka (Zimbabwe)*
Pinnacle: *Mari Ballot (South Africa)*
EGULE (the weaverbird): *Chibueze Obunadike (Nigeria)*
Rekindled: *Athene Nyarai Mutyambizi (Zimbabwe)*
Will Rise Again: *Aleck Kaposa (Zimbabwe)*
New born: *Beven Nebafor Awusa (Cameroon)*
SALAT: *Chibueze Obunadike (Nigeria)*
To Be Named: *Daisy May (South Africa)*
CANVAS: *Dorcas Wairuri Maina (Kenya)*
The Season: *Emman Usman Shehu (Nigeria)*
Midnight sessions: *Femi Ayo-Tubosun (Nigeria)*
PAPYRUS UNDERGROUND: *Kofi Acquah (Ghana)*

The Cat and Cobra Duel: *Samuel Nyachiro Kegwaro (Kenya)*
PROPHESY: *Kofi Acquah (Ghana)*
Locked out: *Alinafe Diana Zalira (Malawi)*
The Believer: *Aubrey Sandile (Zimbabwe)*
A Mother's Song: *Cosmas Mairosi (Zimbabwe)*
FOR MEMUNA AND CHILD:*Ekundayo Asifat (Nigeria)*
We Are Just Humans: *Gerry Sikazwe (Zambia)*
Right to Die!:*Lusajo Kalangali (Tanzania)*
Water, a goddess: *Kelvin J. Shachile (Kenya)*
Coming To Think About It: *Gerry Sikazwe (Zambia)*
Ubuntu: *Mari Ballot (South Africa)*
Things we do not know about death: *Mobolaji Olawale (Nigeria)*
4:*Monicah Lubanga Kuta (Kenya)*
THE HORSE IS BRAYING: *Nkosiyazi Kan Kanjiri (Zimbabwe)*
BP AT THIRTY: *Mujtaba s Abubakar (Nigeria)*
SCATTERED PETALS: *Nkosiyazi Kan Kanjiri (Zimbabwe)*
Spoken River: *Nosakhare Collins (Nigeria)*
THE NEW SINGING SCHOOL BESIDE OUR HOUSE: *Okwudili Nebeolisa (Nigeria)*
SOUNDLESS CAVE: *Okwudili Nebeolisa (Nigeria)*
BODIES AND SCARS: *Paul Oluwafemi David (Nigeria)*
Mother baptise me: *Sinaso Mxakaza (South Africa)*
Find yourself: *Sinaso Mxakaza (South Africa)*
Ode to my mother's friend: *Awodiya Funke (Nigeria)*
New Life - : *Crystal Warren (South Africa)*
FREEDOM/'fri:dəm/: *Benjamin Elemide (Nigeria)*
Forgotten letters: *Fethi Sassi (Tunisia)*
COLOURS OF WATER: *Benjamin Elemide (Nigeria)*
The fingers of the night: *Fethi Sassi (Tunisia)*
my religion: *Goodenough Mashego (South Africa)*
Canticle of an Electric Storm: *Harry Owen (South Africa)*
Heaven is not Closed: *Lwanda Sindaphi (South Africa)*
The Tree: *John Anusie (Nigeria)*

Ero Gospel: *Michael Ace (Nigeria)*
River Rituals: *Sibulelo Manamatela(South Africa)*
Lost: *Ntseka Masoabi (Lesotho)*
Night Bloom: *Zahraa' Raadhiya Khaki (South Africa)*
MONUMENT: *Sipho Mthabisi Ndebele (South Africa)*
Sabrun Jameel: *Zahraa' Raadhiya Khaki (South Africa)*
Mothers who are fire: *Xolani Ntuli (South Africa)*
SEEN: *Adatsi Brownson (Ghana)*
Survivor or a warrior: *Xolani Ntuli (South Africa)*
tattoos are permanent: *Adorn Keketso Mashigo (South Africa)*
Tree of life: *Xolani Ntuli (South Africa)*
mother land: *Archie Swanson (South Africa)*
In the Marrow of a Yellow Bone: *Beaton Galafa (Malawi)*
IN A GODLY WORLD: *Blessing Turvey Damasiki Chimunyapule (Zimbabwe)*
BIND ME NOT: *Charles O. Okoth (Kenya)*
We Shall Rise at Dawn: *Chukwudi Nwokpoku (Nigeria)*
LISTEN!:*Charles O. Okoth (Kenya)*
LOST PRIDE: *Elijah Unimke Aniah (Nigeria)*
Candle Lights: *Fikile C. Makhubo (South Africa)*
Spacing: *Kgomotso Ledwaba (South Africa)*
Oblivion: *Melissa Farquhar (South Africa)*
Absentee Father: *Richard Mbuthia (Kenya)*.
Sewing: *Tatenda Murigo (Zimbabwe)*
The Beauty of Silence: *Richard Mbuthia (Kenya)*

Part 3: Place, Home and Identity...........................116-142

Afu-Ra-Ka: *Mari Ballot (South Africa)*
Ayyoo Tiyyaa (MY MUM): *Leelisa Jacob Sero (Ethiopia)*
A WALK THROUGH AN AFRICAN VILLAGE: *Patrick Hwande (Zimbabwe)*
Annual Virgins' Dance: *Peter Yieko Ndiwa (Kenya)*

When It Rained In Khayelitsha: *Dimakatso Sedite (South Africa)*
Invasion: *Adré Marshall (South Africa)*
Carrion Call: *Emman Usman Shehu (Nigeria)*
Land Of My Birth: *Jabulani Mzinyathi (Zimbabwe)*
Learning to Drive: *Christine Coates (South Africa)*
Beautiful Zimbabwe: *Cosmas Mairosi (Zimbabwe)*
Community Policing: *Daniel Many Owiti (Kenya)*
A PRINCE WITHOUT A HOME: *Ekundayo Asifat (Nigeria)*
Whispers from Home: *Kelvin J. Shachile (Kenya)*
Many of a Morning in Chinsapo: *Yamikani Brighton Imbe (Malawi)*
On the bus: *Crystal Warren (South Africa)*
Blossom at Prospect Field: *Harry Owen (South Africa)*
Grounded: *Crystal Warren (South Africa)*
Fruitsquirt: *Harry Owen (South Africa)*
Accra and traffic: *Awuah Mainoo Gabriel (Ghana)*

Part 4: French Poets................143-201

Comportement excédant: *Josiane Nguimfack (Cameroun)*
Punaise rouge et noire: *Josiane Nguimfack (Cameroun)*
Vicissitude: *Josiane Nguimfack (Cameroun)*
Rendez nous nos trésors: *Nguetcheu Emile Arsele (Cameroun)*
La mal de ce siècle absurde: *Nguetcheu Emile Arsele (Cameroun)*
Il me vient: *Nguetcheu Emile Arsele (Cameroun)*
Profond océan: *Koffi Luc (Côte d'Ivoire)*
Cette Afrique là: *Koffi Luc (Côte d'Ivoire)*
Couleurs: *Koffi Luc (Côte d'Ivoire)*
Morphé: *Gbeada Woungouankeu Maxence (Côte d'Ivoire)*
L'Amour: *Gbeada Woungouankeu Maxence (Côte d'Ivoire)*
Le Desespoir: *Gbeada Woungouankeu Maxence (Côte d'Ivoire)*
L'Entrepreneuriat: *Emmanuel Siffo (Cameroun)*
La Mémoire de l'oubli: *Gils Da Douanla (Cameroun)*
J'ai vu le futur...: *Balddine Moussa (Comores)*

Autre fois Iles des parfums: *Balddine Moussa (Comores)*
Les religions étrangères: *Balddine Moussa (Comores)*
Voyage avec mon prince: *Vita Léo (Haïti)*
revenons au peuple qui se meurt: *Mpesse Géraldin (Cameroun)*
Je veux juste être: *Edouma Nomo Sulpice Oscar (Cameroun)*
Mélancolique: *Edouma Nomo Sulpice Oscar (Cameroun)*
Démon: *Edouma Nomo Sulpice Oscar (Cameroun)*
Aux Enfers: *Ray Ndébi (Cameroun)*
Secoue-toi racine: *Ray Ndébi (Cameroun)*
A Dieu: *Ray Ndébi (Cameroun)*
La Tricherie: *Etty Gnanzoutchi Ange Jonathan (Côte d'Ivoire)*
Mon petit livre blanc: *Etty Gnanzoutchi Ange Jonathan (Côte d'Ivoire)*
Au Bord de la rivière: *Serges Cyrille Kooko (Mali)*
Entends-tu ?: *Serges Cyrille Kooko (Mali)*
Le Pouvoir politique: *Akere-Maimo J. Ano-Ebie (Cameroun)*
La belle ville du Congo: *Akere-Maimo J. Ano-Ebie (Cameroun)*
ma mère: *Galley Kokouvi Dzifa (Togo)*
Deuil: *Galley Kokouvi Dzifa (Togo)*
Instant: *Galley Kokouvi Dzifa (Togo)*
Eclosion: *Ayi Dossavi (Togo)*
Holocauste: *Ayi Dossavi (Togo)*
Je trace: *Joel Amah Ajavon (Togo)*
Eunuque, je pense à toi: *Joel Amah Ajavon (Togo)*
Écoutez-nous, disent les ânes: *Nsah Mala (Cameroun)*
Après le travail au village: *Nsah Mala (Cameroun)*
Un élève exemplaire: *Nkwetatang Sampson Nguekie (Cameroun)*

Part 5: Politics, Governance and Development…..202-259

Them and you: *Aleck Kaposa (Zimbabwe)*
The slums: *Clesirdia Nzorozwa (Zimbabwe)*
Discordant Voice: *Jabulani Mzinyathi (Zimbabwe)*
ZOMBIES: *Ngam Emmanuel Beyia (Cameroon)*

Workers Day: *Jabulani Mzinyathi (Zimbabwe)*
WHEN THE ELECTION APPROACHES: *Ngam Emmanuel Beyia (Cameroon)*
The Interview: *Peter Yieko Ndiwa (Kenya)*
MY GREATEST DREAM: *Tafadzwa Bandera (Zimbabwe)*
University of Knowledge: *Zongezile Matshoba (South Africa)*
HE COMES AT NIGHT: *Ojonugwa John Attah (Nigeria)*
IT'S HIM: *Chenjerai Mhondera (Zimbabwe)*
Zimbabwe: *Handsen Chikowore (Zimbabwe)*
Educate to Liberate!:*Irene Munthree(South Africa)*
Justice: *Handsen Chikowore (Zimbabwe)*
A Democrat: *Lusajo Kalangali (Tanzania)*
A one way economy: *Sonwabo Meyi (South Africa)*
Prisoner: *Sipho hobane Ndlovu (Zimbabwe)*
alcohol& progress: *Sonwabo Meyi (South Africa)*
AFRIKA MY AFRIKA: *Prosper Kavunika (Zimbabwe)*
conversations with a mon/star: *Sonwabo Meyi (South Africa)*
Rainbowality: A call for Change: *Antonio Garcia (South Africa)*
Redemption for Azania and all the winter strangers: *Abigail George(South Africa)*
Coloured In By Society: *Charissa Cassels (South Africa)*
Exit the old rusted chain-saw: *Christopher Kudyahakudadirwe (Zimbabwe)*
the guns fell silent: *Goodenough Mashego (South Africa)*
Sycophants!:*Nellah Nonkondlo Mntanenhlabathi (Zimbabwe)*
Drowning: *Nkwana Joshua Serutle (South Africa)*
our names: *Nkwana Joshua Serutle(South Africa)*
Change: *Olakitan Aladesuyi (Nigeria)*
WANDERING HOMES: *Sipho Mthabisi Ndebele (South Africa)*
Intersectional Superman: *Zahraa' Raadhiya Khaki (South Africa)*
THE YESTERDAY OF TODAY: *Adatsi Brownson (Ghana)*
How we betrayed our Brother: *Beaton Galafa (Malawi)*

STREET NAMES: Blessing *Turvey Damasiki Chimunyapule (Zimbabwe)*
War: *Hlengiwe Bila (South Africa)*
Questioning the questioner: *Joy Odifemenuwe (Nigeria)*
Assembly: *Kgomotso Ledwaba (South Africa)*
Nigeria! One week, one trouble: *Joy Odifemenuwe (Nigeria)*
My mother is a country: *Xolile Mabuza (South Africa)*
Black don't crack: *Ynarus (Angola)*

Part 6: Migrants, Assimilations, Irritants...................260-269

Between Places (A poetic novel extract): *Tendai Rinos Mwanaka (Zimbabwe)*
My country: *Zongezile Matshoba (South Africa)*
On being a refugee in South Africa: *Christopher Kudyahakudadirwe (Zimbabwe)*
Asylum Song: *Valentine Okolo (Nigeria)*
displaced humans: *Adorn Keketso Mashigo (South Africa)*

Part 7: Portuguese Poets...................270-302

Palestina: *Ismael Farinha (Angola)*
Zimbabwe: *Ismael Farinha (Angola)*
África: *Fernando Paciência Luteiro Palaia (Cuba)*
No ventre do Silencio: *Fernando Paciência Luteiro Palaia (Cuba)*
Cansei de mim!: *Fernando Paciência Luteiro Palaia (Cuba)*
APOCALIPSE 1942: *Kalunga (Brazil)*
DADA: *Kalunga (Brazil)*
Eu sou sol!: *Ynarus (Angola)*
Alma zombie: *Adailton Zinga (Angola)*
Professores sem pedagogia afrocentrada!: *Adailton Zinga (Angola)*
Vítimas da Vaidade: *Adailton Zinga (Angola)*
BORBOLETRAS: *Hondina Rodrigues (Angola)*
DECLÍNIO: *Hondina Rodrigues (Angola)*

PARTIR: *Hondina Rodrigues (Angola)*
TACULA: *Branca Clara das Neves (Portugal/Angola)*
MARCHAS: *Ozias Cambanje(Moçambique)*
NADA É LIBERDADE: *Ozias Cambanje(Moçambique)*
A PAZ NO POMBO PRETO: *Ozias Cambanje(Moçambique)*
Beleza feminina: *Morais José Manuel*
ESTAREI LÁ: *Morais José Manuel*
Quem sabe?: *Morais José Manuel*
OH ÁFRICA LEVANTA-TE!: *Roque Jose Pascoal de Oliveira*
TODOS PODEMOS FAZER A PAZ E CONSTRUIR A FELICIDADE: *Roque Jose Pascoal de Oliveira*
POETA FARRAPO: *Canhanga Soberano(Angola)*
À PEDRA: *Canhanga Soberano(Angola)*

Part 8: Poetry, Art and Writing..........................303-315

The Novelist: *Aremu Adams Adebisi (Nigeria)*
A BLANK PIECE OF PAPER: *Tendai Rinos Mwanaka (Zimbabwe)*
BROWN COLLAR JOB: *Joseph Olamide Babalola (Nigeria)*
The poet`s sweat: *Munyaradzi Gibson Bopoto (Zimbabwe)*
In concert: *Adré Marshall(South Africa)*
finger painting: *Aaliyah Cassim (South Africa)*
An Elegy to Kofi Annan: *Odhiambo Kaumah (Kenya)*
Take it from my hand: *Fethi Sassi (Tunisia)*
lying is an artform: *Goodenough Mashego (South Africa)*
the poet's shadows: *Adorn Keketso Mashigo (South Africa)*
Editor: *Awuah Mainoo Gabriel (Ghana).*

Part 9: Love and Relationships............................316-352

DISEMBODIED MATES: *Andrew Nyongesa (Kenya)*
SLEEPING WITH THE MOON: *Chibueze Obunadike (Nigeria)*
253: *Clesirdia Nzorozwa (Zimbabwe)*
Seasons: *Gamuchirai Susan Muchirahondo (Zimbabwe)*

Sun Glow: *John J.J Dongo (Zimbabwe)*
MY HEART'S EARTH: *Joseph Olamide Babalola (Nigeria)*
Fences: *John J.J Dongo (Zimbabwe)*
TWO SPERMS: *Kofi Acquah (Ghana)*
Beyond reach: *Revash Kun Kanjiri (Zimbabwe)*
Bare: *Anesu Nyakubaya (Zimbabwe)*
When all the Water Leaves Us: *Christine Coates (South Africa)*
JUST US: *Monicah Lubanga Kuta (Kenya)*
Chalice of Choice: *Oyoo Mboya Kenya)*
Both Together And Each Alone: *Ismail Bala (Nigeria)*
Pearls of Pain: *Martin Chrispine Juwa (Malawi)*
When we're together: *Modest Dhlakama (Zimbabwe)*
Lightning Bolt: *Martin Chrispine Juwa (Malawi)*
Touch of an angel: *Modest Dhlakama (Zimbabwe)*
that moment I left: *Nkwana Joshua Serutle (South Africa)*
Peas: *Ntseka Masoabi (Lesotho)*
AN ENCOUNTER WITH GRANDMA: *Paradzai Givemore Macheka (Zimbabwe)*
Last time: *Pelonomi Itumeleng (South Africa)*
Blood: *Sibulelo Manamatela (South Africa)*
TO THINK THAT WOMEN ARE DEMISEXUALS: *Amani Nsemwa (Tanzania)*
Hands: *Fikile C. Makhubo (South Africa)*
NIGHTSKIES: *Dennis Omolo (Kenya)*
A traveller's note: *Fikile C. Makhubo (South Africa)*

Part 10: Trauma, Sexual Assault and Gender Issues....353-374

SPARK TO FIRE: *Nnane Ntube (Cameroon)*
THE POND OF DEATH: *Okey Ifeachor (Nigeria)*
The African Girl Child Shall Rise Again!: *Nnane Ntube(Cameroon)*
LIKONI FERRY: *Kariuki wa Nyamu (Kenya)*
THE FIRE IN YOUR BELLY: *Ojonugwa John Attah (Nigeria)*

mirror: *Aaliyah Cassim (South Africa)*
Dark Nights: *Aubrey Sandile (Zimbabwe)*
Help: *Ayomide Odewumi Mitchelle (Nigeria)*
A Falling Bitterness: *Aubrey Sandile (Zimbabwe)*
You take my breath away: *Bilton Boka (Zimbabwe)*
A Feminist Letter: *Kelvin J. Shachile (Kenya)*
The World Was Silent When We Died: *Nosakhare Collins (Nigeria)*
The supernatural tricksters mutual admiration jazz club: *Abigail George (South Africa)*
She: *Kennedy Chege (Kenya)*
Father, listen to the silence: *Lwanda Sindaphi(South Africa)*
Regression / Recession: *Kgomotso Ledwaba (South Africa)*
Grief: *Lwanda Sindaphi (South Africa)*
Under My Sister's *Shadow: Xolile Mabuza (South Africa)*

Part 11: Translational..................................375-414

ÌWÀ: *Luqman Maryam (Nigeria)*
CHARACTER: *Luqman Maryam, Translated from Yoruba by Luqman Maryam (Nigeria)*
Kgatelelo ya monagano: *Mosima Kagiso Phakane (South Africa)*
Depression: *Mosima Kagiso Phakane, Translation from Sepedi by Mosima Kagiso Phakane (South Africa)*
O bolaile ngwana: *Mosima Kagiso Phakane (South Africa)*
You killed a child: *Mosima Kagiso Phakane, Translation from Sepedi by Mosima Kagiso Phakane (South Africa)*
Ke leeto: *Mosima Kagiso Phakane (South Africa)*
It's a journey: *Mosima Kagiso Phakane, Translation from Sepedi by Mosima Kagiso Phakane (South Africa)*
Shungu dzangu Mhai!:*Johannes Mike Mupisa(Zimbabwe)*
Cry of the girl child: *Johannes Mike Mupisa (Zimbabwe)*
Afurika Chidadiso: *Johannes Mike Mupisa (Zimbabwe)*
Africa: *Johannes Mike Mupisa (Zimbabwe)*

Zimbe mujombo: *Johannes Mike Mupisa (Zimbabwe)*
Hornets' Nest: *Johannes Mike Mupisa (Zimbabwe)*
Rufu: *Prosper Kavunika (Zimbabwe)*
Death: *Prosper Kavunika (Zimbabwe)*
Albino: *Adjei Agyei-Baah (Ghana)*
Ofiri: *Adjei Agyei-Baah, Translated into Asante Twi by Adjei Agyei-Baah (Ghana)*
In The Grey Hair of Soyinka: *Adjei Agyei-Baah (Ghana)*
Soyinka Tirim Dwene: *Adjei Agyei-Baah, Translated into Asante Twi by Adjei Agyei-Baah (Ghana)*
CAIO E LEVANTO: *Maria Manuel Godinho Azancot de Menezes (Angola)*
FALL AND RAISE: *Maria Manuel Godinho Azancot de Menezes* (Translation into English by *Maria da Conceição Saraiva*)
JE TOMBE ET JE ME LÈVE: *Maria Manuel Godinho Azancot de Menezes* (Taduction un French de *Anabela Pezarat Correia*)
MIGRANTES: *Maria Manuel Godinho Azancot de Menezes (Angola)*
MIGRANTS: *Maria Manuel Godinho Azancot de Menezes* (Translation into English by *Nuri de Menezes Torres*)
MIGRANTS: *Maria Manuel Godinho Azancot de Menezes* (Taduction un French de *Anabela Pezarat Correia*)
POR ÁFRICA: *Maria Manuel Godinho Azancot de Menezes (Angola)*
FOR ÁFRICA: *Maria Manuel Godinho Azancot de Menezes* (Translation into English by *Licínio Assis*)
POUR L'AFRIQUE: *Maria Manuel Godinho Azancot de Menezes* (Traduction un French de *Sami Marcelino Benzaza*)

Part 12: Poetics..........................415-433

An Interview with Beaton Galafa
An Interview with Archie Swanson
An interview with Oscar Gwiriri
An Interview With Anton Krueger

About the editors

Tendai Rinos Mwanaka is a publisher, editor, mentor, thinker, literary artist, visual artist and musical artist with over 20 books published. He writes in English and Shona. His work has appeared in over 400 journals and anthologies from over 27 countries, translated into Spanish, Serbian, French and German. Find his books here:*http://www.africanbookscollective.com/authors-editors/tendai-rinos-mwanaka*.

Nsah Mala, anglophone multilingue du Cameroun, est auteur de quatre recueils de poèmes : *Chaining Freedom* (2012), *Bites of Insanity* (2015), *If You Must Fall Bush* (2016), et *Constimocrazy: Malafricanising Democracy* (2017). Il a reçu des prix littéraires au Cameroun et en France. Vous trouverez ses poèmes et ses autres œuvres dans plusieurs anthologies et revues en Afrique, en Europe, et en Asie, notamment: *Wales - Cameroon Anthology* 2018, *Redemption Song* - the Caine Prize Anthology 2018, *Best 'New' African Poets 2017 Anthology*, *The Zimbabwe We Want Poetry Anthology* 2017, et *Paradis d'enfer - Hell's Paradise* 2016. Son premier recueil en français, *Les Pleurs du mal*, est en cours d'édition.

BIO NOTES OFCONTRIBUTORS

AtheneNyarai Mutyambizi was born in Zimbabwe in 1988. She did her Primary, Secondary and tertiary education in Zimbabwe. Currently she holds a BSC Honours Degree in Computer Science and is currently an Associate member of IITPSA, certified PHP Engineer and MCSA. She likes to program, read and write poetry during her spare time. She has a passion for gender based issues and youth empowerment initiatives and is working towards starting an organisation that will enable youth to get education and support so as to realise their optimum potential.

Dimakatso Sedite is a South African poet and writer. Her poems have been published in *Aerodrome, Botsotso, Hello Poetry, Poetry Café, Poetry Potion,* and on her blog, *nala4za.iblog.co.za*. Her other poems will appear in *Kalahari Review* in November 2018. She was a finalist in Poetry in McGregor Poetry Competition 2018, and won the Poetry Open Mic Competition at the 2018 Jozi Book Fair. One of her poems appears in an anthology: *'Botsotso 18: From Private and Public Places'*. She studied poetry at South African Writers' College and holds a Research Psychology Masters degree (University of the Witwatersrand).

Adré Marshall was born in the Eastern Cape but has lived in Cape Town for most of her life. Over the years, she has taught English at various universities including the University of Cape Town where she was awarded a Ph.D. She is the author of a book on Henry James and her poetry has been published in numerous journals, including *Carapace, New Contrast, English Academy Review* and *Stanzas*. Now retired, she does freelance translation work.

Aleck Kaposa born 3 April 1975, is a teacher and author of the books *A Bag of Memories* (short stories, pub 2013), *The Big Yellow Train, There was a Fly, After the Rain* (poems) and *The*

*Magician(2017),*which in 2018 got him another NAMA AWARD nomination in the OUTSTANDING CHILDREN'S BOOK category. In 2004 Kaposa founded and edited The New Voices Magazine for which he got his first nomination in the 2008 NAMA AWARDS in Outstanding First Creative Published Work category. In 2009 he founded a private school, Norton Education Centre in Norton in Zimbabwe, which he runs as Principal and Director.

Andrew Nyongesa is a novelist, poet, short story writer, teacher and literary critic. Most of works of fiction are prose with post colonialism as the underlying canon. He is a PhD student of literature at Kenyatta University and assistant lecturer at Mount Kenya University, Main Campus.

Aremu Adams Adebisi is a boy, among five older girls, who explores the themes of gender equality, black liberation, womanism, boyhood, and existentialism. He has works published on various platforms and anthologies. He likes to call himself the Jos-plateau Indigobird which is endemic to Nigeria and one of a kind. He majors in Economics at the University of Ilorin, Ilorin, and shares his time between Lagos and Ilorin. He is a Nigerian writer

Beven Nebafor Awusa is an enthusiastic Cameroonian writer for over a decade, with non-fiction and fiction works. Choosing to concentrate on poetry than prose due to a busy work schedule, he'll often reckon to use the few lines as of a ballad which could summarise an entire story than a voluminous novel to get the same message across.A firm student of life, music lover, adventurer, he now adds 'Agropreneur'- (Agric Entrepreneur) to his list of ongoing accolade.

Chibueze Obunadike is a student and part-time poetry and prose writer. He currently resides in Enugu State and was among the joint-winners of the UBA Africa Day Poetry Contest. When he's not trying to figure out a new poem, he spends his time reading old books and listening to Jon Bellion songs.

Clesirdia Nzorozwa is a female poet, hip-hop artist, short story and script writer aged 20. Her nationality is Zimbabwean. She has poems that have been published in the Zimbabwean Standard News Paper several times. Poems such as The Slums, Primrose, Don't you forget etc. Egypt and Afrika are two of her pieces which have also featured in the "Don't Give Up Africa" anthology by different poets from *Vachikepe and 100 sailors* which available on Amazon. She has also appeared several times on a ZTV spoken word programme reciting one of her pieces titled "Afrika".

Daisy May was born in Paarl, she grew up in Somerset West and was schooled at Parel Vallei High School. Her love for writing was formed at a young age and she has written since she could remember however she has only recently started sharing her works with the public. She has spent her years travelling the world while working in various creative fields. Her love of words and adventure is prevalent in her writing. Her unique life experiences are relatable and honest. While watching local talents on stage she remembers feeling overcome with emotion and realizing that her love of art was no solely as a spectator but that she too wanted a place on the stage hence her perusal of acting. Daisy has been featured in various films both locally and abroad as well as numerous television commercials. She was published in*Best New African Poets 2017 Anthology*. She looks forward to sharing her life experiences and love of writing with the world.

Dorcas Wairuri Maina is a God-fearing lady, who's passionate about arts and protection of animals. She also has a heart for people and on her free time participates in church organized charity activities and enjoys meeting new people. More to her passion for arts she loves singing, writing poetry under the alias Rureyblue and attending art galas. She has a bubbly outgoing personality with a dream of traveling the world. Dorcas holds a Bachelor of Commerce and Business Administration and a Master in Business Administration. Dorcas currently works in the finance industry.

Emman Usman Shehu hails from Maradun, Zamfara State of Nigeria. He currently resides in Abuja, Nigeria's capital, where he works with the International Institute of Journalism. He is also involved with the Abuja Writers Forum (AWF), and is the editor of Cavalcade and Dugwe (www.dugwe.com).

Femi Ayo-Tubosun is a short story author, poet and novelist. He has works appearing on literary websites, including "A Dance With Demons" and "An Ecclesiatical Experience". F.A.T.E. is the self-proclaimed herald of the new generation African Literary Arts. When he's not writing or taking pictures of plants, he is chasing the wind or searching for the seven words to make a woman fall in love.

Gamuchirai Susan Muchirahondo: I am a twenty-year old poet that started writing at the age of eleven. It started as therapy when I found myself going through many changes physically and mentally and began encrypting my anger, frustrations, concerns and various emotions through rhymes. I grew into writing and today, I've written countless poems. My writing is however, broad and most of my content is on feminism, depression, and strong emotion from different extremes. I am currently studying Civil engineering at the National University of Science and Technology Zimbabwe. I am a girl, born and raised in Zimbabwe strongly passionate about expressive art

Jabulani Mzinyathi is a poet of note. He is a self-styled prophet-poet-philosopher. His work is featured in local and international anthologies. His most recent definitive collection is published by Mwanaka Media and Publishing is entitled 'Under The Steel Yoke'. Jabulani calls himself a writer belonging to the *Zimbolicious* stable of writers. He is into prose and poetry. A chiShona novel and another poetry collection are almost ready for publication. An ex-teacher, ex-magistrate, a holder of a diploma in human resources magistrate Jabulani is presently a legal practitioner. Jabulani loves the arts in general and hopes to always work with many budding artists.

John J.J Dongo is a researcher, blogger, poet, spoken word artist. He is also the current country representative of The Human Projects and the Co-founder of Motivate. In his words art in whichever form it may exist in, has the potential to transcend boundaries and speak to people. You can find some of his work at www.wordsbyjayjay.com.

Joseph Olamide Babalola is a young writer and poet, whose heartfelt love for literary creativity has been self-stated as 'insatiable'. He loves to weld words to create beautiful effects. He was longlisted for the 2018 Babishai Niwe Poetry prize.

Samuel Kegwaro is a writer, teacher and Blogger. He has a degree in Linguistics, Media and Communications from Moi University, Kenya. He fell in love with pen and paper while still in Primary School. His teacher of English inspired him to use his "third eye and third ear" to create what has never been curated in order to bring change to his society.He currently teaches English and Literature at River of Life Secondary School in Embakasi Nairobi, Kenya. He has two poems in the book: *Africa, UK and Ireland: Writing Politics and Knowldge Production, Volume 1* and one poem in *Best New African Poets 2017 Anthology*. His poems have also been published in various online publications

Kofi Acquah is a Poet, Student & a Performing Artist from "The Village Thinkers" (a Creative Writing & Art Society) in Ghana. He has been shortlisted twice for Ghana Writers Awards— 2016 & 2017. He has contributed immensely to International anthologies, journals and magazines including the *XXI Century World Literature—India(2016), Voices of Humanity Vol.1—USA(2016), Tuck Magazine, the poets without limit, modernghana, enews gh, The New Ulster journal—issue 62(2017)* etc. Kofi is a co-author of *'Palm Leaves'* (a collection of poems) and hails from the Central Region of Ghana.

Josiane Nguimfack Zeufack est comédienne, metteure en scène et écrivaine. Après plusieurs prestations amateurs au primaire et au secondaire, sa formation professionnelle débute en 2010, dès son entrée à l'Université de Yaoundé I, Filière Arts du Spectacle et Cinématographie où elle est actuellement chercheur (doctorante), spécialisation Production Théâtrale. Elle est présidente fondatrice de la Compagnie Ndem Ti Li. Elle a participé à plusieurs festivals dans la ville de Yaoundé en tant que membre d'organisation. Elle est membre du CLIJEC – Cercle Littéraire des Jeunes du Cameroun. Elle publie en 2014 le recueil de poèmes *Lueur en flamme*, aux éditions L'Harmattan.

Emile Arsele NGUETCHEU est né le 09 décembre 1976 à Bafang, petite ville de l'ouest Cameroun. Il a co-fondé, avec le poète gabonais Patrick ALEPH, Le Club Des Poètes du Gabon où il a été le Secrétaire Général. Il est membre de la Ronde des Poètes du Cameroun, ami de l'association Livre Ouvert. Après avoir exercé plusieurs activités: Représentant Permanent à Wally Agence Hotesse (gabon), Rédacteur en Chef du journal "LA VOIX DES JEUNES" (Gabon), Consultant au Comité de l'Excellence Africaine (Cameroun), Président d'Africa Foundation Awards (Cameroun), Commerçant, il est actuellement Maître de Cérémonies. Il est l'auteur de plusieurs livres de poèmes et de théâtre tels que *Les racines de la résistance* (2016), *Le moi qui parle* (2012), *Le vertige de la parole* (2011), et *La clé des bribes si*.

Koffi Luc, professeur de Philosophie de lycée, est actuellement doctorant de philosophie à l'Université Alassane Ouattara de Bouaké. Il est originaire de Didievi, région du Bélier.

Gbeada Woungouankeu Maxence est doctorant en Géographie à l'Université Alassane Ouattara. Passionné par l'écriture, il a dédié sa plume à la poésie.

Emmanuel Siffo voit le jour le 14 octobre 1990 à Foumbot, où il passe juste 2 ans avant de se rendre à Melong, puis Yaoundé pour mener ses études primaires et secondaires sanctionnés par un

Baccalauréat. En 2012 il entre à l'Université de Yaoundé 1 où il obtient une licence en Philosophie (2015), une Maîtrise (2016) en Didactique des Disciplines, actuellement en rédaction d'un master 2 portant sur la place du conseiller pédagogique au Cameroun. Il a également plusieurs casquettes : entrepreneur, travail en freelance, organisateur événementiel, communicateur, rédacteur web, chef et acteur de projets, conseiller pour voyage d'étude, etc.

Gils Da Douanla, du Cameroun, prépare un mémoire en littérature hispano-américaine. Il est acteur et médiateur culturel entre francophones et hispaniques. Il est également traducteur-interprète indépendant –français-espagnol. Il est membre du CLIJEC –Cercle Littéraire des Jeunes du Cameroun– et collaborateur des magazines de littérature Clijec le Mag' et de culture africaine Lepan África Revista. Il est auteur de plusieurs nouvelles et poèmes publiés dans les revues et ouvrages collectifs. Il est lauréat du concours national de nouvelles pour jeunes auteurs (2016) et lauréat du concours de nouvelles de l'Ambassade et du Centre Culturel d'Espagne au Cameroun (juillet 2018).

Balddine Moussaest né le 25 mai 1989 dans les Iles Comores. Elle a fait salicence en lettres modernes françaises à l'Université des Comores. Apres quatre anspassés sur l'enseignement, ell a eu une bourse d'étude pour poursuivre ses études enmaster ès littérature à Zhejiang Normal University en Chine. En dehors du mondescolaire, elle travaille aussi en tant que carreleur et s'intéresse également à l'électricitédu bâtiment. Elle aime le dessin et la beauté d'une manière générale. Pour elle la vieconstitue un art. Elle a un grand respect pour la spiritualité, elle ne supporte pasl'injustice, mais aime servir les autres.

Vita Léo est le nom artistique de **Marie Vita Léonard**, restauratrice et peintre haïtienne, installée à Perpignan dans le sud de la France depuis 2005. Elle a commencé à peindre en 2008 en raison d'une rupture de sa relation conjugale. Elle fait de la peinture acrylique, mettant l'accent sur les difficultés et les expériences de la vie. Celui-ci est son tout premier poème, portant sur l'amour. Vita parle français et créole haïtien.

MPESSE Géraldin vit et écrit à Yaoundé. Il est auteur d'un recueil de poèmes en langueespagnole. En 2018, il publie, avec les écrivains argentins, une anthologie :*Palabrastabuadas*. Le jeune écrivain a publié des poèmes dans la revue (en ligne) *Le capital de mots*. Ilécrit également pour Clijec Mag'. Par ailleurs, il a été le président du comité d'organisation de la 3e édition du FESTAE (Festival africain des écrivains émergents). Enseignant d'espagnol et étudiant-chercheur en Langues Africaines et Linguistique à l'Université de Yaoundé I, il est actuellement le directeur de publication de Lepan Africa Revista.

Edouma Nomo Sulpice Oscar réside au Cameroun.Il est un jeune poète, membre de l'association littéraire Le Salon de Littérature, organe du groupe NGUEDI Jm Éditions, basée à Yaoundé au Cameroun. La recherche en méthodes de Lecture et d'Écriture est sa passion.

Ray Ndébiest Camerounais, basé à Yaoundé. Écrivain (auteur de *The Last Ghost: Son of Struggle*), il est analyste littéraire, chercheur, traducteur et directeur de publication au sein de NGUEDI Jm Éditions. Passionné de littérature, il s'occupe aussi de la formation des lecteurs professionnels et de l'orientation des auteurs dans l'association littéraire le Salon de Littérature.

Etty Gnanzoutchi Ange Jonathan, ressortissant de la Côte d'Ivoire, est un écrivain en herbe, qui est encore à ses débuts avec la plume.

Serges Cyrille Kooko, poète et écrivain malien d'origine camerounaise, est auteur de *Les Larmes du silence* en 2016 et *A la Croisée des chemins* en 2018 aux ÉditionsINNOV.

Akere-Maimo J. Ano-Ebie is a multitalented poet from Cameroon, aged 37. He is the Communications Expert of PRESEC/SNV Cameroon. He has also worked in different capacities at MC-CCAM, Plan International, and CARE

International. He began creative writing way back in college and university, where he freelanced for local journals such as *The Humorist, The Entrepreneur, The Eden, Cameroon Panorama*, and *Profiles International*. He has more than 100 articles to his credit on varied topics and he is author of an unpublished poetry collection. He is also a gifted songwriter/singer and graphic artist, having released his first album "New Creation" in January 2013. His French poems here were translated from English.

Kokouvi Dzifa Galley est né à Lomé. En 2004, il est titulaire d'une Maitrise en Sciences Economiques de l'Universités de Lomé. Il est membre du réseau d'auteurs *Escale des Ecritures*. Boursier Beaumarchais en 2009, lauréat de Visas pour la création 2016, il participe à plusieurs résidences d'écriture. Il a publié *Arènes intérieures* (Théâtre) In Libre cours au Tarmac, Editions Passage (s), France, 2018 ; *Un pas avant* (Théâtre), Editions Awoudy, Lomé, 2018 ; *bris de vie, bris de souffle* (Poésie), Ed Ponts de Lianes, Togo, 2017 ; *Peau de braise* (Théâtre) in Balade théâtrale 2, Ed. Awoudy, Lomé, 2015 ; *Dés-espérances* (Théâtre) in *Balade théâtrale*, Ed. Awoudy, Lomé, 2013 ; *In-certitudes* (Theater) Ed Lansman, Belgique, 2009 ; *L'Oracle a parlé et autres contes du Togo*, (Conte) Ed Ponts de Lianes, Togo, 2014.

Ayi Renaud DOSSAVI-ALIPOEH est un écrivain (poète, essayiste et nouvelliste) et blogueur togolais. Né en septembre 1993 à Lomé, il est biologiste de formation. Il a publié à ce jour cinq livres dont *Rosées Lointaines* (2015), *Chants de Sable* (2018) (poésie) et Nous et l'histoire (2018) (essai sur l'histoire africaine). En mai 2018, il gagne le premier prix du concours continental d'écriture « Afrique de mes rêves » de la Banque Africaine de développement ainsi que le prix Littéraire France-Togo, et est actuellement secrétaire général de l'association d'écrivains PEN-Togo.

Joël Amah AJAVON est auteur, comédien, et metteur en scène. Il a été formé en interprétation dramatique à l'école Studio Théâtre d'Art de Lomé (2006-2009). Il est est lauréat des Scènes du

Théâtre Francophone d'Afrique Centrale 2010 avec sa pièce *Ma rivale, la mitraille*. Il est co-fondateur de la Compagnie Artistique Carrefour et a dirigé le Festival International de Théâtre de Maison (FITMA) de 2012 à 2017. Il est par ailleurs membre du réseau d'auteurs Escale des Ecritures.

Nkwetatang Sampson Nguekie est né le 06 novembre 1972 à Mmuock-Leteh dans le Département de Lebialem au Cameroun. Il a étudié au Lycée Bilingue de Bamenda et à l'Université de Yaoundé 1. Il est auteur de deux romans - From Village to Town et Hard Way to Fortune, et plusieurs poèmes pours les écoles primaires et secondaires.

Luqman Maryam stays and was born in Nigeria, in the State of Kogi, Local government area of Ijumu. She is of the tribe of Yorubas. She is currently a student

Mosima Phakane is a 22 years old poet, born in a village called Ga-Matlala Kordon in the Limpopo province, South Africa. She's been writing poetry and short stories from the age of 14 and uses every opportunity she can to grow as a poet and writer. She's currently in her second year of study at University of the Witwatersrand studying towards a BSc degree in Civil Engineering. She's a member of a student poetry society at University of the Witwatersrand called "Wits Poets Corner" and a volunteering organisation called Faculty of Best Advisory.

My name is **Munyaradzi Gibson Bopoto**, I am a young man aged twenty one residing and born in Bulawayo, Zimbabwe. I am both a poet and a short story writer who is extremely passionate about his work. Been writing for five years now and I have performed at poetry slams in Bulawayo including hosting my very own arts event which was a learning curve. My topics are about anything that really matters that is Theology, Racism, History, Pan Africanism among other issues.My influences in poetry are Dambudzo Marechera, Chenjerai Hove and John Eppel including many others.

NGAM EMMANUEL BEYIA, Cameroonian born is poet, educationist, and an advocate of socio-political change. His writings address various issues and every reader is likely to find one that suits their interest. He studied in THE UNIVERSITY OF YAOUNDE 1, Cameroon, where he obtained BA in French and English. He then enrolled into Higher Teachers Training College, graduated with a bilingual diploma. Upon graduation has been teaching in local High schools in English speaking Cameroon.

Born as Nnane Anna Ntube, she adopts the penname **Nnane Ntube.** She is a teacher of French and English with a Bachelor's degree in Bilingual Studies and a Bachelor's degree in English obtained from the University of Yaounde 1. She equally holds a Diploma in Bilingual Letters obtained from the Higher Teacher's Training College, Yaounde. Nnane is a Youth Advocate for Peace and Democracy, an activist for change, an actress, founder of Youth Centre for Progress (YOCEP) and Breaking P=oint. She believes in using poetry for change and bringing poetry to life through poetry drama.

Kariuki wa Nyamu is an award-winning Kenyan poet, script writer, film director, editor, translator, literary critic and educator. He earned a BA Education (Literature and English) from Makerere University, Uganda. He is anthologized in *A Thousand Voices Rising, Boda Boda Anthem and Other Poems, Best New African Poets Anthologies; 2015, 2016, 2017, Experimental Writing: Volume 1, Africa Vs Latin America Anthology, The Mamba Journal of African Haiku,* among others. Kariuki, who recently co-authored a Children's Poetry and Short Story Anthology titled *When Children Dare to Dream,* is presently pursuing a Master of Arts in Literature at Kenyatta University, Kenya.

Okey Ifeachor is a writer, author, poet and journalist who has practiced both in the print and broadcast media spanning several years and was privileged to report activities at the Aso Rock Presidential Villa, Abuja. Until recently, he was the Head of News at Dasamal Television Network, Abuja. Some of his poems have been published in national newspapers and magazines as well as in an Anthology *New Voices*. He is currently a doctorate student in Theology. He is a member of Nigeria Union of Journalists, Associate Member Nigeria Institute of Public Relations and Associate Member Nigeria Institute of Management.

Born on 1 October 1975, **Patrick Hwande** is a Zimbabwean poet and playwright. He lives in Gokwe where he is teaching at a Primary School. Most of his literal work has been published in Chishona, his indigenous language. At one time he was a chief poet at Africa Community Publishing and Development Trust. Hwande usually performs his poems and plays at social gatherings in Gokwe Nembudzia. He says he will never put the pen off the paper until his proverbial call to Heaven.

Peter Yieko Ndiwa: I was born in rural Kenya in 1986. I started writing Poetry in 2007 after I enrolled for English/Literature degree course at Kenyatta University. I published my first full volume of poetry anthology in 2014 *'The World Far away and other poems'* and have since been published in various anthologies around the world. I am inspired to write by human suffering.

Born in Harare to a Shona father and Ndebele mother **Revash Kun Kanjiri** attended school in both Mashonaland and Matebeleland. While doing his A level at Dotito High in Mount Darwin, he became a Junior Councilor in the Pfura Rural District Junior Council. During his High School, Revash was much into debating and he won the best speaker award in Mount Darwin 2016. He sees poetry as a way one can use to speak to the world.

Tafadzwa Bandera – Alfred Tafadzwa Bandera was born in Chegutu ,1990 but grew up in Morris Depot, Harare Zimbabwe. He is a social worker, poet, motivational, short story and script writer. He had his works featured in *Tuck Magazine* and *Dear SA*. He spends most of his time writing. He resides in Randburg, South Africa.

You will find **Zongezile Matshoba** in your township or village or school or town or hall or open ground, and wherever there is a literary event for the young and old. His writings narrate the humour and hardships of township and rural life, and interrogates whether it is yet uhuru in people's livelihood.

Ojonugwa John Attah is a Nigerian poet. He also writes short stories and reviews of football matches especially the Premier league. He teaches English and at other times Literature. He has been published by and on: *Best New African Poets Anthology 2015, Kikwetu journal, Afrikrayons, The Muse Journal* at Nsukka amongst others. He has won a few awards for his writing in school and for his behaviour. He loves playing and watching football, reading, writing, listening to music and making new friends.

Aaliyah Cassim:I am a nineteen year old South African currently studying Audiology at the University of KwaZulu Natal, and I live with my parents and younger brother. I have enjoyed writing both poetry and prose since a young age.

Alinafe Diana Zalira is a 4th year student at the University of Malawi Chancellor College, studying Bachelors of education languages. She is majoring in English and minoring in African languages and linguistics. She was born on 17th January 1996. She has passion for poetry and she writes poems during her free time.

Anesu Nyakubaya is a writer, blogger and poet. Her work has been featured in the *Zimbolicous Poetry Anthology: Volumes 2 and 3* as well as *Divas Inc Zw's* website and a number of other blogs. In her words, inspiration is all around us all we need to do is concentrate, as her blog's tag line goes life is poetry. You can check out some of her work at www.soulfulmiss.co.za

Aubrey Sandile Ncube:I am a 25 year old man, who currently lives in Zimbabwe. I love writing literature; prose and poems. I am currently studying filmmaking in Harare, Zimbabwe. My dreams are vast; they include publishing a book in 2019 and building a lasting Zimbabwe film industry. I love poetry and usually recite at Open Mic in Harare.

Ayomide Odewumi Mitchelle is a Nigerian under-graduate. I'm the third of three children of Professor and Dr. Mrs Odewumi. I'm fifteen years old and I like music, researching, reading, designing, swimming and writing.

Bilton Boka: I am a very humble young man who fell in love with poetry a very young age of 15 in high school, started as a small hobby and then many people saw potential in my writing abilities and it gave me fuel to keep on writing and become better. Poetry was a platform that I used to express myself and my emotions

Chenjerai Mhondera is a poet, writers, author, novelist, published in over ten publications to date. He comes from the East, lives in Zimbabwe and is a Citizen of the world. He is Patron and Founder of International Writers Association (IWA) formerly called Young Writers' Club.

Christine Coates, a poet and writer from Cape Town, holds an MA in Creative Writing from the University of Cape Town. Her poems and stories have been published in various literary journals. She has two collections; *Homegrown,* published in 2014, by Modjaji Books, received an honourable mention from the Glenna Luschei Prize, and FIRE DROUGHT WATER published by Damselfly in 2018. Christine's poems have been selected for the *EU Sol Plaatje Poetry anthologies 2011 – 2018, Best "New" African Poets 2015, 2016, 2017 Anthologies.* Her short stories have been highly commended. Coates recently participated in the inaugural Rutanang Book Fair in Potchefstroom and the Cape Town Open Book Festival. She was a judge in the PEN International New Voices Award 2016.

Daniel Many Owiti is a Kenyan creative writer. He writes poems, articles and short stories. His interest is in African literature and most of his poems revolve around Luo culture and contemporary issues affecting youths. He participated in the inaugural Nyanza Literary festival (NALIF-2016) where he emerged a first runners-up. He has also published a number of poems in the Kenyan family magazine PARENTS and a number of opinion articles in the Kenya's leading newspaper Saturday Nation. His poems have been published in *Jalada Africa* and *Kalahari Review*. He is the founder of Eldoret Poets Association (EPA).

Ekundayo Asifatis a Nigerian poet, based in Iwo, state of Osun. He obtained two degrees in Theatre Studies, one from the then University of Ife (Now Obafemi Awolowo University, Ile Ife.) and the other from the University of Ibadan. A man of many parts – he is a teacher, a poet, a farmer, a writer, actor and dancer. He is a principal of a community secondary school.

Gerry Sikazwe is a Zambian poet, literary blogger and promoter. His works have been featured in print magazines, Newspapers, anthologies and Online literary sites notable being *Nthanda Review, AfricanWriter.com, Dissident Voice, Scarlet Leaf Review, The Global Zambian Magazine, Foxglove Journal, Apricity Magazine, Tuck Magazine, African Curators, Creative Talent Unleashed, Tipton Poetry Journal, Zimbabwe We Want Anthology, Times of Zambia (Sunday Edition)*, and *Spillwords.com*.He is the founding editor of *New Ink Review*, a Zambian based online literary journal. Currently a University of Zambia student reading Adult Education, and also actively involved in Creative writing and Spoken-word poetry movements around Lusaka.

My name is **Handsen Chikowore** and I am a passionate human rights activist. I am a poet and believe that through poems I am able to fight for justice and spearhead change for the better.

Irene Munthree: As a Life Coach I am fiercely passionate about the personal development of all human beings with a goal to empower people achieve their wildest dreams.

Johannes Mike Mupisa:I am an upcoming Zimbabwean writer and it's a passion I would wish to spur to greater heights. I feel poetry is the voice of the voiceless. I published my debut novel

Shukukuviri, this year and looking forward to being published in the near future in other literature avenues. I was born in 1988 in the gold mining town of Kadoma. I am currently resident in Zimbabwe where I do three things, write, write and write. I am a proud holder of an Honours Degree in Archaeology attained a Midlands State University in 2013.

Kelvin J. Shachile is a 21 years old Kenyan born passionate writer, actor and poet. He studies Geography– specializing in Geospatial analysis- at Maasai Mara University where he divides his time studying, writing and acting. He has a passion for media studies, creative writing, geography, history and literature. He has been twice published in *Whispers* an online international poetry journal.

Lusajo Kalangali is a Tanzanian poet and teacher. He is from Mbeya region, the southern highlands part of the country. He studied Education at Teofilo Kisanji University.

Sonwabo Meyi: I was born and bred in Grahamstown, from the Apartheid years, right up until South Africa became a democratic country. I was schooled in Grahamstown, went to church there. I know what the National Arts Festival used to be like, & I can clearly distinguish between what it used to be, & what it is now. My being a Black Consciousness Exponent makes me arrogant, however, that kind of a way of thought has also taught me how to be the best version of myself, in all spheres of my life. I read politically & I write in surrealism. Grahamstown has always been a one-way economy.

Mobolaji Olawale practices medicine day and night(literally) in Nigeria. Sometimes, he finds just enough time to pause and write something other than prescriptions. Some of these works can be found on several online journals. He is on twitter @theBolaji.

Monicah Lubanga Kuta: I am a Kenyan aspiring writer. A graduate from Maseno university with a bachelor's degree in Education(arts) wilt IT. A teacher of English and Literature.

Born on the 3rd March, 1989, **Mujtaba s Abubakar** is an aspiring poet. He is a second-class (upper division) graduate in the department of English and Drama from Kaduna State University. He has taught English language and Literature in several private schools in Kaduna, Nigeria where he currently resides.

Nkosiyazi Kan Kanjiri is a South African based Zimbabwean poet of Ndebele Shona decent. He is second winner of Drama For Life National Online Poetry Contest held by the University of Witwatersrand in 2017. He is contributing poet to *Zimbolicious Poetry Volume three* and has poems anthologized in *Eagle on the Iroko*, a collection published in Nigeria in memory of Chinua Achebe. His poems have also appeared in the Sunday Mail and The Standard under the *Up In Arms Poetry* column. Nkosiyazi is a published short story writer too, with stories featuring in *True Lies* and *Outside the Garden of Eden*.

Nosakhare Collins is the author of a chapbook "a pilgrim of songs" (Sevhage Publishers, 2018). Recent poems appeared or are forthcoming in *SEVHAGE Reviews, Antarctica Journal, Least Bittern Books, Dwart Magazine, Youth Shades Magazine, WRR (Words, Rhythms and Rhymes), Poetry Festival* and has widely been anthologized and publicized by eminent global repute. He writes & teaches from Nigeria, and can be reached through social media handle; Facebook: Nosakhare Collins, Twitter: @nosa_collins, Instagram: nosakharecollins

Odhiambo Kaumah is a Kenyan-born teacher of Mathematics and Chemistry. He is a poet and creative writer whose works have been performed at the Kenyan Music Festival to the national level. His poetry has a deep foundation in the culture of the Luo Community of Kenya intertwined with universal philosophies of an ethical African society. His works of poetry have been published by *Kalahari Review* and *African Writers*. He also writes motivational stories based on students' life, some of which have been published in the *Global Students Integrity Centre* magazine.

Born in 1993, **Okwudili Nebeolisa**'s works have appeared in *Commonweath Writers, Threepenny Review, Cincinnati Review, Catapult, Salamander Magazine, Ake Review,* and *Ambit Magazine,* and have been shortlisted for the Gerald Kraak Award, the Sillerman Prize and have won second place in the Okot P Bitek Prize for Poetry in Translation.

Oyoo Mboya is a Preacher of Literature by passion and Teacher of English by profession. He's a Kenyan born, bred and based poet whose works have featured in many anthologies, including the *BNAP 2017* anthology. He's passionate about Art and the ability of Words to break walls and build bridges across eons of time, gaps of distance and abysses of emotions.

Paul Oluwafemi David is a Nigerian Scientist, Philosopher and Poet, he's a student of the art of Professor Wole Soyinka and Ben Okiri. Currently he is a student doctor at the college of human medicine university of Nigeria Nsukka,his poems has been published in AFRIKANA, AFRICAN WRITER,PRAXIS,PRIDE, NANTYGREENS, KALAHARI,WORDS,TUCK, BANGALORE MUSE and THREE DROPS.He's working on some collections of poetry at the den.He can be reached on facebook via www.facebook.com/davidfirstnapaul.

Prosper M Kavunika is a Zimbabwean born Afrocentric commentator and provocative writer whose works have been featured in an online magazine_ *Val tuck* magazine.

Sipho hobane Ndlovu is a Zimbabwean Human Rights Activist, who stays in the United Kingdom. He is a member of the Zimbabwe Vigil advocates for the respect of Human Rights in Zimbabwe.

Yamikani Brighton Imbe is a Malawian writer. He attended the University of Malawi: Chancellor College where he studied Literature. He currently writes from Malawi's capital, Lilongwe. Some of his poetry has appeared on *Nthanda Review*.

Pushcart Prize nominated **Abigail George** is a South African blogger at Goodreads, essayist, poet, playwright, short story writer and novelist. She briefly studied film at the Newtown Film and Television School in Johannesburg. Her writing has appeared in various anthologies. She is the recipient of writing grants from the National Arts Council in Johannesburg, the Centre for the Book in Cape Town and ECPACC (Eastern Cape Provincial Arts and Culture Council) in East London. Her writing has appeared numerous times in print in South Africa and online in e-zines across Africa, Asia, Australia, Canada, Europe, Ireland, and the United States.

Adjei Agyei-Baah is a lecturer and translator at the University of Ghana School of Distance Education, Kumasi Campus, and teaches Academic Writing and Literature related courses. He is also the co-founder Africa Haiku Network and Poetry Foundation Ghana, and currently serves as the managing co-editor of The Mamba, Africa's first international haiku Journal. He is widely anthologized, won several international awards and had his debut poetry collection, *Afriku* recently cited by Professor Wole Soyinka, Africa's first Nobel Prize literature laureate at The 1st Asian Literature Festival 2017 in Gwangju, South Korea. Adjei is an author of other three haiku/senryu collections: *Ghana 21 Haiku* (Mamba Africa Press 2017), *Piece of My Fart* (Mamba Africa Press 2018) and recently *Trio of Windows* (JUNPA 2018), a collaborative haiku collection with Professor Ikuyo Yoshimura and Maki Starfield and published by Japanese Universal Poets Association.

Sinaso Mxakaza is a young South African writer who started writing in 2008 inspired by her love for books. Her poems are about healing, change and finding one's voice in the world we live in. Her work has been published online in sites such as *Voicesnet, Fundza, Poetry Potion, Ja Mag SA, The Pangolin Review, an online anthology (Next Generation Speaks Global Youth Anthology)* and *Africa, UK, and Ireland: Writing Politics and Knowledge Production Vol 1*. She was longlisted for the Sol Plaatjie European Award and the first runner up in the Creative Freelance Writerz competition.

Awodiya Funke is a Nigerian poet, author, medical sociologist, presenter, social campaigner and sickle cell advocate. A Lagosian of Osun extraction, currently resides in Lagos. She is a member of Poets in Nigeria (PIN), active member Association of Nigerian Authors. She's a fellow of Ebedi Writer's Residency, Oyo State Nigeria. Awodiya is poet who believes in using poetry to positively impacts people and societies World wide.(Poetry for service).

My name is **Charissa Cassels** and I am currently studying towards an Honours degree in Journalism and Media Studies at Rhodes University. I am a Coloured South African woman and am passionate about my identity and its complexities. I am not interested in being a voice of the voiceless but rather giving people platforms where their voices can be heard.

Christopher Kudyahakudadirwe is a Zimbabwean freelance writer and poet who believes that the only way to continue speaking to people even after one has departed to meet the ancestors is by writing. Period. He runs a poetry blog at www.kudyahakudadirwe.wordpress.com

Crystal Warren is a South African writer. Her poems have appeared in several journals and anthologies as well as two collections, *Bodies of Glass* and *Predictive Text*. She lives in Grahamstown and works at the National English Literary Museum, both of which are in the process of changing names

Fethi Sassi was born on the 1st of June 1962 in Nabul (Tunisia). He is a writer of prose, poetry and short poems and haiku; translatorof all his poems to English. A member in the Tunisian Writers' Union; and in the Literature club at the cultural center of Sousse. First book entitled "A Seed of Love" was published in 2010,*I dream …. and I sign on birds the last words*, in 2013. *A sky for a strange bird*, a first edition was published in Egypt in 2016, Second edition in September 2018 in Tunisia.*As lonely rose ..one a* *chair,* published in Egypt in march 2017, a poetic book was published in 2018 in Egypt,*I used to hang my face behind the door.*Translated English short poetry book was published in Zimbabwe by Mwanaka Media and Publishingin 2018, *I throw a star in wine glass*

Goodenough Mashego is the author of three volumes of poetry, *Journey With Me, Taste of My Vomit* and *Just Like Space Cookies*. In 2018 he published his first collection of essays titled *How To Sink The Black Ball*. Mashego also has an audio recording titled *Just Like Space Cookies – Listening Sessions Volume One* which is available on GooglePlay and iTunes

Harry Owen, originally from Liverpool, UK, but now firmly established in South Africa's Eastern Cape, is the host of Grahamstown's popular monthly open-floor event called Reddits Poetry. He is the author of seven poetry collections and editor of the international anthology *For Rhino in a Shrinking World* in support of efforts to save the rhino (and the wilderness upon which it depends) from extinction. His latest collection is *The Cull: new and resurrected poems*(Poets Printery, 2017). Harry is currently engaged in compiling and editing a new anthology of poetry by writers who share a strong connection with the city of Grahamstown, where he lives.

Ismail Bala writes in English and Hausa. He teaches English at Bayero University, Kano, Nigeria, where he specialises in modern and contemporary poetry, and literary theory. His poetry and translations have appeared in the UK, the USA, Canada, India and South Africa, in journals such as *Poetry Review, Ambit, New Coin, Okike, A Review of International English Literature* and *Aura Literary Arts Review*. Born and educated to university level in Kano, he did his post-graduate studies at Oxford. He is a Fellow of the International Writing Programme of the University of Iowa; currently working on his first collection of poems.

John Anusie is an aspiring writer who suffers from sporadic bouts of shyness and introversion. He regularly gets invitations to readings and book launches. When he attends a reading and his name is called to read, he immediately hides under a desk. Shyness is one affliction he is yet to overcome.

My name is **Kennedy Chege**, a Kenyan poet mainly preoccupied in documenting the stark and benign layers of meaning in life. My focus is an ambivalent one, ranging from realism, romanticism, surrealism... to contemporary observation

Lwanda Sindaphi is an actor, published playwright, poet and director. He is the co-founder and creative director of Lingua Franca Spoken Word Movement which performed at Northwestern University in Chicago. He is both New Africa (2010-2011) and Magnet Theatre graduate (2012-2016). He is currently pursuing an Advanced Diploma in Theatre Making at the University of Cape Town. In 2014 he was named best poet in Africa by Badilisha Poetry. He teaches poetry at The Cypher, an organisation of young poets. In 2016, mentored by Jennie Reznek and Barbara Kölling of the HELIOS Theatre, he directed Paired which performed at the Cradle of Creativity; and KUDU. He has travelled internationally with War Horse (Handspring Company)

Martin Chrispine Juwa is a Malawian history and literature teacher. Sometimes he writes poetry; sometimes he makes reggae beats in the ghettos of Lilongwe, the capital city of Malawi. He is a graduate of the University of Malawi; Chancellor College, where he studied History and Theology – and how to live with everyone. He loves to read and write about poverty, love and politics.

Michael Ace is a Writer and Poet from Ibadan, Nigeria. He has authored two poetry chapbooks titled *Sermon From A Stammerer* and *Scarlet Silk*. His poems have also appeared or forthcoming on *Praxis Magazine, Brittlepaper, Lunaris Review, Kalahari Review, WRR, Tuck Magazine, African Writer, Wildsound Review, Peregrine Reads, Parousa Magazine* and more. He is a Computer Scientist but with a great passion for Art and Literature. He is a curator of anthologies and contests, including *Pun Poetry Contest, 2018, Growth Contest, 2018, Wakanda: Rewriting Africa, 2018, In my father's house anthology, 2017, Healing Hands, 2016* and many more.

Modest Dhlakama is a Zimbabwean, who is a passionate baker and cake decorator. She is a freelance writer who enjoys writing poetry, short stories, songs and is currently working on her first novel. Her poems have been published in *Poetry Potion* and the *McGregor Anthology 2016*.

Nellah Nonkondlo Mntanenhlabathi is a Bulawayo thorough breed pensmith. She uses her ink to craft poetic pieces and short stories both in English and Ndebele. She has been published in various anthologies. Her words resonate with the reader on some level but the emotional roller coaster her words take you on, reveals emotions that one never knew they had. Beside calling herself a weirdo crawling to greatness, she is a work in progress.

Nkwana Joshua Serutle is a writer, spoken word poet and fine art artist, who was born and raised outside Burgersfort, Limpopo. In 2017 he joined Mzansi Poetry Academy to enhance his writing skill. His work draws more attention on the streets and shifting paradigms on social issues. Some of his highlights in 2017 includes performing at SABC 1, Yo TV. Later on that year he became Top 10 finalist for Leleme La Mme poetry competition. He won the CSP 2018 Open Slam King of the Mic. His poems had been published on *Poetry Potion* online magazine, *Odd Magazine* and *Sol Plaatje European*

My name is **Ntseka Masoabi.** I am a Lesotho citizen. I am an international student at Rhodes University studying towards a Master of Science degree in Geology. I have committed most of my free time in reading books and writing poems and short stories, as a way of vocalizing my inner-most feelings and ultimately, capturing my life journey Two of my poems, entitled *Home* and another piece without a title, are yet to be published in Harry Owens upcoming Anthology.

OlakitanAladesuyi is a Nigerian writer of short stories, poetry and drama. Her writing is mostly influenced by occurrences around her and her belief in the power of stories to create connections and shape perceptions. When she is not creating content for digital media, she is either writing code or actively searching for experiences to make into dramatic fiction

Paradzai Givemore Macheka was born on 18 August in 1962 in Harare, Zimbabwe. Currently he is a business person in the hospitality industry in Johanessburg, South Africa. Givemore is a qualified teacher who taught at several schools in his home country Zimbabwe. He holds a degree in Bachelor of Technology and Education Management. Diploma in Journalism and Professional writing.Diploma in Tourism Management.Givemore is a published writer in 2 Shona Poetry Anthologies in Zimbabwe, namely: *Tipeiwo Dariro* published by College Press (1995) and *Ngoma Yekwedu* published by Budding Writers Association of Zimbabwe (1998)

Pelonomi Itumeleng is a 25-year-old South African mother of one and third year B.Ed student at the Sol Plaatjie University. She is the author of a collection of poems titled *Echoes of the Inclined* (2015) and she is the Study of the United States Institute (SUSI) international exchange program alumna. Itumeleng is a gender-based violence activist. Her current project is *Rape, Consent and Demons,* a poetic narrative of gender-based violence, specifically focusing on rape survivors. She facilitates workshops in leadership, creative writing and personal development. She is the compiler and co-editor of *The Albertina Sisulu Anthology:Reflections.*

Sibulelo Manamatela is a poet, writer and performer based in Johannesburg, South Africa. Her work has appeared in *Type/Cast Issue 5, Poetry Potion Issue 013* and in *The Sol Plaajie European Union Poetry Anthology Vol. VIII.*

Sipho Mthabisi Ndebele has been writing and performing poetry since 2005. He founded the Exodus Klan poetry collective with whom he recorded a spoken word album. In 2015 he released his debut EP: *Dusty Foot Traveler*. In 2016 he staged his first theatrical poetry production entitled *Mosaic Man*. Sipho was a featured poet at the Naked Word Poetry Festival in 2016 and 2017 and Bloemfontein's Litfees in 2017. Sipho traveled to Germany in 2017 as part of the "Agenda 2030: Arts and Culture Makes the World Go Round" project. Sipho can be reached on Facebook at "Sipho Kotobason Ndebele – poet".

Valentine Madukife Okolo is a poet, a film maker, and a social activist. His poems have been published internationally in the literary magazines *Apogee Journal, Origins Journal* and other places. Apart from the world of words, he is also active in the realm of electronic visual media. He has created and produced a couple of TV shows and short films. A lover of nature and art he believes that creativity is the gateway that we use to connect to ourselves and the universe. He tweets occasionally on twitter. His handle: @poetval.

Zahraa' Raadhiya Khaki is an artist and poet currently residing in Durban, KwaZulu Natal. Born a Dreamer, Zahraa' began translating her fantasies into the physical realm from the moment she learnt how to reify her emotion with words. Her parents are both South African citizens, and as her heritage is far too tangled to decipher, she simply identifies as Woman, Artist, and Created. Shespends her days writing The Book that Never Gets Written, weeping over any piece of good writing or newly discovered art form, and occasionally recalls that she is in the midst of completing her Psychology and Literature degree. Her favourite artistic genre is magic realism, the influence of which can be seen in most of her poetry.

Xolani Ntuli was born from Soweto, aspiring writer and performing poet and former student in mzansi poetry academy. Writer in: isiZulu and English. Performed in Siyagiya spoken word competitions in 2017 July and performed "69" poems hosted by UNISA university of South Africa and preformed in word and sound series, currently participant in C.S.P Currently State Poetry Youth Developments,.one of the member on YALE: Young African Leaders initiative 2018 Mandela Washington fellowship program. Performed at Boys and Girls Youth Africa Art and Culture competition in May 2018.He was nominated for the APAPA Poetry Awards: Best male poet and Best title poem 2018

Adatsi Brownson is a 24 year old young reactionary poet from the Volta region of Ghana. He was born in Accra, the capital of Ghana where he lived and schooled. He is a graduate of Chemistry and had been writing for about 12 years now. He is a prolific poet who has written over 200 poems and still counting. His aim is to impact and heal the world with his unique gift of poesy. He writes every type of poem so as to do away with limitations.

Adorn Keketso Mashigo is a short story writer, poet, book reviewer at *Pulp Review*, translator and freelance journalist based in Mpumalanga, Bushbuckridge.

Amani Nsemwa is a junior banker and a writer, aged 25. He holds a bachelor's degree in Business Administration in Marketing Management from Mzumbe University, Morogoro, Tanzania. He is an open minded youth, and has had previously worked with CRDB Bank Plc., a leading bank in the country. He is a believer that all the things will turn out to be good in the end. Influenced by Christianity, he tolerates all the beliefs and wishes to meet his fellow poets in one way or another, through the beautiful forums like *BNAP readings*. He likes travelling, and booze.

Awuah Mainoo Gabriel, hails from Ghana, a poet, playwright and a tennis professional. Currently studying in the university of cape coast.Critics affirm that his remarkable weave of words marks him as a "lyricist extraordinaire". His works have been published online and appeared in most prestigious literary magazines.

Beaton Galafa is a Malawian writer of poetry, fiction and nonfiction. He currently lives and writes from Jinhua, China. His work has appeared in *Betrayal, The Seasons, Empowerment, BNAP 2017 Anthology, Better Than Starbucks, Love Like Salt anthology, 300K Anthology, Literary Shanghai, Mistake House Magazine, Africa, UK, and Ireland: Writing Politics and Knowledge Production, Fourth & Sycamore, The Wagon Magazine, Transcending the Flame, Every Writer's Resource, First Writer Magazine, The Bombay Review, Writing Grandmothers Anthology, Africa Vs Latin America Vol 2, Kalahari Review, The Maynard, Birds Piled Loosely, Atlas and Alice, South 85 Journal, Nthanda Review, The Voices Project* and *elsewhere*.

My name is **Blessing Turvey Damasiki Chimunyapule**. I was born on the 19th February 1982 in Bindura, Zimbabwe. I began writing political essays just for personal amusement, and then began writing poetry in 2016. I have written several poems. My poetry is inspired by politics and the desire to inspire others. I am a Pan-African at heart. I am currently studying with Institute of Chartered Secretaries and Administrators of Zimbabwe. I have written columns for The Soweto Bulletin and The Bulawayo Bulletin, writing motivational articles directed at inspiring high school students. I am currently teaching Matric English Home language in Johannesburg.

Charles O. Okoth: I have written extensively. I have published 13 books, and contributed to an anthology of poetry, *Sing me a Song*, (East African Educational Publishers). I have won the Burt Award for African Literature (2015) for my novel, *High Tide at Shibale*, and was shortlisted for the same BAYAAL this year, 2018, amongst the four finalists nationally, for my new novel, *A feast with the Dragon*.

Chukwudi Nwokpoku is an award-winning Nigerian teacher, poet, songwriter, and gardener. He holds an NCE in English and Igbo Languages from the Ebonyi State College of Education, Ikwo and is currently pursuing a degree in Education/English at the Nnamdi Azikiwe University, Awka. He's involved in the promotion of African Literature through a national poetry movement in Nigeria called — POETS IN NIGERIA(PIN) as he's the Lead Representative of PIN, Abakaliki Connect Centre. His poetry has appeared in *Lunaris Review, PIN Quarterly Journal, Dumbstruck Magazine, Mad Swirl, Libations for Nigeria,* and others. He hails from Ikwo in Ebonyi State, Nigeria.

Dennis Omolo is a Kenyan high school teacher of English and Literature whose poems have been performed at the Kenya Music Festival for the last 5 years. Apart from poetry, the 30-year-old documents the Kenyan Premier League through photos and makes short films and documentaries. He is currently working on his poetry anthology to be released in 2020.

My name is **Elijah Unimke Aniah.** I am a Nigerian from cross river state. Also I'm a student of mechanical engineering with a deep interest in poetry. My inspiration to write comes from pain, struggle and fear. I seldom write about love. My philosophy in life is to contribute to the common store thereby benefiting from the capacities of others.

Fikile C. Makhubo started writing in primary school. She writes mostly in English with a fuse of two of South Africa's official languages, Sesotho and Zulu. She fell in love with performance poetry in 2009 when she was adopted by a poetry movement called SickNatcha in her home town and has not stopped since. She has showcased in a great few shows, won some competitions and lost some equally.

My name is **Hlengiwe Bila.** I am a Journalism graduate from Limpopo. Currently living in JohannesburgSoweto. I was born and bred in a village called Shirley 30minutes outside of Makhado. I am an only child but I grew up in a big family. My love for writing is greatly inspired by the people in my life, and my past life. I write what I feel and in a way this has been therapeutic to me. I one day hope to write professionally, and not just as a Journalist

Dr. Odewumi,**Joy Odifemenuwe** teaches gender, cultural and performance studies at Adeniran Ogunsanya College of Education, School of languages; Department of English Otto/Ijanikin Lagos Nigeria.

Kgomotso Ledwaba: I am one part university drop-out, and two parts future graduate. I also think I need to undo the years of miseducation. So, now you can find me at a bookstore dedicated to promoting African literature. I have learnt more here than I ever did in all my history, life orientation, and literature classes. Now I spend my time writing and loving, it's working so far.

My name is **Melissa Farquhar**, I am a fourth-year education student at Nelson Mandela University. I developed a love for writing poetry at a young age and have since written many poems under the pseudonym "m.c.f".

I am **Leelisa Jacob Sero.** I am an Ethiopian Oromo. I was born in Ethiopia but raised in Kenya in Kakuma Refugee Camp. Been a teacher for 5 years at the camp. I am a social media activist and advocate of equality, justice, rule of law and democracy. I am currently pursuing medicine because of a career switch. I have a passion and appreciation for literature and functional writing while in my high school days.

Elemide Benjamin is a creative and inspirational writer, public speaker, spoken word poet, and events moderator. His short story, *Children of The Street*, won the ChildHero Short story contest, 2016. His poem, *Once upon a dream*, won the 2018 FUNAAB poetry contest. His poems have appeared on local and international anthologies. The young man is a Teacher, Biochemist, and has interest in personal and professional development. He's interested in youth, leadership, and societal impact. He is the visioneer of The Great Minds, an initiative that brings young people together to learn and grow together to build capacities for leadership, and transfer the skills to the younger generation.

Tatenda Murigo is a youthful Zimbabwean poet, steadily rising in the world of art in the African society. She is passionate about writing, mainly focused on areas of self-love, healing, growth and African empowerment. She has been published in a number of journals including *Women of Inspiration* to name but a few. She is an active public speaker and an art activist in Africa.

Richard Mbuthia is a teacher, a poet, an editor and a motivational speaker. He has great passion for poetry. His is passionate about helping to inculcate and develop the poetic craft in children. He is also a published poet in books and in different forums online. Some of his poetry books are: *The Setting Noon and Other Poems* (2017), *Letters of Gold* (2017) and *Bounding for Light* (2018). The last two are children's poetry anthologies he compiled and edited.

Mari Ballot says, I have written my first poem at the age of 5 although English is not my mother tongue? I have had some poems published but is now writing my book? However my passion is saving the planet and doing upliftment and job creation via Bamboo projects in Africa.

Antonio Garcia is currently a visiting scholar at New York University, Centre on International Cooperation. An experienced project and programme manager he has worked in various contexts including international NGOs and the military. As a visiting lecturer he has taught at Durham University (UK) and New York University as well as at various military colleges and schools, He also holds an adjunct faculty position at the University of South Africa and has been an instructor at the University of the People. Antonio has published in academic and professional journals, and has also published in poetry and literature anthologies. He is also a fellow of the Royal Geographical Society, certified Chartered Geographer (RGS-IBG), Project Management Professional (Project

Management Institute) and is a PhD candidate at Stellenbosch University.

My name is **Xolile Mabuza,** and I am a 21-year-old poet from South Africa(Lihawu a township after Nelspruit). I began writing and performing three years ago out of love for the written and spoken word.Growing up, I was always quiet. I believed that my voice did not matter, which encouraged a fear in myself, in my voice. I could not trust my words. But then I started writing and performing poetry. I started speaking. I write about things I couldn't talk about: the pain, the lessons, and experiences that have brought me to where I am now. I'm healing myself through my work, and it has always been my dream to share my healing, my voice with the world.This year August I was a resident writer for Naane Le Moya where some of my short stories where published.

Ismael Farinha: Contabilista, Poeta, Declamador, Membro do movimento Lev`arte, Membro do Chá de Caxinde, Membro da SADIA, começou a escrever poesias por influencias do RAP(ritmo arte e poesia) na infância, em 2013 decidiu aventurar se neste mundo vasto das letras, participou no livro do poeta Zola Vida com dois poemas lançado em 2014 Contemplando o invisível, tem participado na revista ONMIRA do poeta e jornalista Brasileiro Roberto Leal, no prelo antologia de poetas das noite de poesia da fundação arte e cultura, na qual é o mentor da mesma actividade desde 2016 que acontece uma vez por mês.

Fernando Paciência Luteiro Palaia, 23 anos de idade estudante do 4º ano curso de Engenharia em Ciências Informáticas na Universidade de Ciências Informáticas (UCI), residente no exterior(Havana-Cuba). Venho por meio deste apresentar a minha candidatura para fazer parte uma vez mais desta magnifica obra que reúne os melhores poetas de África, dizer que é uma honra poder participar pela segunda vez deste grande projeto bem-haja a vocês, bem-haja a poesia acima de tudo. Saudações!!

Kalunga é o pseudónimo de João Fernando André. Escritor, ensaísta eprofessor de língua portuguesa e literatura. Bacharel em Letras, Língua eLiteraturas em Língua Portuguesa, pela Faculdade de Letras daUniversidade Agostinho Neto. Membro da Academia Oeirense de Artes(Brasil). Vencedor, nas categorias de Conto e Crónica, do 26º ConcursoInternacional de Poesias, Contos e Crônicas e menção honrosa nascategorias de poesia e conto do 27º Concurso Internacional de Poesias,Contos e Crônicas (realizados pela Academia Internacional de Artes Letrase Ciências, Brasil, RS). Tem textos publicados nas antologias "Poesia ComReticências" (Pastelaria Studios Editora, Portugal), «5 Sentidos», noJornal Cultura (Angola), na revista Palavra & Arte (Angola) e narevista eis Fluências (Portugal/Brasil

Ynarus: Angolana. A young Angolan girl who found in her writing the vent she needed to heal her soul from the traumas.

Hondina Rodrigues nasceu a 27 de Setembro, em Luanda, Angola. Técnica média, formada pelo ICRA, e estudante de Direito. Gosta de actuar, cantar e escrever. Participou das colectâneas: "Amor à Sabedoria" em 2008, "Pratica(Mente)" em 2010, "O Canto da Kianda" em 2016, Sementes da Língua – Angola Galiza em 2017.

Maria Manuel Godinho Azancot de Menezes, has portuguese and santomean ancestry, resides in angola and is a pediatrician in Luanda. She's the author of the poetry book "Magic moon", launched in September 2017 in Lisbon, Portugal.Participates in the 2017 VIII anthology of contemporary Portuguese poets "Between sleep and dream", in the "Best New African Poets"(BNAP) - 2017 anthology, and in the first lusophone anthology of the publisher Paráfrase 2018 "I can't defer the heart".Her poems are the reflection of experiences, values, dreams, and appeals to humanity.

Branca Clara das Neves nasceu no Luena, província do Moxico em Angola. Publicou em 2014, Luena Luanda Lisboa: fala de Maria Benta, livro editado pela Colibri e o audio-livro da mesma obra em 2016, com o Estúdio de Filipe Santo. Tem para publicar Zindengono Zi-Buzitu, um conto em Português, Kikongo Yombe e Francêswww.brancaclaradasneves.com

Hosiasse Miguel Cambanje: pseudónimo: **Ozias Cambanje**.Nascido 01/01/1990 em Cahora-Bassa, Tete, Moçambique.Poeta, Professor e Estudante do Instituto Superior de Artes e Cultura (ISArC) desde 2016.

Morais José Manuel, nome artístico "Bestmora", filho de Jonas Manuel Zamos e de Rita José Kanjila, nascido ao 25 de Janeiro de 1995, em Cangola – Alto Cauale, Município de Cangola, Província do Uíge, nacionalidade Angolana. Frequentou o ensino médio no instituto Médio Técnico 17 de Dezembro em 2014. Exerce a profissão de Professor.

Canhanga Soberano nasceu no Libolo, Angola, em 1976.Jornalista, Gestor de Rh e Professor no Instituto Superior Técnico de Angola. Foi assessor de comunicação da diamantífera Catoca e dirige o Gabinete de Comunicação Institucional e Imprensa do Ministério dos Recursos Minerais e Petróleos. Publicou: "O Sonho de Kaúia" (romance-2010), "Manongo-Nongo" (contos-2012), "10encantos (poesia -2013), "O Relógio do Velho Trinta" (romance-2014), "O coleccionador de pirilampos" (Contos-2014), "Canções ao vento" (poesia 2015), "Amor sem Pudor" (poesia-2018) e "Travessuras de Jack" (novela-2018). No prelo: "Mangodinho"

Archie Swanson's poems have been published in *English Alive* (an anthology of South African High School creative writing) as well as the quarterly South African poetry magazines – *Stanzas* and *New Contrast*. They also appear in the *2015, 2016 and 2017 Best New African Poetry Anthologies* and the 2017 anthology - *Experimental Writing: Africa vs Latin America* as well as the 2018 anthology - *Experimental Writing: Africa vs Asia* in which two poems have been translated into Japanese. In 2016 three poems were translated by the Spanish poet López-Vega and published in the Spanish National Newspaper, El Mundo as well as the Bolivian newspaper Correo Del Sur. In 2017 two poems, labour of love and off to africa, were long listed for the Sol Plaatje Award and the poem flashback was shortlisted for the UK Bridport Prize. His poem journey is included in *Absolute Africa!* – a 2018 anthology of poems curated by Patricia Schonstein. For the past three years he has been one of the guest poets at the McGregor Poetry Festival and was also a guest poet at the 2018 Prince Albert Lees Fees (Reading Festival). His collection of 49 poems, the stretching of my sky, was published in 2018. Archie serves on the Board of the SA Literary Journal. He has lived in George since 1978. His involvement in the export fruit business and love of surfing has taken him to many countries.

Cosmas Mairosi is a Zimbabwean Educator ,Performance Poet, Author ,Arts & Chess Consultant (Southern Africa who lives and works in South Africa. His work has appeared in these publications among other: *Che in Verse,2006; Contemporary Zimbabwean poetry(2009); The War Against War: Poetry about stark realities of war(2010); Whispers in the Whirlwind: A Collection of Poems about Socio-Economic Challenges in Africa(2010); We Come From One Place: Poetry about the ills of racism, sexism, ethno-centricism and nepotism(2010); Defiled Sacredness: A Collection of Poems About the Effects of Rape and Sexual Abuse on the Individual and Society(2010); We Come From One Place: Poetry about the ills of racism, sexism, ethno-centricism and nepotism; Voices: Artist testimonials(2011); Zimbolicious Poetry Volume 1 (2018)*

Introduction

Best "New" African Poets 2018 Anthology continues where we left off with the previous edition, *Best "New" African Poets 2017 Anthology*, and its predecessors the 2016 and 2015 anthology. In this fourth volume of these continent-wide anthologies of African poetry we have work from 154African poets from over 30 African and the African Diasporas in English, French, Portuguese, Sepedi, Shona, Yoruba, and Asante Twi languages.

As we have done with the preceding volumes we started off with three collaborations and the three collaborations pretty much summarizes what our focus was on in this anthology. We looked at three areas we thought deserved collaborating around on. In Africa the issue of God, religions and spirituality is a hot topic with so many churches sprouting all over, in fact from the statistics passed around we have more churches than schools, hospitals, industries, and companies all combined together, with a city like Yaonde alone accounting for over 5000 churches. In Zimbabwe in the major cities every small unused ground has a small church using it, there are so many prophets, so many faith healers, so many preachers, in fact to be a church owner is one of the most lucrative jobs in Africa. We have pastors who own fleets of luxury cars, have millions in banks, some are at the heart of all the illegal activities happening in their respective countries etc. Amidst all this madness we decided to investigate what it means tobe a follower, to understand the God practiced in the churches, to tackle issues to do with spirituality. We have another section that continues this investigation.

The other issue we thought was of great importance was trauma. Going back to traditional African world, it was unheard of that a person can be said to be traumatized, or is suffering from depression and its attendant diseases. No one talked about that in fear of being ridiculed or being told they were just weak people. We have poets unpacking all kinds of traumas, and how to deal with them in this collaboration. The third collaboration deals with love, which also always receives a lot of entries in the open call.

There are three remarkable things pertaining to poetry from Francophone Africa that need to be underlined in the 2018 anthology. It was a pleasurable task to select forty-one poems from nineteen Francophone African poets, representing six countries on the continent and its diaspora, namely Cameroon, Côte d'Ivoire, Togo, Comoros Islands, Haiti, and Mali. First, the presence of Haiti on the country list, speaks to our recognition of the complex and rich definition of what Africa is: particularly the power of poetry to unlock new maps and compasses, with its verses and stanzas becoming branches on the African family tree which stretches beyond continental Africa to those places where the sad experience of slavery dislocated some of our brothers and sisters hundreds of years ago. Second, we witnessed a significant increase in the number of entries with memorable novelties regarding poetic experimentation. Some of the poets daringly slice up words and play around with the spatial and structural patterns of their texts on paper in such a way that produces what one might describe as both textual and visual poetry. Reading the poems becomes a journey on many paths, where the reader walks according to poetic rhythms and the hesitating breaks of action verbs and enjambments. Third, the thematic and aesthetic range of the Francophone entries is impressive and innovative. From poetic lamentations on the plight of the African womenfolk to the confession of various forms of love through critiques of undemocratic rule to the poetic reclamation of stolen glories of the African continent, among others, the poems speak to both hearts and minds. Cliched images of the continent as promoted by foreign donors are punctured while the downsides of both domestic and foreign religious practices are lambasted. The poets address the ugly and the beautiful all at once in verses whose aesthetic appeal is admirably rendered.

As can be gleaned in this anthology we decided to focus on the individual rather than the society at large that we have pretty much focused on in the previous offerings, thus the personal confessional narrative tone is predominant in this anthology.

We also have a section that focuses on poetics, a number of interviews from the previous Bnap poets. These interviews also gives a glimpse on what we do as poets beyond the anthology, issues to do with book launches all over Africa, issues to do with online marketing endevours we do, issues to do with groups we are members to that were as a result of this series of anthologies. Our intent is to keep promoting African poetry talent beyond media gaze and connect African poets, thereby connect African people. Unlike politics that dregs on and on without solutions, poetry has that ability to do that with little effort because poetry is life.

Tendai R. Mwanaka
Nsah Mala

TEXTE EN FRANCAIS:

Dans l'anthologie de 2018, il convient de souligner trois choses remarquables relatives à la poésie de l'Afrique francophone. Ce fut une tâche agréable de sélectionner quarante et un poèmes parmi dix-neuf poètes africains francophones, représentant six pays du continent et sa diaspora, à savoir le Cameroun, la Côte d'Ivoire, le Togo, les Comores, le Haïti et le Mali. Tout d'abord, la présence du Haïti sur la liste des pays, témoigne de notre reconnaissance de la définition complexe et riche de ce qu'est l'Afrique: particulièrement le pouvoir de la poésie à débloquer de nouvelles cartes et boussoles, avec ses vers et strophes qui deviennent des branches de l'arbre généalogique africain qui s'étend au-delà de l'Afrique continentale jusqu'aux endroits où la triste expérience de l'esclavage a délocalisé certains de nos frères et sœurs il y a des centaines d'années. Deuxièmement, nous avons assisté à une augmentation significative du nombre d'entrées avec des nouveautés mémorables concernant l'expérimentation poétique. Certains des poètes déchiffrent avec audace des mots et jouent avec les motifs spatiaux et structurels de leurs textes sur papier de manière à produire ce que l'on pourrait décrire comme une poésie textuelle et visuelle à la fois. La lecture de ces poèmes devient un voyage sur de nombreux chemins, où le lecteur se promène selon les rythmes poétiques et les pauses hésitantes des verbes d'action et des enjambements. Troisièmement, la gamme thématique et esthétique des entrées francophones est impressionnante et novatrice. Des lamentations poétiques sur le sort des femmes africaines à la confession de diverses formes d'amour en passant par les critiques du régime non démocratique jusqu'à la récupération poétique des gloires volées du continent africain, entre autres, les poèmes parlent à la fois aux cœurs et aux esprits. Les images clichées du continent promues par des donateurs étrangers sont percées, tandis que les inconvénients des pratiques religieuses domestiques et étrangères sont critiqués. Les poètes s'adressent en même temps aux laids et aux beaux dans des vers dont la propension esthétique est admirablement rendue.

Part 1: Collaborations

To the god of fear
(Best "New" African Poets Collaboration: Mbuthia, Ntensibe, Mairosi, Bolaji, Odewumi, Gwiriri, Malelah The Poet, Guzha, Mwanaka, Ocean Scott, Maina, Swanson, Haile Saize I, Mhondera, Maridzanyere, Mavolwane, Awusa, Agyei-Baah, Abubakar, Jaison)

Joy Odewumi:
Every one is suspicious of everyone. It was not like this before. We used to be our neighbours keeper, not anymore. FEAR in capital letters lives, eat, walk and work with us now, since before our own very eyes over 200 children disappear in silence, walahi! sleep was murdered and peace of mind travel to Kuvuki land, very far and everyone became a suspect. Traumatized beyond reality, God help us to find peace of mind, to see each other as one big family and not as: butchers, kidnappers, fraudsters and betrayers. This collective trauma must end now before we become a nation of fearfulness, because before now we used to be fearless.

Cosmas Mairosi:
Bring me washing powder
I want to scrub clean
The stigma off the backs
Of generations of the dispossessed!
I refuse to be broken
After centuries of back breaking burdens.
I refuse to be broken
After centuries of systematic denigration
My soul refuses to be crushed
After centuries of belittlement
vocabulary coined to turn
full-grown men into 'garden boys'

Mature women who run decent households
Into 'house girls'.
I refuse to be broken
Even after eons
Of being stripped of my humanity.
Bring me bandages of healthy human laughter
To assuage the wounds of my punctured heart.
Bring me needle and thread
I want to sew together
Pieces of my broken manhood.
Bring me a broom
And I will sweep under the rug
Skulls of disgruntled slave-wage earners
Uncompensated workers who have gone under!
I need some pain-killer
To swallow with pride the bitter-nickname
My foreign progeny are growing up with:
Kwirikwiri!

Oscar Gwiriri
Deployment
Oh wife, stop that wailing child,
Her voice evokes the screams
Of Rwandese women and children
Amidst the brutal massacre.

Oh daughter, drop no pot lid,
It throws me into prone position,
As I dodge South Sudanese bullets,
Fall on razor sharp mortar bomb shells.

Yes, its New Year's day Son,
Let no fire crackers crack,

As they explode, explodes
Intestines of my mind
In the DRC deep forests.

Oh neighbour, whisper knock,
To serve my sleeping ears
From night raids in Somalia
Where rebels slit bloodless throats
Fulfilling the ego of shameless wars.

Richard Mbuthia:
So I am black, right?
The colour of my skin causes fright...
Is that why you spit my heart out?
You munch and unthread my humanity
Piece by piece, poking holes;
I am this savage nonentity
That understands no reason -
I enjoy your vile demeanor
As I patiently await
Your return to sanity.

Dorcas Maina:
Fitting out to fit in
The voice that goes unheard
The thoughts that go unsaid
The opinions that meet death at inception
Borne from the confinement of colour, shape and size.
Labels masquerading as liberation
The stretched out arm of impunity offering aid while siphoning the rights of men

Tola Bolaji:

It's dark in the rain
I know I must not drive
But this drive in my brain
Turning off the light of my senses
This fluid drowned me as a child
Still flood me as a youth.
I am a man they say
And so I must die with my tears.

Ocean Scott:
When you die
When your feet are found
Off the ground,
When a rope is found
Around your neck

Will I have
Myself
To
Blame?

I've been shaking my head
At the news of your death,
I see your ghost nodding at me
From the pews of the parlour

Could I have stayed the nights
I chose to leave,
Could I have cancelled trips
To Egypt's tombs

Coz you told me you were suffering
From things only I could save you from

And I said drink lots, sleep lots
And you'll be just fine.

Sheril Guzha
The breaths that I poisoned
I gaze at the wraith-silver disc of a moon that hang in the starry night sky and,
The stars that look like sallow yellow orbs,
Or are they little babies, with tiny hands, tiny arms and tiny feet, oh and a tiny head?
I harshly rub my eyes with clammy palms, yawning lazily
I squint, blurriness fading, surroundings more crisp
And suddenly exorcism memories flood my mind,
The priest holding me down on the metal alter
Or is it a grotesque looking old traditional healer tying me onto a bed?
Mother said it had to be done or else father would whip the demon out of me.
My nose curl at the smell of the incense in the room or is it smoke from a fire?
And then a scream erupts amidst of the silence, from my pain or from the demon taking its first breaths?
My vision becomes blurrier again as my white dress turns red and all I can see is the scarlet blood,
Shuddering dejectedly, heart thudding and fists clenched I am jerked out of the daily horrific nightmare

Mandla Mavolwane
The Wake up call
Like an eagle focused on prey
Eyes carefully look into the photo
As they try to visualise your personality traits.

The visual is all smudged
As i fail to recall the sound of your voice.

Inquisitively probing with curiosity
of a cat
I inquire about your life events.
Looking at the photo again
I link the tales with the image
But i still cannot pin-point your selfhood.

My subconscious constantly recalls the phrase
"He is no more"
Was this a wake up call to reality?
A reality of imaginations
That i will also carry to my grave.

Chenjerai Mhondera
Freedom that never can be
Murdered within, I see still
That body lifeless
Wounded, bruised, inflicted, injured, dumped.
Pools, river of blood emanating from you,
Cruelly, murdered
Their bid, restless to save a tyrant.
Health tears fall,
Giant like raindrops
In that horror, painfully dying an antagonist.
I wreath in trauma, memory play me fear files:
In bits and pieces, you died

Lisa Jaison
Today is the day of escape,

Escaping haunting visions of betrayal from those whose love molests the inner most core of my psych
It's the day of freedom from failure,
A day of escape from the harrowing worthlessness of the unemployed
Today is the day of peace,
Peace from the berating tongue lashing of heart broken mothers
Spewing bile fuelled by resentment of unfaithful abusive husbands,
Just burning my self-worth to ashy nothingness
It`s the day of rest,
A swig of vodka, plastering and muting incessant voices battling for pieces of my soul.
The day of making it to the top floor and leaning tenderly on the ledge of respite
One more step, thirteen floors below, heralding my leap of faith to my final place of rest, only if I jump and end it all.

Haile Saize I
The human race is traumatized
With the patriarchal allegories
Of a bibiblical trinity that replaced a woman with a ghost
Disconnecting a natural family structure
Yet every man came thru the heavens of a womb
A woman is man too; wombman*
A human!
Yes the world is hypnotised
With western political ideological errors
Separating women rights from human rights
Let's put her back to the trinity
So we can start to see her worthy
Without drawing lines of genital advantage
Down with sexism
Man and woman are born with equal privilege

Don't be fooled!

wombman* - is a man with a womb otherwise known as a woman.

Beven Nebafor Awusa.
Gilbert
Sleep in peace dear friend
Dust to earth as your spirit quits
To await the day of the Books,
Ay, I'll see you again
Albeit no idea about when
But I assure 'twill be like yesterday.
You've made your strides during your time
Struggles to make an honest gain
Sacrifice from a peasant home
The dreams, visions and ambitions
We both shared,
Laughed about as we failed
But vowed never to give up,
Here I am, standing in the land of mortals
Lots of offers, for an honest pay
The future looks bright and promising
But now my mind thinks
For how long?
Just as news of your sleep came so sudden
So too we'll be overtaken in our struggles,
No foreknowledge when the fiend would strike,
A quizzical puzzle over ages
To which science and scholars find no answer.

Adjei Agyei-Baah
When a man sleeps with my wife

when a man sleeps with my wife
and knowing well that woman is my wife
I will not kill him,
I will not hold him by his collar
killing is the quickest way to relieve a fool of his troubles

but I will prefer to deal with that stick in-between...
that it may not go to other places
and to rip other families apart

BELOVED MARIDZANYERE
Streams of hot blood
Flow through the patched veins;
Violent vibrations by deep soul cries,
The heart's firmly built walls cracks
'Causing a bloody flood to wash away all the love pillars;
Tears through the deserted and toned heart run pell-mell
Plastering the deep burning ulcer,
With poverty, propaganda, corruption and inhumanity made cement;
Thoughts of already distorted future the mind gush,
Robing hope and of mind, peace;
Imaginations, of bloody wars filled,
Enslaving creativity and visions;
Sight dimmed only no more,
No longer we see the blurry images,
Us the blind.

Mujtaba s Abubakar
Mine Forever

We made ourselves promises
But realised they were indices

Later, there was nothing but hisses

It was another risk to proceed
All the while, we thought we'd succeed
Alas! Our tragedy was to exceed

The first time I met her
My palms could pet her
Never knew I could let her

Why did you pass me by?
You should have let me die
Instead of traumatising me high

Tendai Rinos Mwanaka
She is too fat, no she is too light complexioned, no she is too dark, no she is too thin, no she is too bright, no she is too angry, no she is too calm, no she is too boring, no she is too cultured, no she is too flimsy, no she is too dull, no she doesn't clean good, no she has a hot mouth, no she is too pretty, no she is too ugly, no she is too educated, no she laughs too much, no she drives me crazy, no, no, no, no, no, no, no, no, no, no, no, no,......

Archie Swanson

umatraumatraumatraumatraumatraumatraumatrauma traumatraumatraumatra

[o] trauma [o] blunt [o] force [o] violent [o] pain [o] trauma [o] agony [o] memory [o] re-live [o] fog [o] trauma [o] confusion [o] shiver [o] shake [o] lungs [o] trauma [o] terror [o] pulsing [o] feverish [o] separation [o] trauma [o] loneliness [o] breathless [o] flashback [o]

prison [o] trauma [o] falling [o] tender [o] sensitive [o]
raw [o] trauma [o] nightmare [o] faint [o] reaction [o]
war [o] trauma [o] blow [o] stress [o] ordeal [o]
upheaval [o] trauma [o] torture [o] shock [o] damage [o]
suffer [o] trauma [o] confuse [o] hate [o] jolt [o] hurt
[o] trauma [o] derange [o] stress [o] emotion [o]
psychological [o] trauma [o] enslavement [o] anguish [o]
strain [o] history [o] trauma [o] family [o] race [o]
gender [o] love [o] trauma [o] hate [o] upset [o]
outburst [o] nationality [o] trauma [o] xenophobia [o]
slaughter [o] running [o] panting [o] trauma [o] broken
[o] bloodied [o] generations [o] inherit [o] trauma [o]
disorder [o] syndrome [o] neglect [o] assault [o] trauma
[o] avoid [o] irritable [o] angry [o] destructive [o] trauma
[o] depression [o] guilt [o] shame [o] fear [o] trauma
[o] jittery [o] hopeless [o] control [o] suppress [o]
trauma [o] scar [o] wound [o] bound [o] jobless [o]
trauma [o] hunger [o] disease [o] famine [o] drought [o]
trauma

Note: The words of this poem can be read in any order: horizontal / vertical / up / down / left to right / right to left. They can also be read randomly picking out any word that the eye falls on. The word "trauma" repeats every five words. Besides "trauma" only one word repeats twice - the word "hate". The randomness speaks to the randomness of trauma - that it strikes anywhere and that bad things often happen to good people. The separation icon "[o]" is a graphic view looking down on the head "o" representing the body, mind and spirit of each individual. The icon speaks to how trauma affects people and boxes them in. Yet there is the possibility of escape - to rise above circumstance. The head is boxed in on two sides yet the other two sides are partially open, offering the possibility of escape. The name of the poem is a continuum of "trauma" with the last letter "a" linking back to the first letter "u" and completing what is an endless cycle of trauma.

The Love Song
(Best "New" African Poets Collaboration: Mbuthia, Ntensibe, Mairosi, Bolaji, Odewumi, Gwiriri, Jaison, Malelah The Poet, Guzha, Mwanaka)

Tendai Rinos Mwanaka
Place of Love
If his heart is reliant on the outside world then what primal materials makes up this reliance
Her heart is a weave of charcoal, blue spruce, hymns, incense,
Spider's silk; materials hardly seen as durable
Their love, and the hallows that live within it is best housed in a loose weave
Like woods would feel best when it is raining, barely raining…

Richard Mbuthia
That Feeling
The gushing of fluid from a melting moon,
That which lights a starless night,
Home to a billion flaring comets;
'Tis a feeling of stardom to no star at all,
Suspended on a bottomless pedestal,
Bearing grand, lofty ideas,
To suck in all spears,
For all seasons and times
Yes - no less than a million years!

Ntensibe Joseph:
So she whispers things that swirl my heart
Her eyes speak of hope and a joy so shinning
He diamonds for teeth glitter
And speaks like a melody

The velvet skin is just "ahs and ohs"
Then i smell this heavenly scent
That,that rouses the dead
If i only could write,
I would write of you beauty
Of you completeness
Of you wonderment
Of you that words can't describe
But i can't write
And i leave your sweet love to loom...

Lisa Jaison:
Ours is a smash and grab love
A robbery of hearts for keeps
A do or die, of crashed norms, boundaries, and labels
With longings for each day's end, where I crash in to your arms and soul and die, over and over again.
To wake up alive
If you chance me to rewrite this story a lifetime from now
Then the tale will still tell the same - all hands on deck
Me loving you hard, you loving me strong
Me loving you to smithereens, you forever, my ride or die

Cosmas Mairosi:
It is her gentleness
That sets everything alight
With her ambience.
In her eyes
Nature has bestowed mysteries
Only her kind can reveal to an earnest gentleman.
I drown
Under the gaze of her long eyelashes
I am helpless

a deer caught in her net.
It is her gentleness that sets me alight
As my nose swims in her scent
I ache to explore all her valleys:
I am only blood, muscle and sinew
Yet I must turn into something hard as stone.
I launch my lone missile
Into that slippery terrain
Gliding all in darkness
With no GPS in place
I lose all control
Till I capsize
And find myself again.
It is all her gentleness
That makes me buck, whimper and cry out loud!
It is all her gentleness
That makes me find my centre again.

Joy Odewumi:
This Love
See him, dream him
Lust over him,
Wanted him,
Badly wanted him,
crave for his notice,
Curved for him,
Through fasting for him,
Then he noticed,
Smiled,
Longing in his eyes,
Ran on wings,
Only for him,
To say, "I am married"

Tola Bolaji:
These words from this quill
Bleeds it's rhythm from my heart.
I have always wanted her from yore,
Before words could form in my mind
And love in her eyes.
I was the one who stood by her
Before legs could work and farther.
It was her tears that taught me to swim
And her sigh my fly.
If tonight I could share these thoughts,
And read to her lines of my breaths,
Maybe she will look in the light of my eyes.
But I will tear these notes tonight,
And it's lyrics burn to shreds in my heart.

Oscar Gwiriri:
I love you
How can I gyp you
Telling you I love you
With a mind asunder
Massaging stark mermaids,
My heart sleeping in shacks
Making love to midgets,
Harlots napping on my chest.
I know, but you don't know
Illusions taking me to Orgasmland.
Yes, I must say I love you
To spare your poor heart
As we make hot love
Yet I graze in Phantasyland
.

Malelah The Poet:
September,
Please come soon,
Because under your trees with crimson leaves,
Hearts will learn to love again,
Arms will clasp I pray,
Under the rays that'll peep through your trees September,
She will smile and I'll tell endless tales,
Of how I loved her before I met her,
When she'll tell me she's betrothed,
Or that her heart found escape in another cage that's not mine,
I will look at her crispy eyes and smile,
"I still love you lovely friend"
Because tell me September,
Must love be two ways?
Ask Jesus he'll answer that better,
If she tells me her heart is still tamed in her cage,
I don't know what I'll do,
All I know I'm a man who gets excited easy,
So maybe I'll climb up a bench,
Freeze time and shout,
To let it spread to the poles of the universe,
Sit back and stare at her,
Never have I found so much essence,
Stuck under the skin of one being,
September,
Please let my dreams grow from untouchable to touchable,
September please wake up.
If I could write a love poem

Sheril Ghuza
If I could write a love poem I would sit in the desolate park under the shade of the old baobab tree,

Remembering my many lovers, one and all,
Wind
Whirling in the rain leaving my heart rattling like a roof top on a stormy night;
A gusting chorus, music perfectly sang;
Fire
There was a warmth that she brought but as you got closer to her she devoured and consumed;
Smouldering and licking my wooden soul like a hungry lion;
Water
Her turquoiseness had been lost to the darkness but in the moonlight her ripples twisted;
She was so cold she stung;
Lightning
A bolt that briefly broke the utter sadness of my heart, cleaving my life in parts;
        And in a violent illumination I realised that she did not mean it;
If I could write a love poem I would sit in the desolate park on the rotting wooden bench;
Remembering how wrong I was seeking too much in youthful romance

Human God
(Best "New" African Poets Collaboration: Mhondera, Mairosi, p'Khisa, Gwiriri, Jaison, Nieuwoudt, Mwanaka)

Tendai Rinos Mwanaka
Its like a desperate attempt to gather against the emptiness, the way humanity created God. If he is God and we are humans, there is no way one can become the other and still stays their Godliness or Humanness. Its like the paint at the back of the mirror and the clear unpainted front of the mirror. The paint creates the mirror, the paint is God. The front of the mirror doesn't see the paint at the back. The two even if they work together to make an image, remain separated, none knows the other, what the other is doing. If you paint the front of the mirror, it ceases to be a mirror. Humans can't know the mind of God. Even Jesus didn't now! If Jesus was God and he professed clearly that he didn't know the mind of God, then he was human like Moses. God will know the mind of God. His mind is indecipherable: anyone who is human by any act, physical, emotional and spiritual has no ability to know God's mind. To say a human being knows the mind of God is to make God human, thus an imperfect being. It is to make creation imperfect, which it actually is in its natural ways. If creation is imperfect, if a human being is imperfect, the God the human being knows is imperfect, it's a Human God. Humanity has created a window between God and Humans. Both can see the other thus both affect the other. Its like that space outside your windows becoming your inside thus the two are inseperable. If I don't like my views I change them, the same with my views or viewers, if they don't like me they change me. This is the Human God infested in churches in every border all over the world. This is a God cut into small parts by small minds, we look closer into this fluff, the fluff stracture, the fluff regime, the organized government in the form of

religion with built-in ways to discard the questioners. The bigger question, I mean answer is, if God created everything, and is omnipotent, omnipresent, omniscience, then there is no need to pray to him. He doesn't want our puny noises. He is whole without our prayers. I think its inour juridical(Control) hubris thatwe devised prayer as important between God and Humans by misinterpreting God through our human minds, whetherwe claim spiritual guidance or not. Its just decay we are holding onto. There are no justifications. God has to have his time, his space, his perspectives, his world for him to be God and us Human. Why would he need ours to make him God.The bigger question is, how can a human being know for sure there is God?

Oscar Gwiriri
At Church gate
If I take off this metal jacket,
Wear your church sheath,
Wonder what can be of me,
Excruciated and straightening self,
Oh, what a horrible life style you live!
Morality, in what and whose sense, yet
Tormented by socio-vile moral prescriptions?
Yea, groomed you must be before 'em,
Ignorant of your delusions,
Worshipping a deit you don't know.
Who is sociopathic, me independent on streets
Or you with a whirling agnostic soul?

Chenjerai Mhondera
I think the soul is thin fibre,
Long, shapeless, sometimes lengthless, big, perceived, utopian
Abstract of figurine tall, dark, light shadow, countless feet, height earth into space,

Creation of lord of confusion, illusion and speculation
Who to endear frighten "souls" imaginary yonder
Where conviction illusion a fundamental rule
To decide sane and insane alike,
Moral and immoral in divides such
I am a proverbial chain smoker, with chains of condemnation from a lord of morality,
Whoever made that god a being I don't know,
Imbibe and fuck
Are two words utter disgusting, I for one come between lips mine, man, the man on pulpit
To banish I, entering their parish,
Maybe if I had soul I was at easy.
Man, you can define not if not flesh, mind, heart, blood plus conviction
Unless that conviction is soul, oh I bet convict, conviction, a set of thoughts, daring, is it courage... It's like trying to think yesterday, and you say today is tomorrow,
I guess you got the hogwash in what our spirits feed on from one esteemed, deemed to cross over from humanity to divinity
And in fear you hear hallucinations of Amen,

Cosmas Mairosi
Even there be wretches ready to kill for a penny
Is the love of money
Really the only root of all evil?
A thousand maladies have befallen every human civil
Long before Smaug's blast laid to dust enchanted islands!
The earth was still virgin
When Cain murdered and was murdered
Her gold bullion
Within her bowels was still intact
Her iron, her oil, her coal

Her pearls her rubies unharvested
Her diamonds untouched
Her silver knew no miner's wrenching greed
Yet brother killed brother
On the altar of sacrifice.
There was a puff of smoke
And today humans still smoke
Human flesh for a casserole dish
To the gods of war.
Somewhere on this planet once
Abraham must have sat with his sons
Isaac and Ishmael under a sycamore fig tree
Playing Padder and Nhodo with the boys
Haunched over beatific Canaanite sands.
Thousands of years fast forward
Abraham's children create ghost worlds of each other's boon
Posting souls to recline in the under gloom too soon.
Deliver me from doctrine-doctored nutrition demanding
decimation of my brothers and sisters
I am their keeper!

Jacobus G. L. Nieuwoudt
Try and figure out this smile,
Go ahead,
Try!
What might it hide,
These eyes will
Never tell.
This face of mine
Always looking high
As if this drug
I've been taking
Been making this

Face smile.
Wonder indeed,
As thought becomes
deed. However does he do
It? So free is he?
Wiggle my nose
Roman, Greek
Or Gothic
In my face,
It's plain to see,
No longer a freak,
For if they look like
me, and sound like me
And act like me,
It's kind of hard to convert
me.
It's always my birthday
Where I come from.
Go on?
Inquire about me,
Ask your MOM
How SHE cut my hair
To force my Gods
To run!
How she kept it short
And burned down my temples
So I'd be a slave to your MOM,
But
Alas,
My hair grew back,
And my eyes started to see,
You can't keep me down any longer,
And you can't whip me,

For I am,
Just as they are,
Unfortunate
For You,
And,
unfortunately
For HER,
It's impossible
To keep good Gods
down!

Oscar Gwiriri
Preach nomore
Behalt, Mr Preacher man!
Waste no time and energy
Sermonising to a wanderer
Abandoned by a prayerful mother,
Nursed by morphined monsterous hands
On the sweet streets of Soweto.
Is it the same deit you discourse about
Worshipped day 'n'night by mother?
Oh, let me rot in these drains
Or roast in the dungeons of hell
Than martyrising my soul
On mores never rubbed on my navel.
You evangelise about rebirth
Yet so many times I have died
Mind, soul and spirit roasted on bitterness.
Still roam quasi-alive in Soweto,
Wondering where was that god
When mother nailed six inches of hurt
Right into the inner me?

Lisa Jaison
How can God be God, when you keep being God
The judge, jury and executioner-that's you
Ruling over women, black, gay, and foreigner
Yet you still ask where be God
You who placed God on a pedestal so high in the sky where he can't hear a cry?
You called God man, yet you know men are deaf
Made God white, yet you know their penchant for colonies
And when God would not answer to this you cried foul
Nullified, and relegated God to the oxygen you breath
Good enough to deliver life, but not worth the say
You inhaled deeply and demanded God evidence
A God treated like a faithful, slighted and betrayed good village wife
Only good for home coming when life turns its back
Whose image is rugged, distorted and brutalised by fair weather lovers
Yet still she lives amongst, and within and us

Wafula p'Khisa
when the midwife cut the umbilical cord that bound us to ancestral womb
we scrapped off our tribal tattoos, wore the rosary
and burned the shrines of ancient gods with vengeance
to embrace a new deity, and sail through the rising spiritual tides.
we murdered our gods, and buried them in unmarked graves--
somewhere in the backyard of memory;
never to rise and set eyes upon our travails
then we sold our soul to foreign deities; we kill, rob & lie
for untold favours falling off their plate of benevolence!
so when a messiah, with a thick overflowing beard, was born in our village one morning

a bunch of christian faithfuls gathered at the market place, burned
his effigy & sang hallelujahs
for the holy ghost fire to torch him into bits of ash
They raided our shrine, stripped naked our lord, and dragged him
to jail like a lowlife pervert
scattering us all over, like subdued dreams of winter!

Part 2: Consciousness, Spiritual, Individual, Existential

Artist's Trails
Tendai Rinos Mwanaka

Signs that name objects speak about themselves but do not put the objects into words. When questions, I mean objects, cannot be put into words, when the words to search for the answers, I mean signs, are not actually words, the answers cannot be put into words, words cannot manifest into things, words manifests to themselves.

This Words Tower works its wounds for warnings, it says: In this Words Babel, no one is excluded from the knowledge of the roundness (life) of things, whether dead or alive. Life as a school; why not try to take its curriculum. The first lesson is on human touch, and the experiment is: Microwave your pride!

Here are the results:

Take advantage of the ever-changing point.
Unlike the fixed point where you can huff and puff locating it with your body, the ever-changing point requires the outside-the-body presence. Some might call that a soul, psyche, consciousness, conscience, spirit, *mweya*...
Just locate it!

Allow it to keep changing in the space. Add circular lines around its change fields. Lines that touch these ever-changing *change* points will together become your construction block. Set (put), what others might refer to as input and unset (unput) yourself between these construction blocks- gather yourself by inhabiting the emoticon theatre. Ask yourself, or just answer, "am I reversing the pattern of the physical body."

The art of finding the physical body does not support weight; rather it represents the weight-bearing emotions of human beings. Then ask again, "am I reversing the pattern of the spiritual body"

This is an ordinary enough telling, this telling and this not telling of things. The kind of things anyone may find themselves living with or not telling when talking about things:
Living, so say you what say I, tell of this switchback of shadows, a new organ that grows in your heart.

We trace the shadows of it against the download of itself, chewing just people things... like that; *walk-away-from-your-shadow* play. The shadow swallows him (its you) and it is warm in the inside of him as it keeps him from sleeping. He had no idea it was a burden of all two-sided things, the burden of every wish. What wish?

The stars horizon is an empty line of music, she (its you) basks in the trance of this music, the folded stars of Cassiopeia's dream go down the grid, then up to the nearest bright moment, hip down, and another moment joint up, and then again and again. See, See it. The see-saw, the spin-whirly. *Hmmm.* We are listening to the subterranean lullabies of plate-shift shitting and ordaining the extinction of us.

Selfish is neither sell nor fish. Marita was arrested for pretending to be in a marginal box, an imaginary box. Maryam was hospitalized in a nut house for impersonating longing, okay just attempting to sit on its thighs. Lazarus was jailed for trying to disintegrate himself-he now prays for small things. He now prays to the God of Small Things. I didn't say to the small god, a Buddha! Let this be victory enough, the echoes of us being in our heads against us.

Where are we without this, what are we without this, this is a revision, a beginning, a compromise, an improvisation- we will go our whole life for this and only and only, settling for something, anything, okay everything and then ex(im)ploding. I have made it a word! Feel it smash, shave and smooth away our directional mistakes.
We all owe rent!

Artist's Trails, frozen echoes, pure impressions of the truth! This is now where ideology criticism meets memes. We could give this language a heart. Keep talking; telling, talking: we can see it moves things. Half-half, Ho-hum. This language map.

He is just an average pen, going his normal routines, scribbling nonsense on paper with this black, blue, red…, ink; there is nothing to see here.
Vanquish the script!
Come back!

Pinnacle
Mari Ballot

Here-where in us   beneath us   above us
an indescribable connection an unusual unity   attaches   yet
liberates us
here-where enthralled we bond in wonder
here-where around us   adheres inconceivable consciousness
in purer atmospheres here permeate inexplicable energy
we speak without voice hear without sound see not with eye
touch without hands
here-where we booted-and-backpacked crampon-crawl
cautiously
measure steps   breathe sparingly
past precipitous heights on top off peak we can just be   be being
here-where we man-manacled combine trust and the divine
here-where we link not just with piton surface and rope
not just with one another but through one another
ascend with heights   through heights with and against extreme
weather with snap-ring soil snow mist even eagle-feather
except this sky bleeds blue drinks darkness   narrates rivers
dreams oceans   seeks souls searches spirits yet reveals more
than space
unites unknown unseen worlds
yet releases those that are already free
except sweat and tear even rain hesitates in their drop from here
except these winds toss more than their breaths across
except this boundless expansion holds
holds more than million years of mountain
more than fears   more than fibres of time
more than cliff and cave   somas of the brave
yet bears more than the wear of soil stone and abortive bone
it contains creation universe infinity eternity

it was   it is and it shall be ..... after we
here-where we conquer more than that-knowing   more than
miracle more than meaning more than thought   more than
being…
here the mountain summits us.

EGULE (the weaverbird)
Chibueze Obunadike

in my language, the elders say

"ihe okenye na-ahụ ka ọ nọdụrụ ala, nwatakịrị agaghị ahụ mgbe ọ na-ebili ọtọ,
ọbụlagodi ma ọ rịgoro n'elu osisi kachasị elu ma ọ bu n'elu ugwu."
(what an elder sees sitting down, a child will never see standing up,
not even if he climbs the highest tree or mountain top)

and it worries me,
because I cannot help but think that maybe I was born blind
maybe I was born with both hands fixed over my eyes

because how else do I explain
that all my life I have been walking into walls,
always confusing dead ends for open doors

how else do I explain that I have been living
in search of trees to climb,
like a weaverbird, body bent like a tree branch
just if to see things a little bit clearer

"nwatakiri ga-amalite ihu dika ndi okenye ma o buru na o no n'etiti ha."
(a child will begin to see like the elders if he sits among them)

all my life I have never been able to see
what lies just in front of me.
the elders say I was born blind, with both hands over my eyes

or maybe that's just what it means to be a child—

to be born a weaverbird,
body bent like a tree branch.

Rekindled
Athene Nyarai Mutyambizi

The wind whistles past me to define me
The voices gossip behind me to predict me
The odds play against me to refine me
But here l stand still in the knowledge of who l am
Fully comprehending my potential
In assurance and confidence l apply my hands to war
Like a huntsmen l walk alert
My bow and arrow in my hands aiming at the target
As l walk in for the kill

For a long time l lay in fear
Battling to walk out of comfort
In my mind lay different predictions
And certainly all of them led me to defeat
For a while l was stuck in that reality
It brought me nothing but doom and ill fate
Like a zombie l lived through life
And it just zoomed past me like l was an audience
I no longer can afford this feeling of looming death
I am alive and l come to life
I can no longer stand this doomed life
I am success and it's how l will live

My circumstances are not a part of me
They are the odds battling to refine me

My obstacles do not mean defeat
They are the farmers separating the grain from the chaff
I am in no way against impossibilities
What lies ahead are new mountains unexplored
But who are you Oh Mountains before me
Surely you will be brought low
Your days are numbered

Will Rise Again
Aleck Kaposa

I will rise again
tomorrow
after the stillborn dream
has been coldly dreamt
after the long awaited bliss
has been castrated
after the needle
has pierced the most delicate flesh
after hope's cadaver has been interred
and tears have been shed
after time has washed away the pain
the wounds will heal
and i will dream again
i will be a sun
and rise again

New born
Beven Nebafor Awusa

Under the comely eyes of the sky
As the city starts to rise
To a young morning growing into full bud,
A new star is born in a cold world
Slowly venturing out of the cocoon of the ordinary
Peeking into a small halt on the canvas of eternity.
Happiness is really rooted in simplicity
Complacent parents with no car but big dreams
No gold but a heart full of love
For their precious bundle of joy
Breaking the shackles of the prisons of their past.

In the wee of the very hours of the morning,
Far beyond the prairies of the East
Trees line a path that beckons forward to an expansive vista
Of a coalmine attended to by a retinue of men,
Black faces on svelte bodies, many torn t-shits.
The alarm of a phone blares away
Like a call from the Sistine Chapel
All activities come to an immediate pause
A dishevelled figure steps forward,
Talking on the phone as our minds explored the unusual-
"I just had a son." He shouted
We all hopped with bliss as wrinkles disappeared from our foreheads.

Our two hours' journey lasted just for a moment
When she peeled her sleep-deprived body off the bed
To present to us the new born
A soul trapped in a human form,

Mind as a lush landscape of potential and possibility.
Rarely did I see my brother cry
Though the cares of a sundered family rested on him and his wife,
Satisfied feeling suffused his whole body
Emotions moved him to sobbing.

"You are a child of the world." He said
Stirring into the eyes of the little being who yet had no name.
"By birth right, you are the citizen of the earth,
Let your imaginations carry you hither and thither as far as you dare,
Yonder every valleys and hilltops you set your mind upon,
As you conspire with the timeless laws of nature
Don't forget to do your best in all measure,
Striving to be better than yourself only
Never compare to any other being,
In as much as I should have loved to bask in riches,
I am only a coalminer, but I am happy
Dream and dance along the colourful horizon
You have no limits upon the world's shore."

As the shy moon's crescent appeared neath the narrow window,
We set off home with our new born, bound for glory and hope.

SALAT
(on fridays, prayer is a morning ritual)
Chibueze Obunadike

Friday is a solemn prayer in my mouth

I wake up feeling like I have forgotten pieces of myself behind in a dream

one where I am stuck in the middle of a sun-beaten bush path,
stretching out into nowhere
the bushes so thick and green that they begin to
twist themselves like memories into my skin.

I drag myself to the sink to wash my face and the way the water slips
between my fingers like prayer beads
reminds me of a story where the earth was destroyed in a flood

I want to make this body into an ark
to survive this ruin
but it is seventy percent water and does not know how to float,

which also means I am terrible at swimming

which is why in my dreams I always wake up to find myself drowning
flowing back into the ocean that made this salt-water body
& it is a journey that always unwinds me back to
the stream in my mother's belly.

Friday is the beginning of a cry in my little sister's mouth,
she doesn't want to get up and go to school,

the weather is too cold and her body too hot, in a way that breaks
out in a fever

behind us the day is breaking, and to the east, the orange ball
of the sun is just beginning to rise above the horizon.

downstairs, my neighbour is beginning to pray the salat.

I watch as he readies himself with ritual ablution,
his body slowly unwinding with the softness of the water
becoming a kind of purity, a kind of ruin

he bends his body like a foetus down on his worn mat
and the way the morning sun devours his kohl-black skin
wakes pieces of me up into a dream

I am back on that deserted bush path, drowning
as the first cries of prayer leave his mouth

allāhu 'akbar

To Be Named
Daisy May

At birth our parents choose our name
This is what we are called from then on
We are told not to judge people by what they look like
Yet you gave me a name based on who you thought I should be
Did I come nicely wrapped with all the trimmings like you thought I would be?
Was I disappointing because I never lived up to some false reality?
Moving through this life we are conditioned and taught
What things are and how to be
The only thing I can say for certain is that by naming and teaching me
You took all of me
All of the wonder out of this life
For now, instead of looking up at the rustling leaves the way they move and chatter
I now just see a tree
Because you named it you see
Instead of looking upon the crashing waves and endless waters with their fearsome power and magnetic energy
I now just see the sea
When looking in the mirror at my body
Instead of seeing how time has moved and shaped me
How the curves and the edges come together
How the ripples of age have tugged at me
I now only see fault
Because you named it
It is taking me a lifetime to unlearn the things I was conditioned and taught
It is taking so much time to come back to a state of wonder
With childlike eyes and imagination

And even while I sit here and ponder life and all its meanings
I ask you when you name your child
Remember to leave them with the wonder
For it is worthless this life
If not filled with imagination.

CANVAS
Dorcas Wairuri Maina

It's the canvas that stands out, oh what beauty
But when did I fall in it
I can taste the paint as I try not to drown
I must, I must stay afloat
I need to make sense of this
I need to understand how I came to be in this world
I will not let this entrapment become a reality
I will not let this become my new reality

I try to reach out to my ally but this stretching hand seems but a beautiful contour in this painting
I want her to see me, I need her to see me. I need that unstated promise of your seeing me when others can't to come to life. Right now! I can wait no more
Where's that support? Why are you choosing not to tell me the way out which is clearly visible to you?
But I will not let this entrapment become a reality
I will not let this become my new reality

As I sit on this new found comfortable corner, which must be the most alluring cause all eyes seem to focus on this one point
In my heart of hearts, deep within I only wish for one person that my mind interprets to be the ultimate solution but they're not in the showroom and telepathy is not an option
I refuse to let this entrapment become a reality
I will not let this become my new reality

I have to find a way, emphasis on the "I"
As I listen to the numerous opinions of these onlookers
Become privy to information I never thought I would ever know

And all I want to do is stretch out and become but the viscosity will not allow me
Nonetheless I will not let this entrapment become a reality
I will not let this become my new reality

The Season
Emman Usman Shehu

Out of the walls,
the stones
 wail.

Our of the roofs,
the rafters
shriek.

Out of the earth,
the skeletons
screech.

Out of the skies,
the clouds
bleed.

Out of the universe,
the asteroids
crackle.

Midnight sessions
Femi Ayo-Tubosun

I have heard cries
that break the sanctity of night-
they come in unrepentant tolls
that make breaths too heavy for swallow.
It was in them I learnt
that sometimes the pillars of home
cannot bear the burden,
and the comfort of mother's bosom
cannot heal some wounds.
When watery eyes turn away
from mine, I understand why
children should never see
their fathers cry.
Fire and brimstone prayers
have grown cold on lips
that offer no answers to a girl
who asks why blood has become
pins in her veins.
I understand that sometimes
the only reply to questions is silence,
and that even men of faith
have buried the corpses of prayers
that died on their way to heaven.

PAPYRUS UNDERGROUND
Kofi Acquah

Daughters became scavengers___
A time for the mystery,
They dug, they searched.

The tomb,
Stood night for visitors
For his breath wilted,
Like Sun-Day guava leaves.

The ground cried with him,
The graveyard failed a hymn,
His epitaph,
Was written in him.

Buried underground papyrus
Of intertwined diction and secrecy
Bulged out from a heart
Of misfortune.

O' wombless offspring
Save home in oneness,
For death is a Timeless Tree
It sheds dry or green.

When the star twinkles,
The living takes a leave.

The Cat and Cobra Duel
Samuel Nyachiro Kegwaro

Behind my house,
under that big tree.
A black cat challenges a cobra to a duel,
in the dead of the night.
The cat smote the cobra,
the cobra countered the challenge.
This is a deadly fight,
at the ungodly hour of the night.
That black cat is maimed,
the cobra's poison taking its toll.
As the cobra vanishes into the darkness.
But whose cat is this?
Whose cobra is this?
Perhaps
they belong to the night runner,
who knocked my door yesternight.

PROPHESY
Kofi Acquah

She sat between mounds
Yet,
Sight refused a chameleon-like
Tongue; grasping crown dialogues

Grasshoppers saw her nipple
When a tender enamel
Sifted from a sagging breast-milk

Like a soothsayer, she predicted
Like a prophetess, she prophesied
Giant thoughts bisected her womb
And soon inflected intoxicated voices___
I nosed air
through clapping palms
under thatched hut
On a woman's lap

The rain drips down the cheeks
Of trade winds
I squat to think a leap
Over the speaking jinx

For my eyes
Are fortified
above the smock

Locked out
Alinafe Diana Zalira

So many years
I have been struck with temptations
For a taste of the forbidden fruit
Sweet and juicy it looks

With just a gaze at its captivating beauty
My whole body catches feelings
My Mouth salivates, body becomes numb
And my head loses rationality

Lusting for this dazzling fruit
Like a baby longing for his nursing bottle
To squeeze, and lick its juice nicely with my tongue
To quench the thirst of ages

But Alas! Echoes of divine laws
Bring me back to reality
A taste of the forbidden fruit
Leads to eternal suffering…

The Believer
Aubrey Sandile
Unfit personage.
Ostracised populace.
Minority prayer points.
A bread of poverty.
An understatement small as a morsel
Extravagant coterie of corruptible comrades
Conclusion at the beginning
A leaping kangaroo court.
Something's will never be beautiful
Some songs will never be sang
Some people will never cry.
But someone will die tonight
A cold hearted believer.

A Mother's Song
Cosmas Mairosi

A Mother's joy; a Mother's love
A Mother's care; a Mother's pride
A Mother's dream; a Mother's hope
A Mother's Song ...
Is to watch her child bloom to fullness...

A Mother's heart
is full of unconditional love ...
A Mother's touch
is the gentlest of all touches ...

With her hands,
she weaves the magic that colours the horizons of her unborn
baby...

With her body,
she shields the vulnerable toddler
from all the ravages of the elements of the weather...

A Mother's presence
 inspires freedom, wisdom, warmth, security and confidence ...

To Eve - the Mother of mankind
for her name shall always remain truly a legend ...

To Sarah - the nonagenarian mother
for finding out how it feels like to be a mother at 90 ...

To Hannah - the prayer woman
for the countless prayers a Mother can say before a child is born ...

To Hagar - the concubine
when a Mother is in tribulation and error the hand of God reaches out and angels rush to the rescue...

To Queen Esther - on saving the Jewish nation from destruction; being a Mother of the nation means breaking taboos and taking life-threatening risks ...

To Judge Deborah – the warrior woman
a Mother can be fierce in battle if the survival of her progeny is threatened ...

To Abigail - On turning away David's vengeance on ungrateful Nabal's household,
being a Mother means intercession when destruction knocks on the threshhold ...

To Claudia- on warning Pilate about presiding over the trial of Jesus
A mother's dreams can guide the feet of royalty...

To beautiful Rebecca - Mother to the twins of contention...
Sometimes a mother's influence can improve the destiny of her favourite child ...

To Naomi –
being Mother to a son
also means being mother to a daughter (in-law)...

To Dorcas Tabitha –
being a Mother does not mean giving birth to a child ...
But denying yourself sleep every night making clothes for every child in the community ...

To Bathsheba, the widow of the warrior Uriah
Beauty has its price
But through perseverance, a Mother can loiter long enough
To remind a king to bestow the throne on her son!

To Queen Sheba of Ethiopia
It took a mother's pilgrimage across a continent
To approve the wisdom of King Solomon the Wise!

To Mary the mother of Christ, on willing Jesus to perform His first miracle at Cana;
Secrets can only be kept to a certain extent
Not until there is a crisis and you are mother of God
And know your son has the power to resuscitate marriage songs
And change the destiny of mankind!

To All Our Mothers ...
For every lullaby you have sung to each and every one of us ...
For every tear you have wiped away from our cheeks ...
For every first word you have taught to dance on our lips ...

A Mother's song...
calls to celebration
  the achievements, the selflessness and sacrifice ...
of a mother!

FOR MEMUNA AND CHILD
Ekundayo Asifat

THIS morning I wake up
To the song of weaverbirds
I squat on the ground
My eyes to the path that time treads.

Memuna comes
Dung-heap to the mortal world
Like gossamer, she comes
Stalling thoughts trailing time.

Lazarus comes, her child drooling.
Head is frond to the horde of the weaverbirds,
Flies squat on her back and scent wafts,
Scent of he-goat.

They tell me
She drinks from gutters, sleeps in stalls,
Gobbles fodder and wrestles with scavengers
Rooting life in the earth of misery.

Grains I offer
But none she would,
Craving her place among scavengers
Convention of heads in garbage

Witness now you cymbalists
Witness you town-criers
Witness how life wears dark robes
Because she has no voice in the rooms of debates

Where hands and feet weave human fates.

It cannot be that she comes too early
That we scurry to the summons
To hug a fate of spikes
But earth, we know,
They strive to shrivel
That we may clamor.

Memuna, since grains you will not have,
Seek life with full knowledge
That earth, this earth, is Men's heritage for adornment and succor
Seek the home of the mermaid
Stroll you like a queen
And drink where the gods pine:
Indeed our song will pierce the sky,
We whom fate of spikes trails.

We Are Just Humans
(For Luka Mwango, Zambian renowned creative writer, poet, author and script writer)
Gerry Sikazwe

We are merely human
Flesh and bone strapped together
Blood and air sewn in one
Even though we choose daily to be unlimited
We've climbed high mountains
Most fear to even dream of
As though we are who made them
Even though we are merely human
We've printed smiles bright and wide
And tickled many into laughter
As though we own peace and happiness
Yet we are merely human
We've swum in 'dile and 'gator infested rivers
Not once not twice but many a time
As though these savage reptiles were our pets
Yet we are merely human
We've painted our faces giantly in people's eyes
And our names mounted above the sky
That our talks and walks seem alien
(as if heavenly, godly even)
Yet we are merely human
We are merely human
Not gods for goals we claim
Not gods for gold we pluck
For we break and bleed
For we suffocate and hurt
And eventually, for we fall and die!

Right to Die!
Lusajo Kalangali

What's in love that's more precious than your partner's life?
Your mothers delivered babies,
 BUT
Their mothers delivered mice!
What's in money that's more precious than Albinos' life?
Your mothers delivered babies
BUT
Their mothers delivered mice!
What's in power that's more precious than your opponent life?
Your mothers delivered babies,
BUT
Their mothers delivered mice!
What's in …? What's in …?

Water, a goddess
Kelvin J. Shachile

Water is beautiful and makes things grow,
It is a woman, a goddess.
Water gives and snatches life
It is human, inhuman, a goddess.
There is a time when people wonder of it
But water is life.

Water is life.
In the whispers of the ripples over the polders we get hope.
In the sight of the clear liquid thirst quenches and life softens.
Drink, cook, clean and cool.
But water is lifeless.
And so on this very day, today.
I testify, that the sun won't shine, and even if it does,
I won't laugh and merry in its pretty face of yellow lights.
Because water has done it.

On this day, today. I remember only of yesterday.
When the upper dam burst and broke the concrete wall,
The water rushed with madness and had no keenness.
It neither knew a child, woman, man, cow nor house.
Down it went with them all.
It strangled and snatched life.
In the heart of silent shallow waters life drowns
In the madness of the floods and dam burst tragedy, water comes
And sweeps life along with the ripples.

Coming To Think About It
Gerry Sikazwe

Mother told me
to never fall in love with the night
Father taught me
to never be comfortable with darkness
Pre-school Teacher warned
I mustn't learn to enjoy dancing in the dark
Even Pastor preached tongue-twistingly
that I avoid the night
And now I know why:
There is beauty
beauty only night owns
only night owns
(And it is priceless)

Ubuntu
Mari Ballot

It speaks ....with anguish   a hunger   a heart that seeks ...with plagues   pains of the past   deserted roads of dissident dust   with unjust   with deceased spirits   voiced-words of poets of-old   (not with diamonds and gold)
its homes   hum with a sad song   its trees rustle with violent diphthong   dismal- disgrace that its grass sing   rebel-rain that its contaminated-clouds bring   it echoes with dreaded-disease   cruel-crime's   corrupted-unease   its defiled rivers run old atrocious-tears   new brutal-fears   its wicked-wind howls absurd blows a massacre-message unheard
Africa   once oppressed and possessed   now obsessed   somehow here guilt shoots no arrows   and this long awaited new noon   casts putrid strange shadows   under a liberated moon   the great freedom-wonder   are again torn asunder   'the dark river that moved many wheels' now tolerates those that murders   rapes   steals
land of freedom's greatest son   land of sailing ships in sun   where elephant buck and buffalo run   of shacks and shelters drums and slums   land of laurels of loving   dazzling high rise buildings native land of bush thistle thorn   of diamonds   gold   of animal horn   of mealie and corn   multifaceted   multilingual land amongst native flowers indigenous trees above magnificent mountains amidst nature's wild's that beat that throb along infected eroded bloodspilt roads
hear the babies   the children   the widows weep and sob   listen to aged   the victims   the dejected   the deprived   how much brutality will this future forgive again survive?   other evils sneak faceless in the crowd   so much is overlooked allowed   children no longer freely play   whilst citizens just walk away   just hope   just cope   some gather in steeple churches   visit malls of glass concrete and steel they shop   travel   try to ignore this ordeal   then huddle

home to high-fenced secured insulated fumigated air-conditioned bonded brick-houses…
it is our rainbow Africa that calls with penury malady suffering it begs it cries too many lies infected livers lungs eyes too many deaths festering flies too many prisoners distressed unsafe citizens it weeps it screams with excretion depletion decomposed dreams beg cry drowned in the frenzy flood of what we deny Africa of too many why's it suffocates in murdered blood it speaks it seeks it wreaks it shouts as it dies as it dies as it dies …

Things we do not know about death
Mobolaji Olawale

Its colour:
Is death the colour of burnt bodies or fire?
I get home and pull off my black shirt and trousers
But my skin remains dark and feels like another layer of clothing
If I could peel it off, I would find
A soul too black inside
Yet my heart beats relentlessly.

Its taste:
It may not suffice to infer that death tastes just the same as tears
From the premise that the tongues that have tasted death
Choose not to tell us anything ever again so that we can cry
And perceive something akin to death.
I will rather acknowledge my ignorance.

Its prodrome:
I visit a place death has been
Some seconds earlier than it struck and search around-
I am on a bridge
The polluted air masquerades as clean
I sniff and sniff, there is no stench.
I protrude my tongue like a police dog and taste air.
My face accidentally exudes terror, becomes the face
Of this oil transport tanker driver if he were to realize
He is losing control of his vehicle,
But the other motorists and I don't know that for sure.
Besides, the human body is sixty-percent water,
Fire cannot betray water.
Death is not here.
--- *Otedola bridge, Lagos (2018)*

4.
Monicah Lubanga Kuta.

All I hold on to is my ambition,
Dreaming and working hard to have more.
All we were told was that,
It ain't easy out here
No one told us, it could be this hard.
No one told us which way to take,
When we came to the crossroads
All they did was judging a fish,
From its inability to climbing a tree.
Better challenge a fish to
A swimming competition with a leopard
A good swimmer
And does not fear water nor getting dirty.
It has always had more than its ambition.
All I got in my make up kit
Is my cheap lipstick to help me lighten up
And a sincere smile for assurance
I'mma bring out the best in me
If it is a dream and not real,
Let me just sleep a little bit longer
Then wake me up when it is time,
When the real life wrath is relaxing
Then I'll be fresh with my bags packed
Ready to slap reality on the face
If possible, I'll keep changing Lanes.

THE HORSE IS BRAYING
Nkosiyazi Kan Kanjiri

Tell the chap the horse is braying.
Tell him to mount and ride
And stride into dusk
And disappear into sunset.

The clucks and trots we're waiting to hear
Of hooves raising dust
Disappear into distance.

Who cares where the sun sinks,
Be it in the dungeons of the Dead Sea
Or behind chain bound tongues?
Who cares?
When the chap is gone,
Nobody will shed a tear.
Notes

BP AT THIRTY
Mujtaba s Abubakar

We have so much ambition
Yet knowing it was prohibition

You strain your eyebrows
And blink at Parkinson's house
Repeatedly when you are tapped
Like the door when it is rapped

You can't get it out of your head
Unless you listen to a worm, lead

Times you feel paresthetic
The pins pricking your aesthetic
The needles urging you to go
Zugzwanged at chess, X and Os and Go

Your failure is coming to a beginning
You plan a mondegreen at the opening
And led your legacy astray
Or a dream you will betray

A googlegangster becomes your nick
Or pretend, ignorantly, john the wick
And use it all over Facebook
A model, a superhero…even a crook

Now, in dots, the light appears
When closed your eyes pray by the years
Just press your hands on
The eyelids curtain anon

But if unknown you have a mind
To win unknown approbation kind
Unknown labour will thy reward be blind

After the soap opera, your hands dirty
That's why we have BP at thirty

SCATTERED PETALS
Nkosiyazi Kan Kanjiri

In the hell that has become our homes,
We are scattered petals floating to a tune
That harangues our souls.
In the eyes of many we are dancers,
But the depth of our souls knows our fate
The ground is too hot to be still.
We are torn petals
Our stories are curved in our scars.

Spoken River
Nosakhare Collins

the faces bears the last names
of a broken heart stroke with grief
as we hear the spirit of streams cries
louder with signs of puddles into the heart

tears are weighted with felicity, floating
always on earth, soaked with sudden joy
for happiness obeys the law of heaviness
and gutted like sadness, and become normal

every sound has a height, to face the pap
with sound tiptoeing into a sea, rocking the
broken ribs, and smiling back at a flowing waters
seeking land to calm our fury soul

there are no too much words hold sorrows
the vast need to be broken, stable to tear off
the sound breaking into puddles
as every river break into the spirit of spoken river

here, we hear the river speak of felicity
when it begin to flow more, breaking into
qualified part, and seeking into the land
as earth is waiting to hear the river speaks his language

dum dum dum..
let the world hears of you
& let your greatness manifest
dum dum dum..
& let our heart be the history to be told

perhaps a new dawn
will speak of it.

THE NEW SINGING SCHOOL BESIDE OUR HOUSE
Okwudili Nebeolisa

When they opened shop opposite our house
I enjoyed their song, the lilt in their tongue,
It had a scent to it, decent and clean,
All they did for whole days was to sing.
Sometimes full and blurred images of them
Would come up in the windows where thick curtains
Stood, robed like people who were celebrated
For having finished school, each of them
Larger than life, as tall as the doors we had
In our house, or was it a trick of the light?
They loomed, their heads big as watermelons.
The door to their building was always open,
I knew because the few people who went in
Went in and out of their will, alike
In their slimness and tailored mannerisms,
The very opposites of the silhouettes
That came up in the windows, as if,
Taking on the robes, they were being adorned
With new spirits, their voices now becoming
Pools in which I would have been glad to drown in.
It was hot weather, their songs cooled the air,
Finches moved from the tree in our backyard
To the sill of their windows, daring the sun.
They became a major presence in my life,

Turning my days into daydreaming nights.
Despite the sugar they had in their voice
When they sang I didn't join in their chorus.

SOUNDLESS CAVE
Okwudili Nebeolisa

I could hear it, the quick chugging noise
Of tomorrow, but what was sad was that
I couldn't find myself in it, alien
But not of my doing or undoing,
The engine of tomorrow was crushing me,
Millennial that I was, already
Nestled in my own cosy soundless cave.
This dream my psyche wouldn't wake up from,
Like a vowel that refused to end.
I could hear the fast song of tomorrow,
It was like cancer branching out in my lungs,
I could hear it eating me, small morsel
By small morsel, especially while I slept.
How long would my much admired, much chastised
Perseverance on exclusion lead me on?
Time had wound me to a mighty boulder,
Harmattan wasn't going to spare me,
Didn't consider my young body,
Leaving my privileged mind to wander.
I was ash already but I was a Phoenix.

BODIES AND SCARS
Paul Oluwafemi David

(i)
Home is a drug when you live in it and poison when you embark on journeys like patients.
Bodies are the only stories where beautiful things get their stars from scars.
Our bodies are stories written under the cloud of a firmament and etched out as glowing stars with wounded scars flowing through the jar of the sky to win the war that nights gives with darkness, with diseases or things that knocks the door of bodies
To change its name to illness.
Wounded bodies burn the most, shine the most to invite fire to screen bones and flesh with health.
Wounded bodies faint the most, fall the most to invite help from friends snoring on death.
Dawn is the most beautiful because it has been wounded
by nights,
Days are the most beautiful because it has been wounded
by darkness.
Fire burns through the scars of smokes that chokes out stars to float
rainbows as healings.
You've to understand how bodies burn here, how bodies die here, how bodies drill hole to itself to become scars or wounds with rounds
of vibrations without sounds.
Bodies with scars becomes the most beautiful thing.
You've to understand how bodies shrink here, how bodies blink here, how bodies bore hole to itself to become scars or wounds with pounds
of mesh without flesh.

You've to understand how bodies warn its families, beg his families
or kneel for his families because of the flood coming to silence
bodies who're lost inside the world through genocide.
You've to understand how bodies dig its own graveyard alive to
find rest
inside their bodies instead of embracing the door through their
body
leading to the world.
Inside your body is where you're safe not home, not the world.
Inside your body is where all wounds and scars closes up like the
Venus fly trap to defend you like a seamstress called platelets
stretching away scars into stars.
People don't know how bodies relocate to the hospital searching
for home.
The world lives outside your body like an ectoparasite to drain your
blood and render you lifeless, formless and useless.
You're safe in your words not inside the world.
(ii)
This is a poem that begins from travelling through the bodies of
men
and women who're strangers and passengers to their own bodies
because it was hijacked by terrorists through a nomenclature
brought by microorganisms that rules the world in the hospital and
sick beds to change the name of beautiful things like health to
disease.
I know patients wonder how their bodies left home so soon as a
stranger or
Visitor to forget families.
I know patients wonder how bodies can sink deep like the titanic
down the ocean of love to betray jack and rose and leave scars
widely open through memories and wounds to own bodies captive
forever in sickness and madness.

Moments you didn't prepare for makes love eternal, makes it last like a cast from the heart.

I know patients wonder how bodies leave home like a prodigal to lavish all its health and happiness in journeys only to come back stranded, broken and wounded like diseases called idiopathic.

I know patients wonder how bodies leave home like Abraham to search for the promise land in journeys only to grow old with scars to meet it inside his body.

You should've waited to spell happiness among widows, orphans, paupers and people who've drowned outside their bodies like Lot to become a salt sea.

You should've waited to spell stars among victims, soldiers, warriors and travelers who've drowned outside their bodies with evil marks like Cain.

You should've waited to spell love among thugs, refugees, prisoners, addicts and people who've lost outside their bodies with crime and felony searching for families and parents.

Nobody can search for what he doesn't have already.

This is a sad poem with days and nights running a relay to either pass on the baton of light and darkness.

This is a sad poem with rays and trays hawking dreams to bodies with scars, it's a sad poem with dawn and dusk kissing and vomiting blood from the poison from eclipse.

This is a sad poem with happiness and sadness playing together and departing as enemies at the same time from the poison of diversity.

This is a sad poem with men and women getting married and divorcing at the same time from the poison of closeness.

This is a poem with bodies and scars dying and living at the same time because of the poison from death.

I write fast when am sad, bite vast when I'm hungry, write best when I'm wounded like Africa who went through scars to own the Body of poverty, disease, corruption or under development.

Nobody can be lost without leaving his body, can carry disease without hawking sickness.
(iii)
Bodies wear their scars when they leave home to journeys, when they leave words for worlds, when they leave love for land, when they leave purpose for power, when they, leave religion for atheism, when they leave dawn for dusk, when they leave days for nights, when they leave light for darkness, when they leave faces for ghosts, when they leave minds for money, when they leave confessions for colonization or when they leave beauty for surgery. Bodies wear their scars when they leave their bodies to jump outside it and embrace the world.
This is a sad poem with questions and answers frowning at darkness
to invoke the sun in lieu of the moon that allows disease.
This is a poem that begins from a sad African, from Africa to see fear,boredom,spells,darkness,pain,rust or doubts on the faces of people who're already broke the law of health to be lost outside their bodies and exist as a number working for death.
I'm writing this poem with blood to later suffer from hemophilia, writing this poem with blood to rent my body to nights and live in it forever at dawn
where rapture
reads the scripture
like a pasture
where future
culture
can take the picture
of the bone
like x-rays to give rays to shadows.
Shadows turn on their rays when days are
lowered deep inside the grave of darkness where the moon becomes the only safe casket where nights are thrown to bodies

as dust to say goodbye.
This is a poem that begins from starring through the window of a speeding bus
to recognize lost faces, wrinkled faces, betrayed bodies, ageing cells that has given up or quitted life
to be able to glow as stars in the night because of scars.
This is a poem that begins from opening your love like a tap through the scars of patients, victims and statistics that walks through the street as home because of the pain that calls parents cowards or families as bastards because of tears.
Tears open the door to scars when it becomes a dam rushing through blood vessels like a mad memory that has chosen its fate.
Tears open the crater on bodies when it becomes a geologist digging through flesh like an archaeologist that has found a treasure without a name.
Bodies wear their scars when clothes can no longer cover nakedness, when powders can no longer thunder, when lipsticks can no longer paint, when perfumes can no longer invite insects, when legs can no longer enter shoes, when wrist watch can no longer measure time, when bodies wear scars as a permanent tattoo.
Bodies wear their scars when home becomes covered with war, when land becomes loose like genitals, when health becomes gone like wealth, when nights sharpen regrets like arrows, when dawn exposes scars like artifacts, when goals become loans and debts, when faces are filled with wrinkles without jingles, when dreams knock on homes without doors, when purpose finds strength on a weak mindset, when potentials lose the essentials of victory, when tears replaces smiles ,when words die walking inside the world, when shadows betray bodies in their past.
This is a poem that begins from travelling through bodies with scars where the world turns into a waste land, dustbin and dumping

site where microorganisms lives to corrupt the cell through their
investments that mocks Warren Buffet.
This is a poem that begins from travelling through forgotten bodies
left in the hospital alone to be remembered with another
name that can only be called with silence or whispered
quietly for another man not to be angry, offended or depart
from the anger and smell brought
by just calling a single name.
This is a poem that begins from remembering names that
cannot be called to get an answer without fear because it's a
name of a disease.

Mother baptise me
Sinaso Mxakaza

Mother baptise me with your tears
Send good fortune back to me
Your skin is a bible unread
Our eyes are heathens
Time sits in your pores
enchanting gods that don't know our names
You carry yourself like a forgotten city
Place me together in this season
Life has put too many things over us
Every time we come back to ourselves
We need cleansing
What rituals cure us of sickness and heal families?
I see your mother in your eyes
Maybe that is why you don't want to cry
I am a broken child with a vow to always heal
So sometimes I cry for you
I have come for all the women that my body can't carry
Who will love me like your secure arms?
Mother don't die on me
I have no place to bury you
Baptise me with your existence

Ode to my mother's friend
Awodiya Funke

My mother's friend died of hate,
She was stoned to death from birth
All her life was spent in shame
Because of her bequeath from nature
A skin with no pigment

her crime was tied to her neck like a bell
announcing itself everywhere she goes
her blood is strange for her clan
she was odd to be her mother's child

her siblings hide their bonds with her
enjoyed her wealth murdered her health
her mental slate harbored resentment
she labored till death gave her rest

she struggled to live in a world she didn't belong to
what is her transgression? to be born with a weird coat
she never asked for, golden grasses she learned to accept
blisters stick- on her face, hurling rainfall of stigma

from pool of her mother's blood
resentment welcomed her,
hugging her with tons of myths
turning her to a girl with thorns

life pushed her away to an unknown place
where she found home, silent tomb
in peace, her piece was lowered
to rest beneath six feet

Find yourself
Sinaso Mxakaza

There will never be another you
so sit like you own the sun, find glory in this light
Even with all your disasters constantly tripping you up
The broken state of home is a curse
following you into spaces reserved for love and light
The failing state of our countries wrecks havoc
on people's stomachs and wrinkles their skins
Believe in the simple and natural beauty you are
Your hair is your heritage, wear it with pride
Your skin is a source of your bloodline
Recite your clan names like poetry and get to know yourself
This is how your history has survived
for years on the tongues of each generation
Praise the divine people you have always been
Your ancestors are gods of their own
Black will always be beautiful in its true form
Tune out misappropriations about who you are
Listen to the new voices giving life to the beauty we are
I put myself and my people down on paper
so the young can find documented traces of themselves
Opening new worlds to their eyes
They shouldn't doubt their presence or believe they are ugly
It kills children softly to believe the world doesn't have a place for them
Quote a poet and find trace of yourself immensed in these pages
The revolution will be prioritised and it starts with you and me

New Life -
Crystal Warren

The trees
so severely trimmed
in spring
spring back to life
in late summer
stark bare branches
now covered
by fresh new leaves
so green they shine

FREEDOM
/ˈfriːdəm/
Benjamin Elemide

Freedom (n.): (uncountable) the state of mind
when dreams are undressed of darkness
and adorned with regalia of hopeful realities.
Example: I know why the caged song birds;
it is because air is medium for sound's freedom.

Freedom (n): (countable) the reality of madness
where rags are the glory of youthfulness,
and grey weeds grow on aged head of sanity.
Example: unrestricted freedom of expression makes
nakedness speaks openly on the street of eyes.

Usage: freedom of speech - right that only exist
in lands whose citizens are dumb dumbbells.

Freedom of franchise - right to vote (after which ballot is stolen);
to be voted for as animals (snake that steals,
monkey that loots, and cows that range on the grave of lives).

More examples of sentences with freedom:
We'd know what freedom truly means
when human lives have more value than cows.
We'd know we are free when freedom frolics freely
without fear of being abducted into bondage.

Freedom (synonyms): liberty, wind, madness
Freedom (antonyms): constraint, bondage
Collocation: free, freed-dom, free-doom
Logic: freedom is when a freed dom
is free of doom.

Forgotten letters
Fethi Sassi

Every morning, I sit on the edge of the tree
To learn forgetfulness
Some dead leafs fall on my head
Forgotten letters from the tree
I was really sad when I read them
And I imagined that I whispered a sentence to the wind
The sun is far away from me biting its fingers
Shying from me
Escaping memory
Like an evening sleeping on a stair

COLOURS OF WATER
Benjamin Elemide

What does it means to have rain of colours
bow to lines falling into blank page?

You said it is having beautiful souls
in the cabin of ship bearing memories.

What does it takes to discover doors
to heart whose body houses rainbow?

You said colours are one flesh in many regalia,
and deep into skin we see the colour of love.

I remember how you walked into sky,
merged into one verse of song - black.

You said we should be water, without or colour
or tribe, till we flow into every thing and every place.

The fingers of the night
Fethi Sassi

I am still a child
And I still simply suck my fingers every night
So that the shadow won't sneak into my room
The room that I'm afraid of dropping
And I still like to play with my neighbor
My mother still beats me on my fingers
When she catches me sucking
the fingers of the night in the garden

my religion
Goodenough Mashego

my religion is love
designed by powers above my ability to decode
granted me to babysit til i pass the buck to the next
i got full custody of a feeling some still fail to explain
goes beyond your reasoning tis loss & love all rolled into one
capulets & montagues only gave this gift a human face
i choke in its grasp & know it's time to pray
i cough positive vibes tick a minus make it a plus
for a god never seen who art beyond my reach
me his weakened reflection manifestation of my religion

my religion is love
it's babysitting the amputation of your limb so you can become a pistorius
watching you groan from chemotherapy hoping that gives you more life
please live for the day we shall meet again
i watch you wave goodbye hoping i shared your pain
my religion is love for today tomorrow & forever
taking a cursory look wondering why the dead look @ peace
for tranquility belongs to those who can no longer offend the living
peace of mind in the here is a commodity we transact for with breath

my religion is holding your hand & humming kaddish as you gasp for last breath
i can see through charades so self-mutilation presents a blank canvas
we can paint beautiful pictures hoping censors don't edit
hoping our vulgarity is not AGE RESTRICTED like zuma's spear

we all say what we know while we write what we like
love unabridged for some reserved for after-life
i kneel down with a smile text my wishes to the giver
my religion is looking you in the eyes & seeing my reflection in you
you my mirror when you jolly & when your look tormented

my religion is building castles I'll occupy with the rest
it's inhaling sticky durban poison passing the spliff to the world
never calling nobody infidel though my heart is whiter than your robe
I'm the face of imperfection still searching for my map to Valhalla
my GPS designed by the devil only programmed with brothels & drug houses
i become the face of denial that hate can triumph over love
my religion is love & an admission i might be wrong
i see jews & arabs as two sides of the same coin
I'm lost i know but i see goodness in cruelty

my religion is treating you like a recovering addict
administering methadone with the precision of cyanide
remaining patient when you relapse that's the passion of a junkie
i watch you suffer knowing tomorrow starts our long-awaited harvest
the bitter fruitage will be chucked out to the birds
juicy grapes main ingredient in our anarchist ale
it's being a sentry @ the gate of an abode i shall not enter
a birth i was destined not to witness
me being a midwife as you deliver wild seeds cursed from womb
i give you a torch to navigate that cave after you dropped it in haste
my religion is watching you suffer knowing like gold you'll emerge polished

my religion is not casting the first stone for i deserve a firing squad

what you called a lunar eclipse were my sins being couriered to god
boxes & boxes of my contraventions of the Ten Commandments
i exist for the day when i shall reach perfection
letting the naysayers live so they can witness my crowning moment
calling my ancestors' names hoping for a domino effect
if there was greatness in this clan hoping it rubs off on me
my religion is seeing myself in you without you calling my name

my religion is not churchgoing but keeping the altar on sight
inking tattoos of the crucifixion lest i forget the sacrifice
kneeling down closing my eyes lest the devil interrupt me
yelling AMEN not as an ending but an index to my prayer
my religion is not being colour blind for i know white from black
seeing that smirk on verwoed's face as a smile of defeat
the furher's open-hand salute an honour to souls lost during the passage
zionists an ebola virus in the blood of middle east
my religion is loving my neighbour as i love me since i can't love HIM if i can't love you

Canticle of an Electric Storm
Harry Owen

Tonight's maternal sky licks me, her cub, the way forward,
our evening world a scalpel-tongue, cryptic procedure,

time as surgery, every hot corpuscle engorged.

I watch creation flicker here, twitch in conception,
the horizon naked as a lover – unashamed

Mother Earth asserting her fierce fecundity.

Consensus is our covenant, but I'm the real one
where magic bethinks itself to whisper, where singular

becomes plural, delivering us, delivering us.

Praise then to oceans, darkness, skies for revealing
what I am, what you, we are, what life is, as palm fronds uplift

faces, eyes into the dusk's warm amniosis of rain.

[*First published in The Kalahari Review, August 2018*]

Heaven is not Closed
(A poetic narrative of Bessie Head's short story)
Lwanda Sindaphi

Ralokae,a non-believer
Glathebege,a beiliever
The love between the Galathebege and Ralokae propels the
missionary to close his church doors.
He engenders skirmishes,
cripples the feelings of the poor with holy verses,
loads the obedient believer's tongue with the Trinity,
hypnotises Galathebege's bewildered spirit to not be able to breathe
without a pulpit.
Love transcends fixed dogmas.
Love transgresses boundaries.
Love fails dismally to indoctrinate,
for love indoctrinates itself.

He believes that there can be no place for god and gods
No social cauldron to cook both the blood from the Son of Man
and that from the kraal.
There is no heaven for slaughtered goats.
Cowhide-wrapped bodies;
bellowing cows;
intestines draped around the neck.

The love between the poor implodes heavily.
Leaving internally-scarred bodies, a well of woes:
the godly devil continues to wrench it,
igniting it with heart-piercing quotes from the book of Man
Jesus' blood becomes perennial gasoline.
The fire cannot speak of hate.
It stutters, and stutters,

fails to build gasoline boundaries
for love transgresses boundaries.

Heaven is closed,
but the kraal is open.
the poor chooses the closed door.
The poor knocks on the door resolutely
to beg for a place in heaven.
The missionary closes his doors.
Closed doors mean no spirituality to the poor;
absence of spirituality means no heaven to the poor;
absent heaven means no Jesus to the poor;
absence of Jesus means loss, miseries,
means anti-Christ to the poor.
All of the above means you will burn in hell to the poor.
Her - Galathebe's - heart sags heavily from agony,
disheveled,
deformed.
Her bosom carries colonial boulders.
She holds onto the crucifixion blood
with bleeding palms
and weeps together with the human-lamb.
Expulsion from the man-made heaven becomes a handkerchief.
"Heaven is closed to the unbeliever"
says the bearer of hate,
but then love transgresses boundaries
to *build*
heaven for the poor.

The Tree
John Anusie

There's a tree shooting from the soil.
I have no idea what it is called,
And sorry I'm not giving it a name.
Will it choke the corn,
Given its fearful proximity?
I'm thinking of killing that tree
That the corn may grow.

I am the son of my father, I guess,
For thinking to kill that tree.
How will its death profit me?
Has it not a right to earth as the corn?
Has it not a right to earth as I?
Am I not silly in not seeing its service,
Or in choosing to be blind to it?
Am I not the evanescing silhouette
That tree is trying to save?

Ero Gospel
Michael Ace

my brother's head is an array
carrying the weight of an indexed scripture
you could see how his ligaments John his bones
to build the framework of his body
how his arteries Mark the tunnel
that depicts the Ruth of life's intactness
how he Luke(s) at demons
like the soldiers looked at Christ at Golgotha
yet there is a kind of storm he fought
that lamed the verses he knew
he'd say some wars cannot be won
& a man shouldn't live by the words of God alone
but also by the bread on a woman's chest
he said these words & heaven wailed
then Jesus wept

River Rituals
Sibulelo Manamatela

A green beam hovers over the river
A naked woman stands on the brink
Her oiled black body glistening silver

Under the bloated moonlight
She slithers slowly towards the beam
The child at the bottom of the river opens

Its skeleton face and swallows her scheme
Calls her to sing it a lullaby and ease
 it into the empty crib in her womb

She licks its bones clean of silt
And grooms it in her barren heirloom
It is born genderless before time

The witch bottles the not-yet being
And buffers its form in a smoky fluid
Made of moonshine to smother ageing

She shovels a cross in clay
And buries it for another day.

Lost
Ntseka Masoabi

A while back,
I reflected the journey of my life inside the meeting room mirrors
of my mind.
I whispered to my reflection to come back home
to myself,
to who I truly am –
A winter afternoon motionless wind in my backyard
decorated with patchy green lawns
and wooden benches.

Night Bloom
Zahraa' Raadhiya Khaki

It began at the centre of my palm
A soft, pulsating ache
Evidence of the Passion
About to Tremble
through my Sapphic limbs
That unravelled Upward
-Vesuvian burn
In Ascending intensity
Driving into my chest
And unfurling
s l o w ly
A flower
Night blooming
and torn
Wilt tethered petals

Stretching outward
To encompass
A Change

MONUMENT
Sipho Mthabisi Ndebele

I have always wondered
What it must be to raise children of your own
In a land that isn't
I have never had the courage to ask my father this
Although in my quiet spaces
I have imagined how he would answer me
How he would be silent for a moment
Gasp
Hold my gaze
And with a voice drawn from 62 years of breath
He would say
"Son
There are a handful of days I have spent in this temple
That have made all this worship tangible,
Almost all of those days have been tied to my children"

My father is made of simple things
Of dirt
You can see it in his skin
He knows no way other than sowing
It is homecoming for him
He is sandstone
I have heard it said that the Sphinx
And other ancient monuments
Were made almost exclusively from others like him

How they were chiseled but never collapsed
How they were carried across the wilderness
How they found themselves home
In places they were never meant to be

My father is a monument
Time and other men have tried to break him
But he has held together
Even though defaced
Every bit of debris has gone to make us
Monuments in waiting
My father is a giant towering over foreign lands
You can see it in how he does the little things
How he tills the soil as if it were his
As if molding his children
As if writing in botanical hieroglyphs

My father has been farming for 34 years
All he wants at retirement is space to raise things
A place to call home
When he tells me this
I smile
Hold his gaze
And with all the years of breath I have behind me
I want to say
I pray that this earth is as kind to you
As you have been to it

Sabrun Jameel
Zahraa' Raadhiya Khaki

Sabrun Jameel
Patience is Beautiful
Endurance is Peace
Bind
Your root springs forth
Bind
you are Endure
Bind
you Sprout
But where is my Soul?
Burning and tamped
Bindbindbind
Ropes I lash around
Biting, snarling, digging
Inextricably bound
Post with edges double
Impaling on both ends
Ropes falling, whips rising
Self flagellation
They whisper
Behind the padded door
I can't tear.
My nails are shorn
-feathered razors
that's all I feel
I feel I feel I feel

Mothers who are fire
Xolani Ntuli

It's a full moon the night carry the water with the giving hands to give life
Inside the house the family quench the thirst for their body have turn to be dry lands
For everything is connected we are family brothers and sisters

In Their garden they reap what they saw for mother earth feed all yielding green plant for it to be food in their broken hearts

They don't worry about what tomorrow hold for it had rain and poured seeds in their stomach

I know of a boy who never had time to solve a riddle in this holy book

He is what rough seas left behind

Water comes to freeze in his burning eyes

In his mind everything is swallow by the light that shines bright

His mother's absence is floods and his father has mud inside of his bones.

To heal a bleeding wound

The blood comes out frozen praying

I had a mother who was once fire but water drowned her

My mother is a desert with no trees to house the oxygen

through her I can't breath

Her absence is a boiling volcano in the temple of god

Mother's burn into ashes and smoke up to follow the cold wind with no direction of where to go

In the tradition where Queens don't honour their kings to build a family from the fertile soil together to make gods image out of it

We become children's who are chasing fire for warmth

We seek knowledge wisdom and overstanding in the air for we don't know where our mothers dwell

Only when the teacher left the lesson never learnt
For fire can cook my food
It's flames warm me when misused it's burn me

Somehow I wanted to ask my father
of how my mother heart beat sound like
In my taste buds

I can feel visions of him memorising her in the darkness at night

His eyes burn hell flames for nothing can stop the fire from burning

She has no face her planets is Venus
Orbiting

Next time I see her in my dreams
She will be on my fathers face

Baptising him again with holy flames

I never love again these words remind me mothers who disappear
in the mist

Whose absence is a volcano and has names built out of smoke

When ever is cold my mother returns
Still without a face but a body of planet Venus

She burns our garden and soak into the volcano

She is water in the fire she is never
Coming back all is left is ashes

I don't know if she is out the in the air breathing life

But I am.

SEEN
Adatsi Brownson

For months, mouths spoke and narrated
the ordeal of former days
that are yet to be repeated

My eyes and ears wished
they saw and hear, this days so
but the heart is afraid to bear

Are stories true?
And can threads move through
like the unseen eye of a needle?

I became a sentry, just to see stories manifest
My pens are yet to swindle nature
to meet the synopsis of a dreadful dance in hell

We've seen Rome collapsed
And here you are dancing to the pompous array of words.

When last did I see hell break lose?
But today, I spotted hot stones dine with ice.

Are stories true?
Should I say overcrowded water base
Or simply flood.
The long discussed and awaited unwanted
has arrived, just in my dish plate.

Give me a space, for I have seen beyond hell

I can now clearly see money and blood yell
And anything I say here can be used against me in the Court of realistic fiction.

Now all your stories about the destructive flood
rendering people homeless is seen.

Survivor or a warrior
Xolani Ntuli

I'm not from this universe
Nor A star from the milk way
To drink colours of raindbow
After summer rain
A tribute to symbolise long life
Of the earth
Born from man and woman after being aborted by darkness
I come as a God
Written the trueth in burried scriptures
Black and white

Sometimes i fall like a shooting star at night shading a beam
Killing old habit with the first light
Only to rise again like the sun

I didn't come like a hidden fighter
I came as a soldier
Using my mind as a weapon
Seven seals of solmon
Sacred text in my heart

Blood river for the lost knowledge
Await for the new generation to be taught
How to live like a God

I come like a messiah
Comforter of mourning night
Who am I not to be
Healing the blind to see
Breathing life with my aura raising the dead
Awakening the holy ghost
With my words
The genesis of the book of life written in this temple with the
burning lesser
Blessing all the leaving things

Fire burning
Only the sinners
Because even the mistake can kill

tattoos are permanent
(for prof. peter horn)
Adorn Keketso Mashigo

no man is born of weakness because existence
is strength. some say no man is born of strength because
everything that was born of a woman will one day die,
but when bones grow frail wisdom grows strong,
then from the particles of your grey hair we
build a literary ocean for many generations to
drink from your mystic fountain of immortality,
because when drops of rain hug, like words embracing,
they make for a river with beautiful songs,
like when the wind kisses and caress trees at night the song
becomes an epic poem to last our sleep until morning,
you are music to the deaf, quintessence clay to heal the blind
because your poetry is the divine of all sweetness and joy
it transcend the physical universe of reason.
what wine have you drunk that purified the
potency of your speech and gave your poems
little gaudy wings to fly beyond space and time.
because solomon was given knowledge of the speech
of birds and his existence dominated the wind,
your existence dominates space, just like the butterflies of your
words.
man is composed of water and clay but to age is when the
body observes final stages of human evolution,
it is to be dust, to be water, to be clay, to be the stars,
because selfhood must be abandoned before the poet
can enter in unison with the mystic,
because the fire of the quran teaches us that
when Abraham was cast by Nimrod's orders into the flames,
the fire was miraculously changed into roses, your poetry

manipulates speech into honey, it is like a river in paradise.

Tree of life
Xolani Ntuli

Inside my body, live an organ
That has thousand beat
On hands drum kick in a day

I feel heavy weight in my bones
that make me want to vomit my heart out.

Launched inside my ribs
To be protected and guard against lovers
And drinkers of blood

Teary eyed you will witness when im lonely

Quenching my thirst with tears
Waiting for a saviour

I feel pain inside my chest
Fuel slide down to my stomach
My brain burn my daily calories
But i don't stop swallowing

My belly is full i can't digest or manifest the holy spirit

I love a girl with my mind body and soul last sunny day
It felt like two people in one body
Nakedness surface for the first time on

My eyes
Separated fingers battling to form a feast
But they won't love an abusive boy

I have a bad taste when it comes to sweet things
My mouth won't allow me to swallow
Can't feed what is holy to the dogs

I have a bad smell like a rotten meat

I set on the tables as if it was at last supper with the disciples
I recite a prayer with my heart

Someone will hear this agent voice
Hymns and rhymes screaming inside my veins

At home
We don't only pray
We meditate

mother land
Archie Swanson

somehow we dare to think
that we can own the land
yet land owns us
lures us in
beguiles us with her charms
invites us to place our dead within her dusty arms
to plant our seed deep into her belly
and call to god for rain
we defend our right to own her face
direct the creases of her smile
and mine her frown
we recognize the hill
the familiar mountain
the path of youth
place of our fathers
yet land does not care
does not turn her head to see
or flick her braided hair
does not hear whisper or gunshot
is not thirsty for the blood we spill
exists to be eternal dust beneath our feet
from whence we came
to where we go
impassive holder of harvest and of drought
place of ancestors and of beasts
through which the long wind blows
across the shores of years
of aspirations
epochs
of civilizations

In the Marrow of a Yellow Bone
Beaton Galafa

I was forged from hell fire and disease
That if I licked the world with the tip of my tongue
It would crumble and melt into tiny bits of broken glass
That would be washed to the sea and cut throats of sharks
And dig wells at the centre of the earth to drain all oceans
And leave the world barren and thirsty again.
I fell from the centre of the sun trying to get around the heat
That burnt my skin dark and made the nose and my lips swell
I am a lunatic who thought it wise to denounce my race of apes
The best treatment I deserve is to throw me back into the zoos
On posters side by side with lions and one giraffe craning its neck
Into the future to see on my behalf if there is some light in the bone.
I am nothing but a thousand corpses with sores eating me from within.
I am here to find my way to greatness through ancient walls and temples
Through the poor factory workers and kids eaten slowly by competition
That culminates into long lonely jumps from the 15th floor of restaurants
And echoes of hollowness into the nights that follow
Lonely mothers staring into the eyes of lonely fathers
Their hearts in conversations on what one thing they would have done
If they had the power their country wrestled away from them just once.

IN A GODLY WORLD
Blessing Turvey Damasiki Chimunyapule

A capless structure stands erect.
As builders struggle to install the cap.
It casts a dark shadow upon continents.
The cap's sight like a blade pierces soul,
Pushing them towards their demise,
As mysticism reigns.

The ruling elite works on the structure.
Everyday driving the masses to kneel,
At the base of this monstrous rock.
Conjuring powers from unseen dimensions.
Thus deadening the world's conscience.
Godlessness saturates the continents.

Casting spells upon the masses,
So devoid of illumination.
Dancing to sounds laced with soul poison.
Watching images corrupting the human core.
Corruption of the soul so fashionable.

Dazed, humanity cannot discern,
The tragic broader road,
They are travelling into hades.
The sanctuary is now so desolate,
And difficult times lay ahead.
Abomination that makes desolation,
Is setting up.

BIND ME NOT
Charles O. Okoth

BIND me not to your superficial bounds
Bond me not to your supercilious shackles
Nor yet the superfluity of nations
And the droning din of tainted clans…

For I desire to soar higher
I wish to explore the expanse
That eludes my searching eye;
I hope to unravel the mystery
That keeps nature afloat
And perchance mince secrets
That the gods hold sacred

So, off with your shackles, villager
Pull off the forbidding stone
That my spirit may float hot
And I will tread the expanse
Far from your shattered clans

We Shall Rise at Dawn
Chukwudi Nwokpoku

Dawn shall come anew in our land
with fluffy smiles softening our sour faces
battered by the darkness
that has bedeviled our days

We shall rise at dawn
to commune with *Ámádiōhà, our palms raised northwards
to quash these ravaging wars eating deep
into the flesh of our glebe

We shall rise at dawn
to cross our fingers and tighten our belts
breaking free from the shackling change
slaying pleading throats

We shall rise at dawn
to raise supplicant calabashes to **Ágbàrà
to pour some rain onto our barren fields
for the happy bloom of our greens

We shall rise at dawn
to gather round the dining table festooned with white and green
and 'break our fast' with sacrament of unity
with our rainy days dried by the rays of oblivion

*Ámádiōhà — *god of war*
**Ágbàrà — *god of thunder & rain*

LISTEN!
Charles O. Okoth

Hark! Be keen and listen
Listen to the winds as they churn
Numerous jolly ballads and boos
Keenly hearken to the birds and bees
As they chant in song and buzz

For you know not that they possess a secret
And they gladly wish you to share it
Hear; it comes floating clear and sweet
Painted and tinted like a celestial gift

Listen; even to a fool's rant
For the fool might suffer a slip of the tongue
And wisdom is bound to exude
For who knows if a fool is or made?
Give them time; listen; and judge them a new

LOST PRIDE
Elijah Unimke Aniah

Why do men still fight for this pride
that we lost to a snake long time ago
It came to our first man
with pleading eyes
and soft deceitful wiles.

Consumed by the zeal to impress his own rib
he gobbled his fair share without a backer thought
in the presence of a crawling smiling astute sly,
who was well hidden behind the golden leaves.

drowned in the ocean of this eye opener
gazed down his trunk
only to discover his giant maypole was bare,
unclad,
he struggled with the golden trees,
parting it with some of its own.

In success, the habiliment was organised
for he shielded his maypole,
his rib did same
shielding her young twin roes
and the deadly tunnel opening.
(the drama was on).

The big man came by dusk
everything, to him, seemed unfamiliar
desired an explanation
finger-pointing, haggling blames.
In spleen, did unchurched the man and his rib

from mars mountain,
hiding it immediately in the drunk clouds
this same ones,
staggering before our very eyes.

But we can't see it,
not because we are now blind,
just that even our eyes has lost its pride.

Candle Lights
Fikile C. Makhubo

Mama has always been beautiful.
Always been hot.
The makeshifts of hell.
Her flames flicker like a candle.
So they kneel at her feet, and caress her light in prayer.
Oh they pray, and they hope and they dream.

They become kings in her care and she does all she can.
She wear herself out, in front of the mirror all day to look like a queen for them.
She tires on her toes all day making a meal of herself.
So they can feast. One by one. So they feast.

The curse of a beautiful woman is that she never becomes a home.
Just a fairy-tale that keeps starting over from the end without the forever after.
Beautiful women are happy stories for men.
So she laughs.
For that's what hopeless romantics do.

She laughs even as they keep walking out.
Even as the last one lay hands on her, she laughs right after the tears dry.
She keeps laughing through the confusion of her daughters.
They have her face so, one day they will understand.
But, it isn't understanding we seek.
We need a mother.
We need her to tell us she understand all we going through as she's been here before.
Indlela kwamele ibuzwe kwabaphambili.
(The road is asked from those who've travelled on it.)
Yet she left us behind, so we wouldn't step into her footsteps and get lost with her.
Searching for her, we became the same candles in dark world.
Where men follow our light for what it is.
And they kneel at our feet. And they pray. And they hope. And they dream.

Without realising... It wasn't their attention we were seeking walking the way we do.
Laughing the way we do. Burning hot and low the way she does.
We were looking for her.
And after we've corrected her mistakes, maybe she'll approve.
Just this once, maybe she'll approve.
So I laugh,
even as she keeps breaking my heart.

Because that's what good daughters do.

Spacing
Kgomotso Ledwaba

Some scientists think space is
The nothingness between things
Some others think space is something,
Not just something, some think space is everything

That everything is a part of it
That parts are an illusion

The illusion of separation is dominant and with time it is alienating
My being an alien is familiar and oftentimes natives are alienated at home
Until they speak with "dignity"
Until they eat "properly"
Until they behave "accordingly"

To break bad habits, you must first know that they are bad
I think you told us we were bad so long, we believed you
Some scientists say space is nothing.

How do you occupy nothing?

Oblivion -
Melissa Farquhar

The writing on the wall tells a secret far greater than any great maker,
The fear within of a looming oblivion,
In death, we fear mortal disregard.
Our names but a whisper on a breeze past recollection.

To squelch our panic and demolish our fears,
We write on rock walls and age-old commemorations.
To ensure our memory never ceases to be,
Immortalizing our appellations in creations.

With each etch into the rock side our fear subsides,
We grow more serene with every engraving.
"They will recall" we insist
"The man who did this."

The world scarred with each and every carve,
Our frivolous and subconscious fears calmed.

Absentee Father
Richard Mbuthia

Your face is the midnight sun
Illuminating obstinate darkness
That, with a whisper
Shoos the light away
As celebrants join in the fray.

Your voice a lion's bleat
Amid the verdurous herbage
In the arid patch
Just across the fence.

Your alien progeny smirk –
Hollow laughs paint pastries
Stale on a discoloured sherd;
Discordant half smiles
Ascending hearty half miles.

An absentee father you are,
Your seeds you gave with relish, ecstasy
The story follows a broken trail;
She, your clone you vested –
Your voice and face her unwelcome attire.

Who will teach boys a man's life?
Who will hold their hands in the canyon,
Casting doubt into oblivion?
Who will look into their eyes
And affirm their dejected selves?

On that relay track
A frail baton shivers in the gust
Absent hands pass the switch
A switch grossly hewn
With edges to pick and prick.

Sewing
Tatenda Murigo

My skin is a
Patchwork of ancestry,
And I can only imagine
My forefathers
Weaving each
Ebony-dipped fiber
Together,
Debating with God
On which shade is better,
They thread the needle
With such accuracy,
A melanin so finely stitched
You can't see
The soul beneath.

The Beauty of Silence
Richard Mbuthia

As you amble –
Past the fiery thistles,
Ensconced in sweet bramble;
With mind light,
In heavy thought:
You pause to listen,
To the beauty of silence,
That once stood –
Stood for sanity,
In reckless freckles,
Oozing with unjustified
                Importance;
As the story unfolds,
Culminating in a more –
                Sensible opening:
The much-awaited preamble.

Part 3: Place, Home and Identity

Afu-Ra-Ka
Mari Ballot

I am the voiceless   weeping in the poet's why
I hear my forefathers' freedom cry it echoes   I live with chameleons and geckoes
I dreamt with dinosaurs   I soar with eagles I jump high   walk tall along waterfall
across the vast blue enslaved sky I suffer endless wars   my houses don't need doors
I have the sun on my face the moon on my crop   that never yields
I tend to jungles and fields   have minerals and resources
I ride wild horses across windswept dreams and deserts swollen swamps and raging rivers
ancient stars are my signs   spices plants herbs heal me
I see mighty oceans meet and foam
fear tiny mosquitoes   pestilential tsetse flies that roam
amongst the elephant buck leopard and lion
in this wounded world I am the warrior my ancestor's whispering
as we sing in the foreign violent wind
my body moves rhythmical   I dance I dance   become the trance
the drum beat of raw earth
here is the colourful cradle of human birth   impressive mountains tall grass and rainbows are our mirth
I am the seeds of creation that wing the world's salutation they are my brothers and sisters yet I am depleted stripped bare dying for my tribal survival
I suffer   I toil   my weary restricted bare feet tread fifty-seven conflicted countries   I root in African soil   here in my heaven

rancorous winds howl anarchist prowl I speak   I plead I chant
songs vibrant with a thousand different tongues
amongst the buffalo snakes and crocodiles hope and hunger
haunts me
my red blended bright blood throbs   my grievous human heart
sobs   where are our simple joys? abundance may not be on my
plate but is in my heart
I chop wood   fetch water herd cattle search peace   I fear   I see
so many orphaned children starving   carrying burdens
reflecting guns in their eyes… not toys…!

Ayyoo Tiyyaa"(MY MUM)
Leelisa Jacob Sero

Ayyaa!Ayyoo!Dhageeta Dhageettanni!(Mother!Mother!Did you hear?)
Eeh!I see
You're Soaring Higher Africa:
Rising beyond Ayyoo Africa.

(Corruption and Dictatorship walk in drunk and knock at the door.Sound effects must be appropriate to signal their arrival and knock on the door lovingly and romantically.)

"Open the doors for me wider"

(Mama Africa walks few steps forward inquiringly)
"Who did you say you are?"

(Corruption happily)
"It's me my dear and only
Who makes me warm and homily
Sorry for being intrusive,inimical for long,
My affinity for dictators still tender and strong"

(Mama Africa-Determined and sternly)
To you,
You cancer,I shall stamp you out through this door,
For I have had enough of you fool,
While you get a laugh from my decades battle,
I've devised a way of up-rooting you from the bottom,
Yes,from dawn to dusk,
I turned it into my task,
Cleaning while "Dhaadattattin" like a bee,

So beautiful and magical in MY HOME TO BE!

(Corruption/Dictatorship pleadingly)
"Brag not for victory in this game,
Now that its me you've managed to tame,
Home and dry you've passed your message,
Please allow me to see my mate
For I need a massage."

(Mama Africa-Still determined and firm)
"The sullied souls who brushed their shoulders with you villain,
Are rotting in jail now,
None escaped from the long arm of the law,"

(Corruption/Dictatorship begging for mercy.Must be expressed through appropriate gestures,actions and stage movements)

"Really,It hurts to hear your concluded claim,
To me,my customer, you'll always remain.
By this poem I take the blame,
Forgive me darling and spare my name"

(Mama Africa-Daringly)
"By this poem I vow to fight,
Back you go or bury you alive in dawning light,
Never tired of upholding the constitution,
Democracy,rule of law,equality,justice and liberty,
That reminds me of the protecting and upholding the tenets
Of the Universal Ideals of Humanity,
That fosters love and unity,
Love and affection
As my children are moving in the right direction:
With unity,love and affection,

I soar higher and rise in tremendous transformation,
With the betterment of my nation.

Going down corridors of history,
Of Apartheid and Colonialism,
Post-Apartheid taught the world co-existence,
Slavery, famine and civil wars,
I suffered all these,
And encountered many things,
Overcame all the odds,
Challenges and problems
I did stumble, tramped, trampled,
Never quitting, fully determined,
Faith in my children's iron will
Finally triumphing over them all.
Sweet goals accomplished.
"The World has a lot to learn from "US"-Africa!"

So my brothers and sisters,
The secret is now revealed,
And it's time our ignorance & disunity repelled,
A microcosm of society a healthy family is,
 The custodian and the propagator of societal peace.

A WALK THROUGH AN AFRICAN VILLAGE
Patrick Hwande

Just a walk through an African village,
I am greeted with fascinating scenes:
A monumental man behind the granary,
Passing water as the eye guards the village path,
In front, his spouse is making a meal.
Spotting me, the man jumps up, and his trousers gets soaked up!
The village headman and wife,
Stop me and take their time to meet me,
I suspect they carry a crucial word,
Only to be greeted and asked if everything is ok,
Before they return to anxious-looking subjects,
Don't they know, I have a longing lover at a rendezvous?
Giggling girls in Sanyati River, half –naked,
Manipulating waists to arrest my attention,
Why emulate women of easy virtues, I wonder,
With the agility of a cat, the place I vacate.
Brother`s wife by the well, keen to talk to me,
She subtly takes umbrage at my growing impatience,
She wants to know why I am skirting Rumbi,
Her beautiful sister with budding breasts.

A platinum girl from a beer party, its twilight,
If you greet her from a distant,
She won`t let you go without a handshake,
Never mind fresh mucous on coarse palm,
"Whose son are you?" She interrogates you,
Before letting go of you.
The Children I teach,
Greet me, hidden in bushes,
Craning my neck to have better view of them,

They scamper off like cornered rats,
Now I know, I just wave at them as I go.
A barbaric baboon in Dewe mountain,
Teases and tantalizes me like a bully.
Beyond the mountain, in a lushly forest,
African canary oozes serenading melodies,
To tickle hearts with diminished gladness.
Just below the sacred Valley,
The inquisitive eye feasts on a richly greenery panorama.
Livestock abound on grassy lands,
But why are the boys trading barbs and blows?
Bad boys are barely believable!

A squirrel crossing my path in front of me,
I spit and curse to block the bad omen,
Nut shells spread at cross roads,
I jump: I don`t want to argument someone`s yield.
Aren`t these nonsensical theories, I wonder,
A honey badger treating self to sweet staff,
Beat it once it dies, another and beat it wakes up!
On my way home later,
I meet a little girl in terrific speed,
Her siblings has had a snake bite,
A healer gives her roots to chew,
After a while, we are told,
The victim`s pains have all evaporated!
A wealth of African experiences,
Gives me a billion reasons to dream about Africa,
Amazing and mesmerizing African ways could be,
I find them very rich and rewarding.

Annual Virgins' Dance
Peter Yieko Ndiwa

Bare-breasted, young, juicy
Thousands of women, as young as five
A celebration of chastity and unity
United in what? Poverty.
Posh, pomp, lavish week long dance
Trampling already dusty, impoverished country.

Tributes sounded from virgins
Beaded, mini-skirted and branding machetes
Modernized too with mobile phones.
Reed dance, a celebration
of womanhood and virginity.
Virgin legs from distant villages
Shook the royal ground in a dance.

Tourists' and journalists' cameras clicked on the topless
Topless hearts raced in anticipation-
Who is going to be lucky this time?
to move from hovels to own palace,
receive a classy car and delicacies
Away from abject poverty and meager meals
Travel overseas for shopping in royal trips entourage

Police kept vigil, rebuffing the nosy journalists
Hundreds of millions dollar worth king smiled
Long singing and foot stamping sounded
Trashing away the weary populations' hope.

When It Rained In Khayelitsha
Dimakatso Sedite

Our shack is sun-soaked and warm,
 the chatter outside muffles the murmur
 from our radio.   Krok-krok on our roof,
our cracked door hisses, is flung to a thud —

Our eyes are seeds stuck in half-sliced avocado.
We rise like flowers opening in slow motion,
and rush towards the pelting window.
After days layered with dryness,

rain rustles our leaves again.

The sky is a grey cloth that folds into fists of clouds.
Lightning cracks heavens like heat slicing frozen ice.
Rain dabs powdery soil, men stop drinking,
and babies swallow their cries.

Neighbours gather at their limping gates.
Our eyes are a spray of car lights
in the coal of night, gazing at the rain;
cats long swallowed by mountains crawl

back into our shadows.

My three-year old son asks why the sky is leaking.
 —   To him rain is a stranger —
Khabonina the cow gallops into the wind
to the quiet orchestra of sprinkles.

Dogs rouse from their endless sleep, tails erect

like rods, chins sturdy as a soldier's pose.
—   A scene from a screen-less movie —
Paper and twigs gurgle down gullies

like confused boats, towards the skull of a dam.
They tumble to where trapped puddles cannot…
My father stutters in laughter, a cracked cry
stuck in the creases of his heart.

Water slashes his ankles into scars,

clacks into tubs like stone on bone.
Basins dot streets of Khayelitsha
like a carpet of African flags
on the toe of Africa.

Invasion
Adré Marshall

As they walk down the hill,
a black bat silhouette against
a bedroom window alerts them.
They tread softly nearer;

its outstretched wings fray
into ragged edges; spikes of glass
bare their claws around the hole
where the stone swooped through.

They push open the front door; splinters
shower over the chairs and carpet, long slivers
stab the jumble of clothes,
plates, random objects hauled
out of cupboards and strewn across the floor.

A block of concrete lies beside a table
split right down the middle.
The wide window that once
held up a view of beach and bay
is scattered in a hundred shards.

This space is alien now, a house despoiled,
the harmony of blue sea, sky, white beach
now dismembered. Fangs of ice
shred the picture of the waves,

shingle beach, and the small stream
creeping now to hide under the rocks.
In their world, chaos has come again.

A world they never can resurrect.

On the hill, a shape moves behind the bushes
and they startle. What is crouching there in wait?
It stretches upwards, grows a long neck, a pair
of horns – and a bushbuck ram slips out of sight.

They step outside, turn their backs on this sign
of a fractured world, look out at an ocean
unconcerned; an otter slips into the gully,
the black oyster catchers, perched

on their favoured rocks, still wield sharp
orange beaks to dislodge black mussels;
all carries on exactly as before
except for them

except for them

Carrion Call
Emman Usman Shehu

The vulture spanfully hovers
to carrion call of left-overs.
Another drought drift of despair
stretches the Sahelian nightmare.

Dust bowls harass beige barren land
  hanging on ledge of extinction.
  Survival key is predation,
  instinct honed to meet a demand.

  He powers down efficiently –
a parachute of black feathers,
  jinks off from sparse wilting heathers
  to mixed flock at work efficiently.

The rapidly dwindling carcass –
a once elegant, endangered
gazelle, scholarly tagged Dorcas.
Chip tracker broken, disabled.

Land Of My Birth
Jabulani Mzinyathi

The land between those rivers
The Zambezi to the north
The Limpopo to the south
The land of my birth

The land of those stone structures
The great architecture of the VaRozvi
The land of shungu namutitima
Stolen by queen victoria' subject

The land of many tourist attractions
Too numerous to mention
Land of the enigmatic Chinhoyi caves
Land of the enticing cool eastern highlands

The land ravaged by misrule
The land of that thwarted dynasty
The land of the coup that was not one
A land brimming with book learning

Zimbabwe land of my birth
My umbilical cord there embedded
The land brimming still with hope
Where hope still refuses to die

This land of stunted growth
In dire need of chemotherapy
As the cancer of corruption gnaws it
Land of securocrats and benzocrats

A land brimming with human resources
Peace loving in the face of adversity
A land of unimaginable resilience
Like the study walls of Dzimbahwe

When all the Water Leaves Us
Christine Coates

Agapanthus unfurl,
proteas torch,
everywhere the frenzy of cicadas.
All I can think of is
how terrifying summer is.

The sea sings a high-pitched flute,
the wind whips up waves,
hangs fences with plastic,
papers streets with
chip wrappings and polystyrene cups.

The verges turn brown
like Joburg winters, clouds fly north.
I watch weather reports,
the dam levels drop,
a weak cold front teases on by.

Out there feels dangerous,
temperatures soar, heat hazes the Flats,
I keep glancing upwards,
hoping the south-easter will turn black, with moisture.
Then February brings its worst.

I flee the city.
Along Baden Powell the gulls
all face one way, whirlwinds sandblast the car.
A helicopter carries a magnetic scanner,
searching, searching.

Beautiful Zimbabwe
Cosmas Mairosi

Beauty is my song
My song is beauty
Beautiful people, beautiful places,
 beautiful Zimbabwe!
Beauty is the mountain paradise of the Eastern Highlands
A mosaic of undulating panorama
The epitome of diverse visual riches
A sensual metaphor of valleys, streams, waterfalls and plateaus
The peaks of Inyangani and Chimanimani
Reaching up to the heavens like pilgrims paying homage to the gods
Mist shrouding them like a bridal veil
Vumba Botanical Gardens- forever the domain of subtropical flora
Boasting a unique collection of modern and prehistoric blooms
On stone-terraced bossoms
Burma Valley – a tropical anathema
Chinyamakwaramba – the hill that sat down
Chirinda- a primeval virgin forest of unspoilt jungle
Where the lianas tangle in glee
Lofty Pungwe, endless Mutarazi Falls –
A sing-song splendour

Plunging into the mesmerising Honde Valley and Pungwe Gorge
Beauty is my song
My song is beauty
Beautiful people, beautiful places,
Beautiful Zimbabwe!
Beauty is the story of my nation written on walls of stone
At Khame and Dhlodhlo ruins
Beauty is the mystery surrounding the ancient citadels of stone
Masvingo eDzimbabwe,Dzimba Dzamatombo,Dzimbabwe
Great Zimbabwe! The throne of royal kingdoms
Throbbing with the pulse of our present and past
Beauty is a hilarious song sung by
the shriek of a fish eagle
The shy laughing hyena
The hiss of a sly slithering snake
The towering giraffe, the trumpeting elephant
The graceful eland,the flamboyant kudu
The roaring lion, the lunging leopard
The bullying buffalo, the snorting rhino
Beauty is the baffling Zimbabwe sunset
Bathing everything in breath-taking glory
Beauty is the immense aquatic haven of Lake Kariba
Swelling with the legend of Nyaminyami
Beauty is Zimbabwe's well-designed cities:
Accessible by the safest and most efficient transport networks
Mutare, sits cradled in a granite cage
Dappled by aloes, flamboyant and cycads
Harare, the city that never goes to sleep
City that sits in the sun, sparkling always, like a diamond
Bulawayo, the city of kings
Gweru, the heartbeat of the midlands
Kadoma, the city of gold and textiles!
Beauty is summed up in the colourful and majestic splendour

Of the Victoria Falls
A mammoth wonder of mist,spray and thunder
Mosi-oa-Tunya – the jewel that crowns our national heritage
Beauty is the tranquil hills of Matoposi
A natural gallery of granite boulders
Balancing in a frieze of miraculous wonder
Exquisite Bushman rock paintings decorating
 the caves of Nswatugi,Bambata,Silozwane and Gulubahwe
Malindidzimu – the place of spirits!
Awed by the commanding stillness, and world view
The spirit of a wanderer found rest among these hills
     Such beauty…
  "the peacefulness of it all…"
  "scenes so lovely…"
are fit to "… be gazed upon by angels in their flight!"
Beauty is my song
My song is beauty
Beautiful people, beautiful places,
beautiful Zimbabwe!
[Note: the words enclosed by quotation marks were spoken by Cecil John Rhodes himself. Even though he had the whole of southern Africa under his foot,he chose to be buried in Matoposi Hills.]

Community Policing
Daniel Many Owiti

There is a new man loitering around here,
A Stanger,
We fear things might start to disappear,
We sense danger,
So we have reported him to the chief,
We suspect he might be a thief.

A private developer,
Is hastily putting up a high-rise apartment,
We think it is improper,
So we have reported to the government,
Regulatory authority,
To be sure the construction meets threshold quality.

Someone is putting up a perimeter fence,
Around the basketball court,
We think it is an offence,
We took her to a law court,
The case might delay,
But we know our children have a right to play.

A night club is playing loud music,
We sought for the owner,
Complained the noise irritates us sick,
Presented him with a restraint order,
When he ignored our plea,
We locked his club and made him flee.

A PRINCE WITHOUT A HOME
(After a Visit to Ogere Remo)
Ekundayo Asifat

Straw, metal or concrete
A home bears no other name
The dwellers are the rafters and the props – the spirits
That primes its breath.

A prince without a home
I seek and find my roots among folks whose homes
Pulsate with love.

In our ancestral dwelling
Urchins pose a tribe of nuisance-flies that lick sore on feet
of travelers
Their noise pierces Quiet in homes of thatch
In calm dwellings, love blunts the pains of living

At Ogere where love possesses limbs
My host turned a minion
The neighborhood awash with smell of delicacies
'Meals are best had on table of idle talks;
Fingers turned shovels probing 'plate bottoms'
Thus the host stood by Spurring his guests urgings:
'Until the guest is sated with cuisines the host remains mute,
starving'
Home or out
Love possesses cat paws
Thrusting peace to guests
And those who give unabashedly

Whispers from Home
Kelvin J. Shachile

Missing home? Comes the whisper.
The hillside hut I grew up in.
Enjoying the birds chirp on the mugumo,
The sounds of water at the water falls.
The scenic view of the green carpets of grass
Where we played in our childhood days.
Memories that I whisper, to stay with me.

Sitting amidst the silent wilderness,
I feel the emptiness that comes with the breeze,
The calm and soft breeze carrying a voice.
Asking me if I enjoy the new place.
I am not, because the watchfulness and worry,
Keeps me yearning.

Whispers from home asks me a question.
"Do you think you made the right decision?"
I yearn to tell it they forced me into it,
And for so long I have had human souls to eat.
In the heart of heartless terrorists,
I am a new recruit, they promise money
But home is honey.
I long to leave Kismayu for home.

Many of a Morning in Chinsapo
Yamikani Brighton Imbe

As usual
Warmly greeted by the 5am chilly breeze
Echoing the walls of his tiny box,
He grudgingly breaks out of his cocoon.
Outside
The Snoring of yester-today drunkards
Melodiously choir with the cockcrows
Their piss ardour
Forcing women out to yet another market day.
On his way
Multicolored and half-naked bodies cruise past
Engulfed in morning innocence
Yet, tampered upon by many a night vampires
Sucking from their veins until they are dry and dead.
At the depot
Raspy and hoarse voices outwit each other
In rather harmonious disturbing tones
Invitations escaping from smelly mouths of touts.
On board
He listens silently to the rattling engine
Swaying them on the once tarmac-now-dusty road.
On one of the empty windows – like home
He enjoys the beauty of filthy bins and litters
As the bus touches down Labour-Town Depot.

*Chinsapo is a squalor settlement in the outskirts of Lilongwe, the capital of Malawi

On the bus
Crystal Warren

Returning from a long holiday
I watch the familiar landscape,
enjoying the recognition
of hills and valleys.

It is dusk, dark clouds
are tinted with the dying light.
Animals aplenty to be seen
at the side of the road.

Apart from the usual horses and cows
I see springbok, kudu, zebra, giraffe.
I keep my eyes peeled
ever hopeful of finally seeing

one of the lions
whose existence is promised
by the warning signs
and double fences.

We quietly pass the game farms
but my fellow passengers
do not lift their eyes
from their phones.

Fruitsquirt
Harry Owen

Up above, the trees are eating themselves:
hear them chew. Every leaf is a fruit bat
budding from late summer darkness
a winged leather rasp, a raining of figs.

Trunks creep, clenching their cork-
veined muscular definitions
of hot mammalian fruitsquirt.
Each eruption of noise is movement,

the night garden depixillating
into a mulch of footsteps,
the empty squawk of human
backbitings in the student digs below.

Yet how I love this crazed wild magic!
Make merry, all you squatters up there,
down there: embrace while you may
the batshit rapture of being so alive.

[First published in Grocott's Mail, 19 May 2017]

Grounded
Crystal Warren

An earthquake in a mining town
sends tremors across the country.
Not for the first time
I am relieved to live
far from the centre
in a small town
whose arid earth
remained stable today.

Accra and traffic
Awuah Mainoo Gabriel

Snore
Sigh
Sneeze
Prayer
Shower
God, listen to our prayers
Amen!
Happy
Honey, is coffee ready?
Bread
Butter
Cheese
Thank you dear I love you.
Kisses
Peg

Hug
I love you kids.
Have a nice day.

Seat belt on
Bad roads
Potholes deep as Mississippi
Oh Ghana.
Here, my license officer, everything intact
You keeping me too long!
Sorry, I don't have one Ghana cedi
Police and bribe; Savage!
Dumb man with three eyes
What?
I always love to see your green sexy eyes
Please excuse my vehicle
I am so late to work.

God thank you for safe arrival
Good mourning everyone
 I saw Ghana in an ambulance
"Good mourning gentleman,
We love your necklace"
Oh thank you thank you
I only know it'll turn into a tight rope soon
"Gentleman you're fired"
Oh boss you know Accra and human traffic.

"Sweetheart welcome,
Daddy welcome"
Please do not hug, thorns all over my skin
Sorry, lemon in my mouth
Excuse my pain;

Hold on honey
The necklace is strangling the testicles
I cannot bend to weed your front yard tonight.

Part 4: French Poems

Comportement excédant
Josiane Nguimfack Zeufack

Je me suis déjà résignée
A passer tout mon temps à me manier
Devenue une simple plume
Qui prend plaisir dans la brume
Je me laisse porter au gré du vent
Vacillant de branche en branche
Je ne manque plus de cran
Car toute mon existence change
J'attends impatiemment mon sort
Pour mes multiples torts
C'est fini le rêve de la demoiselle
Je fais désormais usage de mes ailes
Pour m'en sortir d'un seul trait
Bonne pour représenter la copine de fer
Mais jamais la belle mariée
Bonne à écouter les pleurnicheurs
Sans toutefois s'apitoyer
Eh bien ! Fini à jamais ce leurre
Essayer de faire bonne figure
J'en ai marre
Plus que marre
Et je signale de ce fait ma cure

Punaise rouge et noire
Josiane Nguimfack Zeufack

Transformés en Hommes intègres
Durant une formation d'esclaves nègres
Vous avez hérités de palliatifs
Ensorcelés par la drogue
Comme si cela était en vogue

Réagissant aussi brutalement qu'un primitif

L'alcool et le tabac

Sont devenus votre aimable ingurgitation
Au point où s'en fait un tabac
Vous ne vous sacrifiez plus pour votre nation
Mais pour l'ensemble des racoleuses
Qui sont des éternelles saboteuses et radoteuses
Vous vous foutez de celles qui ont une encoprésie
Si malgré tout vous leur faites une intérieure euthanasie
Vous ne tuez plus les ennemis d'État
Mais vous assassinez vos concurrents
Ceux qui goutent à votre dépotoir
Ceux qui redonnent vie au transparent
Les amants de vos épouses
Qui hument quotidiennement leur bouse
A l'aide de vos baladeurs doigts
Vous violez toutes les lois
Misent en vigueur par vos supérieurs
Ceci sans verser aucune sueur
Vous traumatisez la population
Que vous êtes censés protéger
Sans contextuellement songer

Aux injustices qu'elle reçoit de sa condamnation
Vous escroquer de pauvres gens
Qui sont déjà assez miséreux
Pour qu'ils deviennent piteux
Et qu'ils manquent de sang
Jusqu'à la moelle de leurs os
En ne les offrant qu'un joli tétanos
Vous faites usage de violences physiques
Vous êtes des virus psychologiques
Vous broyez sans relâche et sans risque
Vous retombez sur les têtes comme des briques
Vous vous noyez continuellement dans la nique
Avec vos engins semblables à une pique
A la moindre difficulté, vous vous suicidez
En prenant des excuses bidon en dé
Et après avoir fait un de ces carnages
Sans tenir compte de votre voisinage

Vicissitude
Josiane Nguimfack Zeufack

Je porte en moi le sourire d'un nouveau-né
Heureux d'avoir traversé l'étape fœtale
Pour enfin profiter d'une jouissance annale
Et d'une succion libre sans tonner
Je porte en moi la joie d'un enfant

Qui a reçu des bras de sa famille
Un amour unique qui cille
Avec ce dont rêve tous gens
Je porte en moi le malaise d'un adolescent
Qui a été pendant longtemps la risée
Des personnes à la langue aiguisée
Soutenue par un enthousiasme passionnant
Je porte en moi les blessures du passé
Qui ont raisonné en moi comme un fla
Laissant place à un trauma
Qui ne s'est jamais effacé
Je porte en moi la douleur d'une jeune femme
Ayant vécue la perte d'un être cher
Qui n'avait rien d'un humain infâme
Lisant en elle comme dans un livre ouvert
Je porte en moi la déception d'une dame
Qui s'est faite dégager gracieusement
Par un homme sans âme
Se comportant lascivement
Je porte en moi le désir d'une future épouse
Souhaitant bercer des bébés sans blues
Résultante d'une relation fusionnelle
Faites de respect, de fidélité et de dentelle
Je porte en moi des douleurs

Me remettant toujours à l'heure
Et qui font que je suis moi
Et que tu es toi

Rendez nous nos trésors
Nguetcheu Emile Arsele

« Pour réclamer tous nos objets sacrés volés … »

Ce matin
Sous une pluie averse
Qui se verse et bouleverse
Tout Douala
Le pas alerte
Je traverse
Les rues de Bele Bele
L'History Town
Les yeux, le cœur lourd
Mon spirit
Comme un véritable coup de pilon
Dans le mortier de ma grand-mère
Pile pile l'oubli
Jusqu'à satisfaction

Et c'est en assez
Que je perroquette
Une igname de bonheur
A tous ceux dont je croise le chemin
La main
Hors de la poche
La bouche

Qui taquine la voix
S'élève
Haut
Plus haut que notre Fako
Notre Kilimandjaro

Et c'est en assez
Que je réclame
Requiem pour un continent assassiné
Que nous soient rendu
Nos trésors
Qui souffrent barricadés
Dans vos tristes pénitenciers
Que vous nommez pompeusement musée.

Rendez
Je dis bien rendez les nous
Nos trésors
Rendez
Rendez-les nous
La proue princière de sa majesté Kum'a Mbape
Rendez-les nous
La statue d'Afo Akom
Rendez
Rendez-les nous
Les os Ishango
Rendez
Rendez-les nous
Les reliefs historiques du royaume d'Ifé
Rendez
Rendez-les nous
La pierre de Rosette
Rendez

Rendez-les nous
Le zodiaque Dendérah
Rendez
Rendez-les nous
La statue de Ramsès II
Rendez
Rendez-les nous
Le buste de Néfertiti
Oui
Rendez
Rendez nous tout
Tout ce que vous nous avez lâchement volé.

16 juillet 2015, Sur les côtes du Wouri
Note : Extrait de *Les racines de la résistance*, Editions Afric Avenir, 2016

La mal de ce siècle absurde
Nguetcheu Emile Arsele

C'est une multinationale
Parmi les multinationales
Dont la gueule hante l'avenir du monde
Au quotidien
Elle ouvre grande sa vanne de puanteur
Et déverse indifférente dans la nature
Tous types de déchets inimaginables

Des dégâts que cela provoque en cascade
Sur la santé de la nature
Et dans le corps de l'être humain mon frère
Elle s'en moque pas mal
Comme on se moque d'un habit chiffon
Dont la marâtre a voulu nous cadeauter

Demain
Quand cette multinationale
Parmi les multinationales
Aura finit d'enterrer
Le plus de monde possible
Quand des dépouilles de nos parents
Elle continuera à constituer le fumier séminal
Dont elle a toujours rêvé
Pour mieux engraisser son capital social
Domptée et dominée par le mal de ce siècle absurde
Elle s'en ira gaillardement en Suisse
Cintrée dans un costume sur mesure de trois pièces
Et cette fois-ci enterrera dans les coffres forts helvétiques
Des milliards et des milliards de dollars.

Note : Extrait de *Sur le dos de la terre rouge*, Inédit

Il me vient
Nguetcheu Emile Arsele

« *Pour prendre en dérision nos envies.* »

Il me vient
Une envie de tuer
De sauter le Rubicon de tous les interdits

Comme si ma vie en dépendait
Il me vient
Une envie de faire l'amour aux mots
De sodomiser un poème
Comme si ma vie en dépendait
Il me vient
Une envie de tutoyer le vide
De méditer sur le silence
Comme si ma vie en dépendait
Comme si ma vie en dépendait
Il me vient une envie

De rire

Rire de tout et de rien.

16 août 14, Sur les côtes du Wouri

Note : Extrait de *Les racines de la résistance*, Editions Afric Avenir, 2016

Profond océan
Koffi Luc

Profond océan aux vagues houleuses
Aux oiseaux multicolores
Agité que sidéré.
Je ne peux que te traverser
Même si tu engloutis toujours nos âmes,
nos espoirs.
Des gens venus de loin passant ici
Sont arrivés chez moi
Ils ont vendu mes pères
Ils ont brulé mes terres
Ils ont emporté mes ressources
Aujourd'hui
J'ai besoin d'un peu d'eau à boire
Laisse-moi passer
Profond océan
Tu es témoin de l'histoire
Je mourrai mais je reviendrai ici
Car derrière ton lit réside la Vie heureuse.

Cette Afrique là
Koffi Luc

C'est cette Afrique là qu'ils aiment,
Ce regard desséché de guerre,
La famine qui vole sans fin sur cinquante-quatre âmes
Une Afrique à genou.
C'est cette Afrique qu'ils aiment,
Ces sébiles envahissantes,
Les lupanars à la sueur sombre,
Ces enfants sans vie,
Ces regards desséchés par la guerre.
Ceux qui aiment l'Afrique l'aiment à genou
Et nous, nous en sommes plus qu'heureux.
Où irons-nous si l'Afrique vole en fumée ?
Si la famine nous extermine ?

Couleurs
Koffi Luc

Le noir le jaune le vert le rouge
Il y a trop de couleurs qui nous diversifient
Trop de couleurs qui nous séparent
De nos frères, nos semblables.
Mais il est un seul cœur
Qui unit un monde si beau.
Le noir le jaune le bleu
Il est trop de couleurs qui nous rendent
Et maitres et esclaves
Mais un seul regard
Qui exprime la joie l'amour.
Certaines races sont jaunes
D'autres noires ou blanches
Mais un cœur nous est commun
Pour nous accepter et nous aimer.
Mais un même regard pour être joyeux.

Morphé
Gbeada Woungouankeu Maxence

A la véranda de ton seuil, je te vois t'en aller
Où vas-tu cher ami?
Vouté dans la verdure de l'adolescence une voix foudroyante
évinça mon cœur et mes larmes comme une tornade inconsolable
pleurais ton splendieux corps vigoureux, agonisant s'en aller.
Ton âme captive dans une geôle sombrait
dans un sombre cauchemar nocturne.
Où vas-tu cher ami?
L'heure de ton départ est il proche?
L'alarme de ta réincarnation a t'elle sonnée?
Me laissant dans ce pathétique tragique départ sans retour,
ma conscience hante mon esprit et terrorise mon âme,
de t'avoir laissé seul paître ton âme

L'Amour
Gbeada Woungouankeu Maxence

Dans la bruine de ma tendre jeunesse,
Dans la plus tendre enfance de mon souvenir,
Je penserai toujours à toi,
Je penserai à ta voix de menthe suave,
Je penserai au minaudement de ton aura,
Je penserai à ta démarche de statuette,
A ton sourire qui m'enivre l'âme
Ton sourire si éclatant, si sobre, si doux
Qui vivifie mon âme pour une renaissance paisible.
Dans la bruine de ma tendre jeunesse,
Dans la plus tendre enfance de mon souvenir,
Je me souviendrai toujours de toi.
Regarde au plus profond de mon âme
Et tu verras l'extase scintiller dans mes yeux.
Contemple le soleil et tu verras l'éclat de mon sourire.
Saches que ces vers libres proviennent
De l'amour que je porte pour toi.

Le Desespoir
Gbeada Woungouankeu Maxence

Pourquoi tant de tumulte dans ton cœur?
Pourquoi tant de désespoir dans tes yeux?
Penses-tu que la divine providence t'as oublié?
Penses-tu que l'univers t'a renié?
Non, je n'y crois pas.
Regarde au plus profond de toi et tu verras cette source divine,
Cette lumière infinie te sourire
Regarde la baute de la nature et tu verras la réponse à tes préoccupations
Ecoute le chant des oiseaux
Contemple la beauté de l'aurore
Admire la lueur des étoiles et tu verras que chaque jour suffit à sa peine.
Pleure tant que tu peux
Rie tant que tu peux
Saute tant que tu peux
Mais fais les tous avec amour
Car c'est de cet amour que tu trouveras la joie de vivre

L'Entrepreneuriat
Emmanuel Siffo

Concept en pleine mode,
Tu es par ailleurs cette copule qui valorise les jeunes dans le monde.
De toi vient le nom entrepreneur,
Qui a pour radical preneur
De toute occasion qui se présente ;
Dans l'optique de la rendre profitable
A toute personne déplorable.
Tu es une voie mnémotechnique ;
Qui exclut des formules scientifiques !
A toute personne battante.

Tu es la solution de nos dirigeants,
Qui ne savent où mettre tous ces gens !
Avec des backgrounds bienfaits
Qui ont fait des écoles sans effets.
Qui ont monté des projets sans financement ;
Qui ont commencé des recherches sans dénouement ;
Qui ont crié sans être entendus ;
Qui ont dépensé sans eu avoir un dû ;
Qui ont fait des parcours décisifs ;
Sans concours définitifs.

Le départ d'une ère révolutionnaire ;
Tu ne connais pas les anniversaires !
Tu ne connais pas les excuses ;
Tu ne connais pas les tables rases ;
Tu ne connais pas les procrastinations ;
Tu ne connais pas les lamentations ;
Tu ne connais pas la défocalisation !
Mais tu aimes la concentration.

La garantie d'une liberté financière !
Tu permets de vivre son paradis sur terre !
Tu ne connais pas les fins du mois !
Tu permets d'affirmer son propre-moi !
Tu prends une personne qui hier était zéro !
Tu la rends par ses efforts aujourd'hui un héro !
Tu ne laisse pas toujours l'employé entrepreneur esclave !
Mais tu le rends patron de ceux qui jadis le qualifiait d'esclave.

La Mémoire de l'oubli
Gils Da Douanla

– I –

La nuit se déploie sur les jours sans mémoire
Je traverse l'arrière monde onirique
Je remonte la haine mémorable des braises
Le sang et les larmes encore inondent

Pour édulcorer le gris qu'il fait
Le vent les grave dans la mémoire de l'oubli
Il germe des décombres du temps
Pour grandir les destins chétifs

Alors les souvenirs de l'histoire sans traces
Retracent les contours du passé amnésique
Et j'avance balbutiant et ignorant
J'avance vers l'être qui fut et je me découvre
Je ne l'ai jamais connu mais il est tellement moi

Son cri trouve écho dans mes entrailles
Les vies sont des ritournelles de l'existence
On est tous des êtres de mémoire
Au fond reflété par le miroir de l'histoire

– II –
Les hiboux cherchent maintenant leur maître
Dans les tumultes d'exaspération que gouvernent les ténèbres
La race décalée et les hommes au sang qui n'émeut
Peuplent les nuits de l'humanité sans astre lumineux

Tu es là au cœur des désillusions de la multitude
Tu regardes s'assombrir les destins que tu hypothèques
Les bribes de sourires pathétiques éclatent sur toi
Tu te sens aimé pourtant la haine sourit parfois

L'histoire qui s'écrit de rouge vermeil
Rappelle la mémoire amnésiée par ton nombrilisme
Tu as surgi où rien n'avait jamais existé
Et tu as donné vie à un mythe et à des créatures

Le crépuscule se dessine sur tes pas
Mais tu rêves encore comme une fleur à l'aurore
L'histoire se souviendra sans doute de toi
Elle n'oublie jamais ses malheurs

- III -
Femme, je sais que le monde t'a oubliée
Tu cherches ton chemin à l'ombre des attentions
Ta vie s'effrite dans le silence des malheurs
Tu es une honte pour la vie que tu donnes
Et tes entrailles généreuses se moquent de ta patience

Femme, je sais combien tu aimes
Tu fais de ton sein le verger de l'humanité
Mais tu n'enfantes ni fleurs ni ronces
Tu mets au monde des cœurs innocents
Et tu récoltes le mépris du destin

Femme, je sais que la lune a disparu hier
Mais ton corps est lanterne dans la nuit des épouvantes
La source et l'aboutissement des rêves fondateurs
Ton corps est histoire et mémoire du temps
Et ton désir l'étoile des nuits sans lune

Femme, je sais que tu n'es pas l'invention de l'autre siècle
Tu n'es pas le mensonge que raconte la phallodémence
Ne te laisse pas regarder par les yeux morbides
Tu es le sourire qui traverse le souvenir et l'avenir
Et ton visage maternel la promesse du futur

J'ai vu le futur…
Balddine Moussa

Ah! Si seulement on pouvait se taire
Discrètement mettre la colère sous terre !
Mais comment se taire alors que les cœurs
Se meurent ! Que faire de telles horreurs ?
Comment justifiez-vous cette indifférence?
Ils ne craignent rien de leurs descendances !
Pendant que ces Têtes abord de l'oiseau volent
Pour l`étranger, pour des aventures folles :
Aller se traiter une acné, ou se maquiller !
Se faire les ongles, ou plutôt pour skier ;
Ou juste pour quelques millions passer du
Bon temps ; attraper le temps perdu,
Offrir des vacances à leurs enfants chéris !
De l'autre côté elle ne vaut pas grand-chose la vie
Si la famine ne tue pas, c'est la guerre !
C'est la machette du voisin ou du frère !
Ils ont joué au ballon et au domino la veille,
Ils se bombardent à la bombe au réveil.
Ils ne sont plus du même parti ni de la même tribu,
Ni de la même religion; le lien sacré n'est plus
Ces spectacles plaisent aux organisateurs
C'est pro, ce n'est pas un spectacle amateur
C'est un moyen de se faire gratter un billet.
Ils ont brisé des familles et des amitiés
Des années durant et le danger perdure :
Des villes et villages se crament sans futur.
J'ai vu le futur quelque part, corps figé
Sur le sol. On voyait les yeux bouger,
Pas les membres. On dirait une petite fille !
Autour d'elle pas d'amis ni famille !

Elle ne lui reste que sa tête et ses os
Sur cette terre de cendre sans nourriture ni eaux.
Le soleil se régale sur la peau grisâtre
De celle dont on ne verra le corps accroître.
Des yeux embarrassés pleuraient d'impuissance
Pendant que des caméras tournaient dans tous les sens.
Ces yeux à peine ouverts cessent de regarder
Elle ne pouvait plus continuer à regarder.
Sa famille était victime de quelques ennemis.
Il n'y a pas très longtemps ils étaient tous amis.

Autre fois Iles des parfums
Balddine Moussa

J'entends un peuple danser sans musique
Des cœurs en colère, des discours iniques.
J'essaie de m'imaginer un quelconque bonheur,
Qui alimenterait ces pauvres cœurs, à une heure
Où on chanterait liberté, et danserait tête baissée !
On compterait des détenus et des blesses !
Des opposants politiques soupçonnés de…
Ou d'autres qui aurait osé parler de…
Des propos semblant à des mensonges purs !
On oserait même parler de dictature !
Quelle folie ce peuple est en train de verser…
On justifierait des délits par quelques versets.
On raconte qu'on aurait retiré le droit
A certains, lesquels se seraient passés de la loi.
On pourrait croire que tout cela est vrai,
J'espère en fait que tout cela ne soit pas vrai.
Parce qu'on connaitrait mieux que ça,
Ce pays serait le pays du Gombesa,
Ou cœlacanthe, comme on dit en français.
Mais où est parti ce pays que j'aimais ?
Ce pays autre fois « aux iles de parfums ! »
Qu'a-t-on fait aujourd'hui de son pauvre destin ?
Pauvre mais riche par son flambeau de paix.
Est-ce dans le sang qu'on recevra la paie?
Qu'entends-je de là-bas, pauvres citoyens ?
Des rires ou des pleurs, ô peuple mien ?
J'ai du mal à croire à ce qu'on raconte !
Que cette histoire ne reste qu'un maudit conte !

Les religions étrangères
Balddine Moussa

Frères dont la colère éclaire la conscience,
Et dont je ne remets pas en doute la science,
Je sais que vous êtes des êtres dotés de sens.
Le mal du continent accroit votre souffrance
Surtout ceux qui sont victimes de la France.

Mais ne faites pas de vos frères des ennemis,
Ils sont comme vous, victimes et soumis.
Les pointer du doigt ne vous fera jamais amis,
Etre ce qu'ils sont, en soi n'est pas une infamie.
Mais de grâce n'ayez pas les cœurs endormis !

Tels que vous, ne sont-ils pas des Africains ?
N'avez-vous pas en commun un même destin ?
L'orgueil vous fait oublier votre ultime faim ;
La liberté et l'indépendance sont votre dessein.
Pour un même combat, s'exige un même chemin.

Traditionalisme, christianisme ou islam,
Telles sont les religions qui animent vos flammes.
Que chacun fasse de la sienne une puissante arme,
Pour lutter contre les destructeurs de nos âmes ;
Luttons pour cette unité qui nous réclame.

Vous chantez le refus des religions étrangères,
Alors, croyez-moi, votre sagesse exaspère !
Croyez-vous sortir l'Afrique d'un enfer ?
La religion a un côté sombre, et un clair.
Gérons avec sagesse au moins ce côté clair.

Une Afrique unie, une Vision de Nkrumah !
La réconciliation des Races de Nelson Mandela !
Anta Diop et la Conscience noire comme combat !
Les audacieux Sékou Touré, Nasser et Lumumba !
Les Dignes Kadhafi, et Thomas Sankara !

Quelles idées ces Hommes avaient pour l'Afrique ?
Pas comme les vôtres, des idées à sens unique !
Le net larmoie de vos discours haineux et comiques !
Oseriez-vous projeter une fin autre que tragique ?
« Nous sommes et vous êtes » est un projet satanique !

Votre intelligence nous a appris beaucoup de vous.
Pour vos délires, comme Leader, on ne veut pas de vous.
Au pays, laquelle des langues étrangères parlez-vous ?
« C'est pour communique et unir les gens » dites-vous !
 Alors les religions n'en font pas autant, je l'avoue…

Voyage avec mon prince
Vita Léo

Comme la chaleur de l'été,
j'attendais mon prince
pour venir refroidir mon corp
avec son brumisateur.
Avec lui, je voulais aller explorer la planète Neptune -
cette planète que j'aime tant pour sa couleur bleue
comme la mer Caraïbes.
Je voulais emmener mon prince
loin de toute ces femmes affamées.

revenons au peuple qui se meurt
Mpesse Géraldin

ma bouche est un rifle dont les mots
acculent le haut qui renifle l'oxygène
et crache le carbone
sur le macadam du rêve cimenté

je traine dans mon carquois
les vingt six lettres de l'alphabet
j'enfante les vers que les flammes
voraces avalent

je mar
        che
                somnolent
je marche ivre des cochonneries du capitalisme
et sillonne les rues désertes

je mar
         che
                  somnolent
sur la merde des politiques
sous les yeux impuissants de la mère violée
la mère patrie qui n'offre que
les festins faméliques au peuple

je marche
         je marche somnolent
et t'appelle ma belle

viens
viens voir le rêve qui se meurt
viens voir le rêve échapper
la mémoire de l'errant qui le fermente
viens voir le rêve
s'écraser sous le poids des flammes

et je t'appelle ma belle
viens
viens avec ton compas d'espérance
qu'on retrace les contours de la mère
que Um avait voulue
la plus charmante parmi les six du harem central
viens avec ton équerre
qu'on retrace la trajectoire du rêve piétiné

Je veux juste être
Edouma Nomo Sulpice Oscar

Je ne veux être
ni le mouton ni le berger
de ces doctrines
Il faut m'en éloigner
Non ! Le bonheur n'existe guère
La souffrance par contre est
cette terre, cette planète
revêtue d'un immense voile bleu
Ô couleur qui me fascine
Cadet du noir ténébreux
Peins en moi la voie du Non-être
Comme une toile d'océan et d'abysse.

Pourquoi désirer si tout est impur
Pourquoi espérer si le trépas est...

Combattre la réalité a-t-il
jamais convaincu

Pourquoi des questions qui
ne trouveront aucun écho

Je ne veux être
ni le mouton ni le berger
Père ! Ton enseignement
est pour moi une trahison

Si je te regarde et te supplie
Qui pries-tu à ton tour
Si je dois obéir et périr

Qui t'impose ses lois et ses désirs
Et mes frères et mes soeurs
Pourquoi ne peuvent-ils pas
Le temps d'une minute
soutenir la furie du Soleil
« Lui qui te ressemble tant »
Ô Soleil ! Roi des ténèbres
Que caches-tu ?
Quelle est cette lumière en toi
portant autant de noirceur
Et ce noir que tu protèges
de toutes tes forces
Quels secrets renferme-t-il

Je ne veux être
Ni le mouton ni le berger
Demander
m'a écarté de la générosité
Recevoir
m'a privé des biens
Écouter
m'a propulsé dans la métasphere
Voir
m'a caché toute beauté
Que faire...

Mélancolique
Edouma Nomo Sulpice Oscar

Nulle sensation, nul sentiment
ne décrit cette entité qui se balade
un temps frivole, un temps maligne
en chacun de nous
Et, tout comme le bonheur
le monde à ses côtés
est un insaisissable enfer

On croit vivre le meilleur pourtant
Ce n'est que le pire qui se mire
On s'y attache, s'y accoutume
On s'y accroche... Puis on s'en lasse.

Quel ennui !
J'aimerais ne plus la subir.

Pouvoir résister à l'extase
que chacune de ses caresses me procure
serait un grand pas vers cette tristesse.
Dois-je m'en éloigner
Elle qui, en tout, renferme une partie
Dois-je suspendre mes sens
Siège de son règne.
Oui ! Je ne suis pas l'ami de la joie
Je lui en veux... son infidélité...
À peine s'est-elle invitée
Que seule, toute seule, s'éconduit.

La souffrance
Fidèle et ô combien oppressante compagne

Jamais ne te trahit
À ses côtés, tout est réel
Point d'espérance, que du supplice
J'aime les couleurs et les formes
que prennent les choses lorsqu'elle nous tient
Ainsi, tout est unique et authentique.

Démon
Edouma Nomo Sulpice Oscar

Aucune prière en ce monde n'aura suffi
pour te chasser de mon existence
Aucun feu n'aura réussi à te consumer
Aucun liquide n'aura su
jusqu'à ton monde te transporter
J'en suis épuisé !
Tous les jours, toutes les heures et toutes
les secondes, tu es présent
À chacun de mes pas, à chacun de mes gestes
Dis-moi, je t'en supplie, lequel de mes péchés
m'a tant lié à toi
pour que ni ma foi ni ma volonté
n'aient réussi à te déloger de ce lieu funeste
qu'est mon corps !
Dis-moi pourquoi par lui tu manifestes ta joie
Mes os ne parviennent plus à supporter ton poids
Ma chair perd peu à peu de sa fraicheur
Mon coeur s'est assombri et mon esprit s'est ramolli
Ma famille, mes amis, plus rien !
Que dois-je faire pour mettre un terme à tout ceci
Devrais-je mettre un terme à ma vie
pour que cesse ce supplice
Hélas ! Je l'ai déjà essayé... trois fois...
Rien. On dirait que même la Mort
A décidé de m'abandonner, seul
contre toi, seul, contre mo...i
Pas un jour qui se lève sans ce besoin
de devenir quelqu'un d'autre... Mais tu es là
C'est toi ! Oui ! C'est toi qui diriges mes pas
C'est toi qui dictes quoi faire et quoi choisir

Mon regard hautain et dédaigneux est le tien
Ces manières et ces actes discourtois sont les tiens
Non ! Je ne suis pas faible ! J'aimerais le crier haut et fort
Mais tu me l'interdis... Dieu sait comment
J'aime tout ce qu'il y a de beau en cette vie
Seulement, avec toi, tout est dépit
La fraîcheur de l'eau, la caresse des flammes
n'ont plus aucun effet sur moi
Que sais-je encore de la Nature et des valeurs ?
Que puis-je entreprendre si tu m'as tout pris ?
Cette petite voix qui me prêtait ses mots

quand je n'en avais plus
Ce compagnon qui me guidait par les nuits sombres
et me possédait lors des combats d'enfants
pour qu'il ne m'arrivât rien de pire
Que s'est-il passé ?
Les démons sont-ils la forme évoluée
de nos anges gardiens ?

Aux Enfers
Ray Ndébi

Me voici, enfers, prenez tout de moi
Ne laissez rien, ni ma voix ni ma voie
Elles ne sont d'ailleurs miennes que par cette chair
dont j'ignore tout, sauf qu'elle va à la terre
Prenez tout, puisque de ne plus rien être
Là est ce qu'il faut… Faites-moi disparaître
Qu'il ne me reste plus aucune couleur
Pas le moindre esprit, ni joie ni malheur
Allez-y, prenez-les et brûlez-les
S'il le faut pour aller au paradis
Alors brûlez jusqu'au dernier avis
Il y a bien assez, en mes certitudes
de houille pour l'usine des pâles habitudes
Consumez de vos feux les plus voraces
Les plaisirs de ma race, leurs seins rapaces
Je n'ai droit à rien, si ce n'est à rien
Sert-il de connaître le mal et le bien
Il est du bien dans les guerres pour beaucoup
Et bien du mal dans les prières des fous
Ceux-là qui croient dur comme fer en la paix
Et sans le savoir, entretiennent l'ivraie
Ne sont-ils pas, eux, cette mauvaise racine
La griffe qui donne de la chair aux canines
Et ils tonneront encore les canons
Tant qu'on voudra de la paix sans pardon

Non, je n'en veux pas ! Enfers, me voici
Vous êtes déjà parmi nous, chers amis
Vous êtes chacun des airs que nous humons
Quand nous avons des désirs, nous brûlons

Oui, nous fondons comme sous la canicule
Il n'existe rien ici qui vous recule
Ne soyez donc pas pudiques, ni timides
Vous, nus par essence et mus par le vide,
Videz-moi de la liqueur de mes veines
Asséchez toutes les sources qui les contraignent
Au néant, aujourd'hui, que l'on me livre
Qu'enfin je connaisse l'extase du Libre.

Secoue-toi racine
Ray Ndébi

Secoue-toi racine, sors de ta patience
Ce baobab ne s'est que trop assoupi
Que tombe et que se casse son inconscience
L'arbrisseau nouveau sera son répit

Secoue-toi racine, je t'en laisse le choix
Fais-le comme l'enfant sans terre ni parent
Continueras-tu de geindre sous ce poids
au fruit qui ne donne d'avenir au temps

Secoue-toi racine, la terre t'en supplie
Ne crains pas d'être maudite par ce vieil âge
Le soleil lui a donné de sa vie
Et il n'a pas vécu à son image

Secoue-toi racine, sors et viens le voir
Il n'a pas offert de cette grande lumière
L'herbe autour n'est que tristesse et mouroir
Ne le laisse pas tant haut et tout en chair

Secoue-toi racine, car si ce n'est toi
C'est la terre qui le fera, et très fort
Elle te brisera jusqu'au bout du doigt
Et ton arbre et toi, serez bien vite morts.

A Dieu...
Ray Ndébi

Quand n'est ni soleil ni lune ni étoile
Ni bal de nuages entre la terre et son voile
La vieille veuve savoure sa plénitude d'ombre
Son visage baigné de l'intense pénombre
n'a plus besoin de masquer sa tristesse

Elle est splendide ainsi, l'obscure déesse
Le silence de son errance qui jadis
fut un chemin tracé du paradis
est aussi paisible qu'un glaive au fourreau
Loin de la taille et des mains du bourreau
…
A ces moments où Dieu n'est qu'une question
Peut-être le rêve tremblant de la passion
A ces moments où le temps n'est lui-même
qu'une vague couronne, déchue et plutôt blême
Les saisons perdent chacune l'air de son nom
La terre n'est plus la reine au bras d'Orion
Plus de jalouse alors pour la pousser
dans un trouble qui voit sa chair se creuser,
ses veines éclater, ses yeux exploser,

ses fleurs se flétrir, ses monts s'écrouler
C'est quand la mère n'est plus d'aucun attrait
qu'elle découvre la Liberté et la Paix
…
Ô vous, dieux des lumières et des couleurs
Antres de l'hésitation et de la peur
La Terre n'est plus une toile de votre musée
Jusqu'ici, elle ne l'a que trop été
Le temple de son âme l'appelle, elle y va
De grâce laissez-la, ne l'y suivez pas
Vos atours s'en trouveraient fort ternis
En même temps que vos prétentieux esprits

De toute évidence, vos serres s'y accrochent
Et les joies de vos bonheurs s'y embauchent
Nul doute qu'il vous serait pénible d'y être
Ne serait-ce que l'infime instant d'un spectre
…
La Terre s'en va, elle ne reviendra plus
Avec elle, j'aurai aussi disparu
Là-bas, il n'est plus ni ange ni démon
Il n'est plus d'inconnu ni de renom
Le soleil et la lune ne sont plus qu'un
Le moi, déjà orphelin, est défunt
Personne ne le pleure ni ne le regrette
C'est ce que le tain de la mer reflète
…
Alors adieu. Oui, à Dieu, s'il lui plaît
de vous préserver, un soir, des regrets.

La Tricherie
Etty Gnanzoutchi Ange Jonathan

Nuitamment son ressentiment est tenace contre le savoir,
Et il se découvre nu de connaissance
Quand l'aurore galope sur des nuées de montagnes dans les mains de l'horizon
Il se décide à voiler la face de ce qu'il ne connait pas, ce qu'il n'a jamais connu
Toute honte bue, il se couvre de regards usurpateurs
Ses mains tiennent les fourches de la ruse
Ses sandales couvertes de combine
Son cœur vomit de la tromperie
Telle est la tricherie.

Près du champ du tricheur
Je suis passé voir
Dans sa vigne rien que du déshonneur.
Sa bourse grince des lamentations
Car ses mains ont refusé de travailler.

Le travail le lasse
Sur lui, la paresse fait tomber un profond sommeil
Mais une âme tricheuse et nonchalante est vouée à la faim.

Je suis retourné voir sous le soleil,
Le poisson se pensant malicieux va se réfugier dans le profond le plus proche
Se retrouve enveloppé de filets
Et l'oiseau qui s'hasarde dans le grenier du chasseur
Est confronté à son piège,
Ainsi les tricheurs sont dévoilés en temps funeste.

À cause de l'Hiver de la souffrance, le tricheur ne laboure pas longtemps
Mais la récolte le châtie de déshonneur.
Va vers la fourmi, Tricheur,
Considère ses voies.
Bien qu'elle n'ait ni Commandant, ni Préposé, ni Chef,
Elle prépare sa nourriture durant l'Été,
Elle amasse ses vivres pendant la moisson.
Et toi Tricheur, dis-moi, Homme impétueux,
Que thésaurises-tu sous admonestation ?
Sauf la débauche et la honte enveloppées d'empathie des contemporains.

Jusqu'à quand, Tricheur, resteras-tu couché ?
Encore un peu de sommeil,
Encore un peu d'assoupissement,
Encore un peu de croiser les mains,
Et ton indigence semblable à un Homme paré de désespoir.
Ressaisis-toi, cher Tricheur,
Sois toi-même, sois juste à ta manière
Car la course n'appartient pas aux Hommes rapides
Ni la bataille aux Hommes forts
Mieux vaut la justice dans le labeur
Qu'une grande richesse mal acquise.

Mon petit livre blanc
Etty Gnanzoutchi Ange Jonathan

Plusieurs livres articulent son contenu.
Quarante auteurs y ont travaillé parfois toute leur vie.
Plus de mille deux cents ans, pour une seule naissance,
Confirmant son immortalité dans le temps.
Bibliothèque géante et modeste de soixante-six livres.
Encyclopédie de paroles réconfortantes.
Chaque livre, chaque époque, chaque auteur.

Sous la dédicace du Grand Auteur invisible et immortel
Qui me parle à travers les pages répressives de ce livre.
J'ai le cœur à ses sages conseils prodigués.
À travers ce concentré de plumes avisées
Je trace mon chemin en sillon.

Les paroles du livre, tranchantes comme une épée à double tranchant,
Transpercent mes pensées en acier de frénésie.
Sous sa coupole j'occulte une consultation matinale avant de franchir ma porte
De peur que mon cœur ne se durcisse encore plus.
Sur les rives de ses pages
Un arsenal de sagesse baigne
Le firmament de l'avenir.
Face à un arc-en-ciel de difficultés,
Lorsqu'une baie de soulagement lorgne l'horizon,
Mon petit livre blanc me parle.

Sa voix suppléante me rappelle le regard d'une mère éplorée :
« Mon fils, réjouis mon cœur et consoles mes larmes emperlées,
Afin que je puisse répondre à celui qui me provoque. »

Ô combien de fois ce livre m'a sauvé la vie ?
Combien de pièges j'ai dû esquiver ?

En période de dépression, il sait me consoler.
En période de solitude, il me garde du mal.
Un remède contre le mal
Voilà ce qu'il est.

Amis, parents et connaissances
Me font souvent défauts,
M'abandonnent trop souvent même.
Mais mon petit livre
Reste mon meilleur allié.
Dans les moments de détresse
Il me soutient.
Dans ce monde aux multiples voix tortueuses
Il est mon unique rempart en tout temps, en toute heure, à tout moment.
Ses pages ne se lassent pourtant pas
De mes mains trop baladeuses, de mon cœur assoiffé du savoir.
Et le Grand Auteur ne s'irrite point de cette consultation ininterrompue.

Cette bibliothèque géante en miniature me parle.
Je l'entends vanter ses mérites dans ma vie.
Ses paroles coulent comme un leurre d'espoir dans mon cœur.
Mon cœur autrefois en pierre,
Se ramollir au contact brûlant des douces paroles contenues dans
Mon petit livre.
Cette encyclopédie vivante dissout mes tristesses les plus fécondes.

L'histoire suit son coup.
Tandis que le coût de la vie me piétine inlassablement,

J'encaisse les douloureux coups,
Par l'armure protectrice de la sagesse du Grand Auteur
Qui transforme mes larmes en eau douce.
Mon cœur noircit par l'amertume
Épouse des rayons de joie.

Sur les sentiers battus par les difficultés et les pièges de l'ennemi,
Ce livre me procure des bottes en acier
Capables de les déminer
Sain et sauf.
Tous mes tracas rassemblés
Je les déverse sur les feuillets fertiles de bienfaits de ce livre.
Ses pages ne se ferment jamais à mes nombreuses sollicitudes.

Terre difficile,
Hésitation facile,
Étrange personnage,
J'ai préféré son confort à la luxure de ce monde.
Ce livre étrange
N'est plus vraiment étranger à mes yeux
Nous nous connaissons comme de vieux mondes.
Qu'il est bon d'avoir pour petit livre blanc la Bible…

Au Bord de la rivière
Serges Cyrille Kooko

J'étais assis là-bas au bord de cette rivière
Que les nôtres appellent le Niger
Les poissons qui nageaient avec insouciance
Semblaient porter le poids de nos inconsciences

L'eau s'écoulait en pente douce
Emportant quelques êtres de la brousse
Qui par malheur s'étaient retrouvés
Dans ce torrent infernal et débridé

Cette eau jadis bleue
Portait en elle le signe de nos haines
La couleur sombre de notre déveine
Et le désespoir qui nous assène

Que de débris de tout acabit
Que d'ordures toutes pourries
Que de selles déversées à la pelle
Les nôtres sont vraiment cruels
Au bord de cette rivière
Grande mamelle nourricière

Au bord de cette rivière
Jadis si propre et fière

Les vagues semblaient transporter
Le futur de notre terre bafouée

Les vagues semblaient transporter
L'avenir des peuples de la mer

Les vagues semblaient dire
Ici, plus de place pour amerrir

Dans ma tête retentissait le slogan
« l'eau c'est la vie »
Pour nous, il vaudrait plutôt dire
« l'eau c'est la mort »

Au bord de cette rivière
Que les autres appellent le Niger
L'humain aux manières peu cavalières
Efface sûrement la vie sur terre !

Bamako, le 15 octobre 2018

Entends-tu ?
Serges Cyrille Kooko

Entends-tu le bruit de mes larmes
Qui s'écrasent sous le poids de ma peine

Entends-tu le vacarme de ma douleur
Qui se fracasse sur le mur de ton indifférence

Entends-tu le charabia de mon cœur
Qui se fissure de ton inconstance

Entends-tu tous ces silences
Que je t'adresse sans cesse
Et que tu jettes au gré des hasards

Entends-tu les échos incessants
De ce glas monocorde
Qui défait les cordes de mon espoir

M'entends-tu périr
Me sens-tu dépérir
Sous le fardeau indicible
De cette passion irascible

Entends-tu le bruit de mes pas
Qui s'éloignent lentement
De ton infernal cercle vicieux

M'entends-tu partir
Pour ne jamais revenir…

Bamako, le 29 septembre 2018

Le Pouvoir politique
Akere-Maimo J. Ano-Ebie

Il perce l'air comme un tonnerre bourdonnant,
En annonçant d'une grande pluie de la crise, la paranoïa, l'incertitude,
Et puis les grands ambitions...la force de l'expérience!
Ah OUI, le pouvoir est sucré comme le miel!

Les meneurs politiques se font les dents
Pour une autre campagne politique plein de l'ambiance
Avec leur ventre bombé et les mâchoires à double couche,
Ils se nourrissent de l'argent de l'Etat et se noient dans l'alcool comme des fous
Ils s'amusent dans des limousines chics et nichent dans de beaux châteaux...
Ah OUI, le pouvoir politique c'est la folie totale!

Ils se délectent de l'orgie de la danse nocturne
Avec les prostituées politiques qui blanchissent leurs libidos...
Ah OUI, le pouvoir politique est sucré jusqu'aux os;
Ils s'exclament dans l'orgasme volcanique depuis tant d'années au pouvoir ;
Ils boivent le sang et ils mangent la chair humaine comme des chats zombies
Tout simplement pour gagner en puissance, puissance, puissance!
Ah OUI, le pouvoir est sucré surtout avec l'influence du diable!

Les acteurs politiques vivent dans des peaux de vipères,

Ils échelonnent leurs actes répréhensibles dans un lieu public sans honte.
Ils perforent les ânes puants de leurs ennemis politiques,
Les courtiser dans un mariage impie de folie politique ;

Ils se cachent dans le noir à la recherche de chair et de sang... beurk!
Ils consultent des cercles secrets pour trouver des ingrédients frais
Afin de résister à tout tsunami politique et ainsi s'accrocher au pouvoir !
Alors, le pouvoir politique est éternel à celui qui veut mourir au pouvoir!

Une terre inondée de misère et de l'angoisse,
Mais le palais du président organise les fêtes inutiles ;
Une économie paralysée par la corruption,
Nos leaders en voyages de loisirs en Europe,
Pas de routes mais autant d'accidents.

Ah OUI, le pouvoir politique peut dévorer le monde entier,
Rendre la société dans la guerre, trouble...le feu, la fumée, la mort...
Le pouvoir politique est imprévisible et les hommes politiques imbéciles!

Note : *écrit et publié pour la première fois en anglais en 2000*

La belle ville du Congo
Akere-Maimo J. Ano-Ebie

Dans le réveil de mon espoir,
Je vois avec toute la gloire
Toute une richesse verte du bois -
La belle ville du Congo ;
Sassou Guessou qui pleut la mort
De son vieux beau fils, Omar Bongo !

La beauté d'une ville,
Le soleil charmant qui brille ;
Un lac des étoiles pendant la nuit
Avec beaucoup les électrogènes qui font du bruit ;
Un peuple accueillant qui parlent avec trop du sourire ;
La belle ville du Congo-Brazzaville de ma vie !

Une économie qui dépend du pétrole et du bois ;
On dit : « il n'y a pas de quoi… »
Il faut beaucoup des moyens pour changer la loi.
On se plonge dans des grains du sable partout
Mélangé avec les plastiques jetés dans les rues ;

« Mbonte nayo » en Lingala on te salue !

Note : *écrit en 2009 pendant ma visite à Congo-Brazzaville*

ma mère
Galley Kokouvi Dzifa

la voix de ma mère
délice d'une mangue mûre
en ma mémoire

***

la sève d'une mère
un amour immaculé
comme une berceuse
averse d'un sommeil qui coule
et qui ne laisse éclore qu'un petit
visage épanoui

***

chaque nuit
elle sort de son corps
drapée d'une percale blanche
étoile filante
engouffrée dans l'intime
d'un monde mystique

Deuil
Galley Kokouvi Dzifa

une ligne immobile
couchée
autour
des larmes essoufflées déplorent
ton dernier exil

***

le mal en robe noire
te donne son bras
devient ta demoiselle d'honneur
ses pas t'emportent
malgré les cœurs morcelés
le ciel coupé en deux
les portes de l'horizon ouvertes
se ferment
traversée ultime

***

une morsure
et la rage souffle sur la bougie
qui illumine ta vie

***

les amis d'enfance
disparus
cicatrices indélébiles

comme des visages
figent le temps

***

un bois flottant!
ho! des pieds! des mains!
un visage
que portent hurlements d'enfants

***

l'odeur a un nom
celui des mouches qui vrombissent
affolées,
excitées telles des guêpes bavardes
bouillantes telles des laves

Instant
Galley Kokouvi Dzifa

un instant
ses envoûtantes déhanchées
et mon trop-plein érode
le terre-plein de ma piété
et ne reste de moi que la symphonie
des monstres intérieurs

***

des envies de brisure
de brûlures
de lignes directrices tordues
pour d'éphémères caprices
bercées au creux de tous mes vœux

***

parer les mots anciens
avec le sourire des lèvres hier tristes
la mémoire
n'était plus qu'une fêlure

***

des rires
dans le jardin de Tokoin
des murmures
s'écrivent sur les murs
nos corps y mêlent
rires étouffés et regards coquins

***

le flambeau approche
donne-moi ta main
un rayon de lune éclaircit
un boulevard au devant de nous
fait monter la sève
à iriser nos cheveux
en une bleue tendresse

Eclosion
Ayi Dossavi

Et le doigt
Démiurge
Forge un mot-monde, un mot-bocal
Pour y loger sa folie créatrice
Se tailler une parcelle de Dieu
A même la chair infinie de l'imaginaire
Un brin d'éclosion pour tromper le silence

Une façon comme une autre
De dire « je t'aime »
A une plume égarée
Tombée de l'assiette du Créateur
Pour dompter l'impétueuse virtuosité
Du monde,
Qui se maquille devant la glace
Qui se dit et se redit sans cesse
Comme un murmure phosphorescent
Qui survole et nargue le néant

Lomé, 09 avril 2015

Holocauste
Ayi Dossavi

J'ai vu la terre rendre son souffle
En garantie à la banque
Puis compter ses morts après le festival de la faucheuse
Dame-Mort, juchée sur nos bipèdes arrogances
Fait ripaille de notre chair
Le sang généreux s'est donné à verse
A la lame revendicatrice
A l'urne démocratiste
A la lune hypocrite
A l'alternance Hippocrate
J'ai vu la terre manger l'Homme
Le gober comme un œuf à moitié cru
Dans sa gueule garnie d'or
De diamants
Et de sang
J'ai vu la fureur sourde du silence
Après l'humanité dépeuplée
Vidée de sa sève et de sa verve
Mise à la diète sèche
Au nom du grand nettoyage d'automne
Un harmattan prévaricateur a nettoyé les derniers os
Et tweeté, les doigts sur son IPhone :
« Le renouveau, messieurs, se fera sans vous. »

Lomé, Tokoin-Hôpital, 08 avril 2015

> Ma poésie va nue
> sur les sentiers du monde
> A la recherche d'un brin d'herbe
> d'une parcelle d'innocence

Pour y graver un sourire
ensanglanté et revanchard
Des douleurs oubliées
et des pleurs des faibles

Lomé, Tokoin-Hôpital, 08 février 2015

Je trace
Joel Amah Ajavon

Il faut que je trace
Traverser la frontière
De l'autre côté, le soleil est tendre
Il fait beau!
Les nuages ont des seins
Il y a du miel dans la pluie.

J'ai écouté ta voix
Elle a plongé là... dans la vague à l'intérieur de moi
Et me balance sur des flancs inattendus.
Comment fais-tu pour entrer dans mes yeux et déconstruire mes rêves ?
Regarde-moi, ne me fuis pas.
Je n'arrive plus à tracer
Je ne sais plus quel rêve j'ai rêvé
Je n'arrive plus à poser le pas
L'un derrière l'autre
Tu es dans mes oreilles et dans mon ventre.
Que cette voix devenue atrabilaire s'éteigne! Tracer ou mourir.

Tracer, c'est mourir un peu. Puis ressusciter. La résurrection qui happe la mort,
arpente l'arpège classique de vie et dégouline dans les égouts des sentiments.
IL FAUT QUE JE TRACE !

Note : Paru dans *Je trace sur la musique de la vague...*

Eunuque, je pense à toi
Joel Amah Ajavon

Eunuque, je pense à toi
Debout, assis, couché
Je pense à l'épice de ton soleil
A tes rues sonores
A la déferlente des klaxons
A la poussière-miel
Aux sourires-amènes
Aux visages-benoîts.
Tenu aux viscères, je chante ta splendeur moite
Loin de mon essence, je suis haret
En proie à l'étreinte de l'incertain
Mes brisures claironnent des cantiques-vins
Résidus douloureux du filicide
Pourtant je te porte à l'éternité.
Ma colère telle une pomme adamique
Sonne le glas de mon silence
Et accouche un azur auroral
Qui rend au Soleil son sourire
Et fait de nos plaies des lueurs
L'odeur de la terre en moi remonte

Je retourne à elle, fécond.

Écoutez-nous, disent les ânes.
Nsah Mala
(Pour les ânes de Dakar et ailleurs)

Ecoutez-nous les êtres humains ;
Pour vous nous œuvrons dans tout domaine.
Mais vous ne nous comprenez jamais ;
Il faudra nous écouter et nous respecter désormais.
Sous le soleil et sous la pluie, nous souffrons
Pour vous ; comme des esclaves, la sueur au front.
Nos pieds sont durs, ressemblant aux pierres,
Mais n'en sont pas. Suivez au moins nos prières.
Vous nous faites marcher sur le goudron chaque jour
Et nous perdons les souliers de nos pieds toujours.
Le goudron écrase nos pieds en poudre dans le sable,
Et pour cette injustice vous êtes coupables.
Vous nous laissez sous le soleil, de grosses charrettes
Sur nos dos, parfois pour aller boire et fumer vos cigarettes,
Et à nous de nous rassasier de poussière et de rien
Bien que ces bagages sur nos dos soient pour votre bien.
Merci de dire que des âmes nous n'en possédons point !
Nos pleurs et nos cris, vous ne les comprenez point !
Notre bruit est un vrai silence pour vous, n'est-ce pas ?
Quand vous bredouillez entre vous, nous ne comprenons pas !
Vous nous transférez comme des prisons au ventre de la nuit.
Nos activités oisives et rendez-vous de la journée dans la nuit ?
Merci de ne plus compter nos âges sur les mains de vos horloges ;

Notre monde n'a pas d'heures, nous comptons l'âge en éloges !

(Perpignan, 13 novembre 2016)

Après le travail au village
Nsah Mala

Boire de l'eau fraîche, je veux,
Dans une grande feuille de taro
A côté de notre champ ; je peux
Puiser dans la petite rivière au bord
Du champ de ma chère mère ;
Mes pieds nus plongés dans
Ces eaux me faisant trembler comme la terre
Alors que le courant froid monte jusqu'aux dents.

Après une longue journée débroussant
Parmi les tiges du maïs frais,
Je veux laisser la rivière laver mes jambes
Comme elle lave celles de ses poissons
Avant que je ne charge sur ma tête
Mon bois ou mon maïs ou mes pommes de terre.

(St Andrews, 9 juin 2017)

Un élève exemplaire
Nkwetatang Sampson Nguekie

« Voici un eleve exemplaire, »
Dit le Proviseur au Propriétaire
De l'Ecole Christelle Secondaire.
« Dans ses mains ne manque jamais un dictionnaire
Français-Anglais de conjugaison et grammaire. »

« Il a donc l'avenir d'un secrétaire
Au Ministère des Affaires Étrangères
Ou au Département des Affaires Sanitaires, »
Repond le Proprietaire.

« Bien sûr ! » exclame le Proviseur en piétinant la terre.
« Il est tres populaire
Au milieu scolaire.
Voici son bulletin ; il les moyens extraordinaires
Et aussi un bon caractere. »

« Programmez moi une rencontre avec son père.
Il faut que cet élève exemplaire
Devient un fonctionnaire
Avec un grand salaire, »
Conclu le Propriétaire.
La Poesie de l'Ombre

Le 30 octobre 2018.

Part 5: Politics, Governance and Development

Them and you
Aleck Kaposa

They fart
And you smile, licking your dry lips
They lie
And you ululate
Dancing in the pain of the reverberations
You build
And they come rushing to destroy
You cry
And they laugh,
You beg
And they simply look the other side
You sing the blues about the blackness of the night
And they cheer you on
You ask
And they do not answer
You listen
And they don't talk
You talk
And they don't listen
You write
and they don't read
you ask for how long this will continue
and they assure you tomorrow will be better
you ask when is tomorrow
and they tell you tomorrow is tomorrow
you wonder and wonder what kind of people they are

and they too wonder and wonder what kind of people
you are ....

The slums
Clesirdia Nzorozwa

Slimy little world.
Under the card board where it feels warmer.
She sleeps and dreams "heaven can never be any better!"

Torn clothes in winter they are warm.
Rainy days our cardboard homes stand firm.
Like toads in the muddy water we sleep.

The streets are safe.
Stray dogs are our friends.
When the darkness comes we hug,
The trees
They always rock us to sleep.

Mother moon said never to be afraid of the shadows,
For she gave birth to an army,
An army of millions of brothers and sisters to watch over you and
me.

Food is scarce.
That's the new anthem for the rats and mice.
The ants taught us food hoarding.
Survival of the fittest, it's a jungle out here!

In a tiny hole we live.
It's never too little every mouth and stomach is always full.
Only these skeletons tell the truth.
My sisters are no longer curvy.

Discordant Voice
Jabulani Mzinyathi

When you sing the sweet melodies
Mine will be the discordant voice
Hold you by the scruff of your neck
Repeatedly shaking the conscience
The conscience you now trample
Under the jackboot of your gullibility
Drenched by the water cannons of fear

See the rising storms of abject poverty
Desperation walking along the streets
Hunger thunder rumbling in the bellies
The mountains of hopelessness rising
Lives decimated by scythes of diseases
Hoping that the sun will shine once more
That there will be reverberations of laughter

ZOMBIES
Ngam Emmanuel Beyia

Zombies in zombine gatherings, gather steam.
Buried behind secret microscopic pots, screening
Overflowing basins of freshly sucked blood.
Telescoping with rare anxiety
 lists of next victims.

Fear, horror sweep through an antagonized
neighborhood.Shows of public brutality
initiated and executed with gross impunity.

Screams….pandemonium …Folks
wrapped-up in commotion that eats
up the silence of the cold calm morning.

Abductions, brutalization,
arrests is the fate of daring
lashers against demonic
monarchies planted in place.

Vampires in vampiric gatherings,
gather steam. With brand new
blades, sharpen their deadly fangs
To suck the life energy from
socio-political critical opponents.

Transformed into wolves and bats
dressed in soutanes. Occultic display
of the inner core, poised to drink blood
of fellow albinos. Poised to exterminate
those who are hurdles to their path to fame,

Change being their most dreaded Dracula.

Hydra in its conference room,
in top secrecy, assemble.
Brewing up virulent poisonous
breathe, blood and fire fomenting
strategies, conspiracies to silence
checkers of wrong burn falsified
accounts and official documents.

Like the hydra, regenerate several
heads of bribery and corruption.
Nepotism, tribalism, mediocrity,
embezzlement. Swimming in luxury
while the hands live in the diehard poverty.

Workers Day
Jabulani Mzinyathi

Drenched to the marrow
The acid rain of pulverising poverty
The dropping napalm bombs of hunger
Vibrations of despondency everywhere
The quicksand of mass unemployment
The deafening silence of factory sirens
The debilitating emasculation gripping
In the stranglehold of uncertainties
The shrinking and uncertain pay packets
In illicit brews vainly drowning sorrows
Trapped in the hyacinth of escapism

WHEN THE ELECTION APPROACHES
Ngam Emmanuel Beyia

The Pharisee spends blank nights with countless
manipulative strategies spiraling the web of his
corrupt mind. With messianic zeal this Sanctimonious
political bootlicker combs countryside nooks
in flashy limousines as if to mock the foot users.

Bearer of nude promises of hope,
fussy of rival's activities, stages
fake shows of fame to canvass support.

Mesmerizes local populace
with temporal tranquilizers.
Resolute to remain up there,
while the wretched down here.

Election fever attains pitch, his
melody becomes mellower and
his tongue sweeter, and attitude
humbler. In a hurly-burly of a political
party, the plaster saint magically
entrances the bewildered masses
with a litany of envisaged projects.

Dust settles on hope, vicious cycle
restarts on the rails of stagnation.
Catapulted to glory, he turns eyes
to the skies. Ghetto dwellers rehearse
same songs of sorrow wallowing in
mud of poverty, smiles buried in high
mortality. Health, education, economy

depreciate in the wicked hands of greed
and self-interest. Roads remain death's traps .
Downtrodden licks deep wounds of deception.

The Interview
Peter Yieko Ndiwa

Wheezy voice cut through the transistor radio
Transmission from far across the sea
Riding the air to the black continent.
News from and around Africa.
"How is the situation at the mines?"
Whining followed the thick British accent
Morning sun shone greyly, mourning.

"I have been at the mine since five
in the morning and…" A pale voice.
Young. Twenty something, late twenties, black.
"In the background you can hear the miners
Chanting slogans, homemade spears and
Other crude weapons in their hands…"
Grisly violence, police opened fire in confrontation
By the hillside lay several dead, injured
Shot, short of breath, policemen keep watch.

"In earlier interview, field executive said
reasons for strike remain unclear. What's
your take?" British accent. Experienced, fifty something.
Thick silence. Whining transistor. Sun hiding
behind a cloud; afraid of violence.
"Tension has remained high here and it's really
been difficult to get a comment from the striking miners…"

Whining transistor, fading waves, complete silence.
Slap on the transistor. Silence. Slap! Slap! Slap!
A cough, creaky, "…wages negotiations broke down…"
A cough, creak, silence, slap "management called…"
Silence. Slap. "…unlawful and unprotec.…" cough
A sputter, tender touch on the transistor.
Please, speak, say these things. Deaf silence
Gentle slap. Silence. Hard slap, Hard slap
"…peace accord had been signed but key
Unions had not agreed to the deal."

"That is our correspondent from South Africa…"
Miners charged with murder of colleagues,
Murder charges against miners dropped,
Arrested miners appeared in court, released
Clashes, illegal strike, deaths, walk off the job…
"In world news, United States presidential elections…"
Transistor suddenly fluent. Switch off. Save cell-power
Sun re-emerged from behind clouds. Silence.

MY GREATEST DREAM
Tafadzwa Bandera

Everything was perfect like the garden of Eden.
People were free like the Israelites
There was freedom of expression.
No chaos, racism, xenophobia nor oppression.
Like Pharaoh and his army, all despotic governments conceded defeat.

The new governments were responsible like a caring father.
They were like a camera, focusing on what's important.
They captured everyone's heart.
Ministers were humble and putting people first like Joseph.
MPs were no longer missing persons, they were honest like a religious song.

Poverty and human rights abuse was a thing of the past like the great depression of the 1920s.
Africa was a developed continent.
Unemployment rate was on zero percent.
Investors from all corners of the world were permanent on our continent like a tattoo.

Infrastructure and recreational facilities were out of this world and our continent was the hub of tourist.
No one was living abroad.
Africa was like Canaan the land of milk and honey.
United Nations, World Bank and International Monetary Fund headquarters were based in Africa.

The youth were aware that they are
Royal, powerful and limitless.

No one was nurturing the ideas of poverty, competition and want.

Girls realized their values. No one was inflating them like a balloon or pushing them like a vacuum cleaner.
Being a pastor, prophet and prophetess was not sexually transmitted.
Satan was defeated Everything was right.

Mother earth was bright
Everyone was living right. It was like Utopia.
Then l realized it was only a dream. A dream…a dream.

University of Knowledge
Zongezile Matshoba

The quarry
A lecture theatre
Breaking the shiny lime
Lessons of life were drilled

Political prisoners unified
The cells
An auditorium
Spirits modified
Souls consoled

Even during death in family
Pieces of papers
Rolled soccer balls
Pieces of papers
Lecture notes

Scholars of university of life emerged
Alcatraz of South Africa
Makhanda perished
Stuurman was Steve McQueen
The Island became a world heritage site
Administrators and leaders emerged
The University of Knowledge
where the human spirit triumphed
Alas, some leadership
Mastering, well, tyranny and corruption
Years of one-party rule collapsed the state

HE COMES AT NIGHT
Ojonugwa John Attah

He comes at night
To plunder
To rape
To desecrate
To pillage

He comes at night
On foot
On his bike
In his raggedy costume
In his bloodthirstiness

He comes at night
In silence
To ambush
To tear down
To make a bonfire of people
He comes at night
To burn down
To cut people down
To occupy the land that is not his
To acquire the properties of dead men

He comes at night
Like a wild beast
Like a mad dog
Like a buffalo
Like a wounded elephant

He comes at night

Unseen
Unnoticed
Unannounced
Unsolicited

He comes at night
To awaken fear
To awaken impending disaster
To awaken the bitterness
To awaken the shrill cries of a thousand

He comes at night
The night cap is asleep
The boot-wearers nowhere near
The airfighters baptized by weariness and
The government has waved play on.

IT'S HIM
Chenjerai Mhondera

It's him I sing
In dirges
And wars that ravage mankind.

It's him I sing
In wars that make his folks dependant

It's him I sing
In wars that make his kindred wretched.

It's him I sing
In wars that make his people, destitute.

It's him I sing
In wars that impoverish his people.

It's him I sing
In wars that make his adversaries a victor.

It's him I sing
For selling out.

It's him I sing
For saving not mass.

Zimbabwe
Handsen Chikowore

A nation endowed with undoubted heavenly treasures
Yet drink from the drains nurtured by rains from hell
A territory tipped on the terrains where hope is ploughed
But still torture the pregnancies that promise hope to flourish

A state that is still further from violent mindsets
Yet set incidents that steal the presence of peace
A country that countless trees grow without any effort
Yet the harvests from the farms are heavy to fathom

A jurisdiction that preach free and fair elections
Yet the addiction of injustice is still engrained in the blood
A land that command the quest for agricultural excellence
But still yield to the status that reside in desert culture

Educate to Liberate!
Irene Munthree

Education crisis, a threat worse than ISIS
SA placed last in literacy test… Yesses
We need a power stronger than?
Jesus, we have got to make every child the genius they were born to exist,
so they may fulfil their own mission and purpose.
If we are not in hot pursuit of our ultimate truth
with minds wide open, then may I offer a little insight?
Mahatma Gandhi demonstrated a peaceful hunger strike
but how do we do that now when you taught us how to fight?
Using guns and bullets, teargas and whips;
teaching us daily to remain still and shut our lips.
And with every strike, you took away my freedom from me,
locked it, buried it deep and you threw away the key.
Thanks to the powers that be, we are now free.
But are we? Are you free. Am I free to be me or am I just free to
live in fear of crime and poverty?
You see the very ones that helped us liberate, now are the one's
causing hate, inner fighting and they dictate.
Keep the masses poor don't let them educate, less they take away
our votes, our power and disseminate.
We have children to feed and tenders to bait; I don't insinuate, I
merely state.
Fees must fall else 27 years in jail was in vain. Of what use is
freedom if I have no job and no food to eat?
I feel like a rat trapped within an inch of the cheese, while the fat
cat laughs as I beg and plead.
We have more than enough resources but not for everyone's greed.
Education, that's our most dire need.

If we can focus on that then maybe, just maybe, we have a shot at unity and dare I say prosperity?
Wait a minute, did I just say prosperity if only that were the mandate, poverty may dissipate,
but wait.... Information overload!
Steps comrades, one at a time begins the journey of a thousand miles.
First let us Educate.
Let us educate so we can liberate those hearts trapped in hate and those minds stuck in a past time.
Let us educate so we may annihilate sheep breeding with closed minds and blind eyes.
Let us educate so we can disintegrate apathy and the belief that we are powerless to change this.
Let us educate so we can dedicate our lives to the restoration of a united rainbow nation.
Let us educate so we may discriminate between wrong and right, not black and white.
Let us educate so we can grow our own economy for a hike in the Rand to see.
Let us educate so we may navigate back to being healthy, wealthy and free.
Let us educate so we may interrogate: job creation, rape reduction, crime destruction and
corruption conclusion.
Let us educate so we may imitate the dreamers and believers who fought with courage and hope
throughout our history.
Let us educate so we may contemplate a clear path to efficient service delivery.
Let us educate so we may meditate on our state of mind and address the state of our nation.

Let us educate so we can resurrect understanding, tolerance,
acceptance, forgiveness, empathy,
love and happiness.
Let us educate so we may levitate above a third world country.
Let us educate so we may as Bob Marley sang "emancipate yourself
from mental slavery,
none but ourselves can free our minds".
Brothers and sisters, don't hesitate, let us educate so we may free
our minds from slavery!

Justice
Handsen Chikowore

With unjustified sewage imposed on our innocence
We jump onto your waist where purity is not wasted
We sing within your unperishable reservoirs
Where sounds of vexations are quashed

Even the poor pour belief in your leaves of fairness
Which see forever and ever the pinnacle of peace
You gather all errs and surrender them to fresh air
Which aim to overturn floods and foams into fairness

You divorce all misplacements of facts
And crash miscarriages of justice into ashes
Shouting within the realms of victory
And nourishing from the mother of all equality

A Democrat
Lusajo Kalangali

He brags boldly a democrat;
He buries his opponent.
He brags boldly a democrat;
He swallows every correspondent.
He brags boldly a democrat;
He dehorns the parliament.
He brags boldly a democrat;
He votes himself president.
He brags boldly a democrat;
He sings ethnicity most.
Badgers are not so mighty;
In rocks make their resident.

A one way economy
Sonwabo Meyi

clock alarms go bang as they ring
bodies numb blood dumb brain hanged
tongues want to speak but the song has already been sung
you are a one way racist economy
only serving a capitalist demi god
who sucks blood of little infants
& rapes naïve widows

wind viral structural it collapses windows
beats & pieces of drums to fight for peace
black bodies take risks & through dark holes they scream: freedom
moles thick as fake white madam's fur with lice in her hair
they interchange roles with petrol bombs
welcome to this shitty town with its one way economy

born & bread to run not for fun
but from a whiteman's gun loaded with furry
bastards blurry eyed punch drunk from old wine
breathing venom abnormally very sacarstically
he forgot I was not the typical Kaffir boy
me i am a son of a soldier
born in a warzone
i saw a petrol bomb-blast before i held a pencil

we create fiery storms & move like mobs
watch the clock as it moves like a ticking time bomb
in this one way economy: where will you find God

Note to Editors: the word Kaffir was first used by so called Arabs, to refer to the Whitemen they met in North Africa. Then, it meant 'Heathen or Non – Believer', as the Arabs believed that the Whitemen were Heathens who did not believe in Allah. When Apartheid became systematic Law in South Africa, in 1948, Afrikaners began to use the term Kaffir to refer to Blacks, especially Black Men.

Prisoner
Sipho hobane Ndlovu

I am a prisoner in my own homeland,
The ability for me to enjoy my freedoms and rights, is all but just a façade.
The moment I raise my voice to protest, the police and the army, hunt me down to silence me.
For fear of my life, I have no choice,
I jump into the sea and hope not to drown.

I see a lot of injustices, committed,
By the powers that be.
My grievances can only go as far as the walls,
in which I am kept like a criminal.
I am a prisoner in my own country because I fight for my basic human rights

alcohol & progress
Sonwabo Meyi

you must be drunk in order to run these streets
you must be a bitch and a half in order to survive here
make sure you are a son of gun in order not to be harmed there
it is a motherfucker of churches & schools yet Apartheid lives where?
streets & national arts festival things but only certain bank accounts click
some lick dick just so they can pose with cocaine sniffing drunk so called celebrities
you asked for poetry
this is my truth it rattles like a loaded gun because i am tired of living in exile

potholes deep as graves they ooze puss & dust & drunk priests come in them
pockets are empty bellies swollen electric boxes silent eskom is dead again
tadpoles falling from unfixed taps this is no rap this is reality
they hate a man so much over there they hit him with a brick while he was talking & drunk
busy walking home
traffic cop sees who did it yet he tells lies at the police station
you shall one day reveal to us: who gave the order

you politik bullshit & fucking nonsense just because you buy the most alcohol
young children laugh & dance & cry: money for housing gone missing
pink skinned men in exotic suits cruising in expensive cars

some prefer to sip while some gulp it down & rush to the second
round or was it a screaming sound
this language is not spoken
they prefer to hush it in undertones while playing goD with a doG
& grumble that the money end quick

most were not born here nor did they ever plant corn there or
wherever
teargas was never manufactured then nor was donkey piss ever
served at the Cathedral

AFRIKA MY AFRIKA
Prosper Kavunika

Afrika you are known for your thousand warriors
You are known for your thousand legends
You are known for your thousand kingdoms
You've are known for your thousand dynasties
You are known for your thousand tribes
You are known for your thousand tales
BUT......
While you were busy slaughtering each other to become warriors
While you were busy feeding each other with superstition to become legends
While you were busy conquering and tearing each other to form kingdoms
While you were busy enslaving and abusing each other to have strong dynasties
Whilst you were busy splitting each other to form those thousand tribes
Whilst you were busy taking turns to utter to each other those thousand tales
THEY....
Were busy casting lots amongst themselves to see who gets the bigger portion of Afrika
Were busy harvesting yOur acacia, palm and bamboo trees
Were busy clearing up yOur equatorial rainforest
Were busy grazing yOur savanna grasslands
Were busy deflowering yOur virgin land
Were busy digging trenches and deep holes uprooting all yOur gemstones
Afrika my Afrika
You were overpowered by your quest to give birth to many warriors

You got carried away by your will to be known for legends
You drowned away in that pool of many kingdoms
You were so zealous in becoming a strong dynasty
You caused more confusion within yourself with your own tongue
Your tales blinded you
Many decades even after their footprints have since long disappeared from the paths in the equatorial rainforest
We are yet to heal from the scars they left on us
Many years even after their tracks have since vanished from those windy deserts up north
We are still yet to recover from the anguish we endured
Many seasons even after their scent have since melted off from the savanna grasslands
We are still yet to identify ourselves
Afrika my Afrika
Look at your triplets Somalia, Ethiopia and Eritrea
Libya has been drained out dry
Restrain your children Rwanda and Burundi
Reason with your son Nigeria
Protect your daughter Congo
Remind your son down south that we are all Afrikans

conversations with a mon/star
Sonwabo Meyi

it is a huge thing my son to be a leader especially when the tides are high
some will smoke alcohol & most of them will drink drugs
it is a must that you remain resolute but be prepared
they are going to hate you for it & at night they will ride baboons & strive to make you bleed
seek ye a witch from the east & hide under her shadow while you sharpen your swords & mind

secret codes are written in the face of the sky while poor black children work and toil with no oil
yours are hidden under ancient scrolls that you stole from the south & sold them to Satan's mermaids
now you run around screaming "illuminati" yet it was you who stole the African talking drum
bullets bombs guns you found peace here yet you saw it fit to tear this place into faeces
there was once a spiritual bond here but you built a church & never went now the children are hungry & dying & your God does not give a fuck & your Bible does not solve the chess board

they play tag with their own umbilical chords & struck a high pitched note sending hymns & eulogies to the African nomadic spirits who graced earth & made love with the stars & gave birth to suns
theft of identities is what your system brought here & you cursed this place by your presence
rape & maim & kill & burn to Hell is the language that arrived walking behind you yet you stood there & told lies

there is no man whether born of wizardry or via the message of
Gabriel who does not know where his blood is

it is a one way economy down here
clock alarms bang against hunger pangs & leave fangs forcing an
attention from all men
women don't scream there they cannot they are too drunk they piss
inside their own underwear
you have a church & built a school then you give birth to a multiple
taverns
the biggest robbery the mother of all heists is the 1820 Settlers
Monument
watch as it gets full to the brim during the National Arts Festival
but nobody knows where the money goes except those that have
connections with Stellenbosch & later take flights to Dublin

Rainbowality: A call for Change
Antonio Garcia

With a rainbow South Africa once led the world
Our influence did not come from guns, money, oil and power
It was the magic of the cry for freedom that all people heard
We believed in a better future and the world watched our brightest hour

Our father Nelson Mandela led us, a giant of a man, a hero
The evil of Apartheid was overthrown, and for the first time we saw our true scars repressed
Our people spoke as one, trembling and excited we were ready to go
We echoed the words, never again will our beautiful land be oppressed

The Constitution was created, the manifestation of our new ethic
The truth was needed for reconciliation, thoughts of generations captured in writing,
The highest law of the land, it embraced our people eclectic
The blueprint for South Africa's future completed, human-rights first for all our kin

We unite behind a concept, Ubuntu, we seek humanity in all things
The high-minded words are just – but they now ring empty
We need access to education, security and investment - the promise of what the future brings
This is a call for change, a long-term plan for sustainable development -it won't be easy

The landscape of the past is still uneven, the wounds remain unhealed

After a quarter of a century we face shocking crime and deprivation
Poverty and unemployment fissure our society – is our fate sealed?
We need a change, to give hope to the next generation

Progress is stifled by corruption and public service is lethargy
We want a true leader, a product of our history, not an antiquated remnant
An inspiration who can make the vision of our country a rainbowality
This is a call for change – not of our position but our mindset –
Coelum non animum mutant qui trans mare currunt

We cannot change our past – we can only change our future

Redemption for Azania and all the winter strangers
(for the poet Diana Ferrus)
Abigail George

I want to see the clowns. Cerise-
red lips underlined. Bloodwork
is familiar here like the stream-
stream flowing into the river. I
smoke bucket lists. I'm self-ego-
controversial like that. I step into
you. I step outside. The night air
moves through me. First its silence.
The claustrophobic silence of the
magical trees. Then the silence of
the birds. I am the moonlight while
insects fold and unfold their
crowns and angel wings. Making
sudden waves with their angel ways.
And all I have to do is reflect. Yes,
reflect! Everything is becoming
misty or is it the drink I am having
going straight to my head, the
company I am keeping. Listen to me.
Politics etched into wooden bone
tasting like the false-dream of a
pharmaceutical. Discontent for so
many is a permanent assignment
of life. I imagined her as a heat wave.
Making waves wherever she goes.
With her noble hair smelling of rain, and the
future habitats of river-ocean-sea.

Coloured In By Society
Charissa Cassels

I am Coloured in by society
My shades have been given to me
Through Apartheid
Where I was not White enough
Yet now I am not Black enough

I am coloured in by
The thickness of my lips
The texture of my hair
The melanin in my skin
The colour of my eyes

I am coloured in
Pages that I never wanted to be boxed in
Blocks that I never wanted to tick
Forms that placed me as an afterthought
Applications that were denied

I am coloured
In a society
That has placed me
As a footnote in our history
That has attempted to erase me

I am
A disruption
An inconvenience
A raw throat
A clenched fist

I
Defy what they want me to be
What they need me to be
What they have constructed me as
Their idea of me

I am Coloured
In by society
That does not know what shade to use.

Exit the old rusted chain-saw
Christopher Kudyahakudadirwe

Who will tell Dambudzo Marechera
That those trees of this city
Have all forested in the streets
Their branches swaying this way and that
As their leaves waved goodbye
To the old rusted chain saw
That gnawed at their broken souls
For thirty-eight teargas filled years?
The trees of this city,
Those that had kachasu blood
Running along their potholed veins
Have unclenched their fists
To show they have nothing to hide.
And those fly-ridden promises
Issuing out of the public lavatory
Could soon be wiped away forever.

the guns fell silent
[for palestine]
Goodenough Mashego

"if an elephant has its foot on the tail of a mouse, and you say that you are neutral, the mouse will not appreciate your neutrality" – archbishop emeritus desmond mpilo tutu

1.
the israelis send cellphone text messages
they drop evacuation orders from fighter planes
they send in arabic an automated warning to your voicemail
they knock on your roof & give you no option
"die slow or die fast. be a refugee or martyr"
they then bomb your house & say it was used by militants

the palestinian mother chooses to die slow
she carries her two little boys & flees
the israeli sniper hits the older - five-years-old son
dissecting his stomach
spilling his guts
red crescent rushes to help
the israelis fire @ them too
the young boy lies bleeding
not crying. numbed. @ peace.
god works in mysterious ways
green flies scarvenging his guts. laying their eggs
two hours later paramedics arrive
"i want water" he begs
stomach torn.
guts leaking
water not an option

the boy wants water

twenty minutes later he dies. fast.
of thirst. not loss of blood.
"you'll drink from an eternal well in heaven" the father comforts the corpse
"you're god's martyr & we'll meet in paradise" the new refugee/mother
sobs.
the boy; like four of his peers playing soccer on a gaza beach
like three playing on the roof of their parents' house – is killed
while the world watches. israel says it will investigate itself.
"israel has a right to defend itself" says barack obama
as he vetoes another resolution to investigate the genocide

2.

the eight young men were slaughtered
when the sayeret matkal got high on hatred
brethren bundled in a bathroom
shot in cold-blood
sons of al-naraf
non-combatants
of military age – birth to death
killed for refusing to suck bibi's pipi
butchered for refusing to kneel & take it from behind

3.

a wrecked wheelchair by the roadside
a rotting corpse a few feet away
wrapped in bloodied cotton duvets
a town wiped from the map – with american artillery
erased as if drawn with a pencil – rubbed off

impunity can only stretch so far
CNN can only hide so much

4.

this one doesn't have a head
blown away by an israeli howitzer
the other one's identity is unknown
face mutilated as if in a judaism ritual
the 70-years old imam is buried under rubble
when he was pulled out a limb tore loose from the hip
a rescue worker kneeled & puked blood

5.

israel has a right to defend itself – david cameron
israel has a right to defend itself – barack obama
israel has a right to defend itself – catherine ashton
israel has a right to defend itself – john kerry
israel has a right to defend itself – francios hollande
israel has a right to defend itself – hillary rodham clinton
israel has a right to defend itself – stephen harper
israel has a right to defend itself – susan rice
israel has a right to defend itself – tony abbot
israel has a right to defend itself – paul kagame
israel has a right to defend itself – US Senate
israel has a right to defend itself – US Congress

6.

"who doesn't have that right" - i ask
apologies - i deviate from the script
for the nine killed in west bank

for three killed in east jerusalem

Blossom at Prospect Field
Harry Owen

I see dogs, the prospect of canine disagreement,
so we walk. Too old now, each of us, for true prospects,
just a few old bones in the car park, though you're happy enough
to recline in warm sun on the grassy bank to chew.
Discovery is half the fun, it seems, at least as much as taste
so no need, Blossom, to look so guilty. You're a dog
without prospects who has found a sudden life to live
and is fearful I'll snatch it away. I won't, I promise.
This is mid-winter: the sheerest delight for both of us.

[First published in Stanzas, No. 10, October 2017]

Sycophants!
Nellah Nonkondlo Mntanenhlabathi

So-called dogs of the war stabbing us from behind with bayonets.
The muckety muck has decreed!,they will say

Let your knees kiss the dust
Wheedle our buskins
Till the hoof sprog

Bend down,
Twerk,
Shake the booty
Coition is swift that way

The Authoritarian snithed off our tongues
We just hit the dirt
Petitioning to the gods with red,yellow and green Barrets
Not because our Jah forsook us
But because
The autocratic god of the camouflaged men
With filthy, nasty,stinking maroon boots
Had laid with our feeble bodies

Because the AK47s
Danced with the clitoris,
Cuddled with the labia
And drank from the well of life

We move to the rhythmic sounds of bullets
Fearing the furnace their eyes breath
And the aversion in their voices

Fear not their bullets,
Nehanda said
They will be like waters in you flesh!

She lied
That deceiving whore!

Our fathers and their fathers before
Have unpeacefully rested on the barren land
Which will send a youth of us
six feet under
For we can not produce

Are they not possessed of wrath?
Or
Are we not bone-idle?

Do not leave a pintle that indulges your poon with blue-balls
He will preach

But....
What if the cock performs miracles no more?

"Let them starve to death!
How dare they question The Sovereigns word?",
The dogs will latrate

The same dogs
Whose puppies we defend when bullied
Whose wives we share crumbs with when hungry

Earthly father,
Thy Zimdom we shall depose

Like that of Louis xvi
Thy tongue we shall guillotine
And thine balls we shall serve to the bulldogs

drowning
Nkwana Joshua Serutle

it's hard telling a black boy
to lift up his chest after drowning

black boys drown in everything black
he drowns in his face
in the mouth of others
who calls him black
for being black

black boy know not
how to use his gills
he opens his mouth
but suffocates
he tries to scream underwater
flickering his eyes for sight
but still he suffocates

he is drowning
drowning in his own voice
losing his tongue to acid rains
that pluck from western to southern

black boy know nothing
of how to save himself
so

he drowns in anything light
like words
powder
smoke
and alcohol

hoping it's the closest way
to escape drowning

our names
Nkwana Joshua Serutle

we should scream
our names in victory,
to those who stutters
pronouncing them,
we should feed their tongues
with our forefathers' clicks
we should make them choke
until they chant to our names -
to whole lot others;
to remark and stamp
our prints to their hearts -
that gods lived in their mouths.

Change
Olakitan Aladesuyi

As always, it starts with a promise;
I will fight corruption with my last blood. no, last breath
what does it matter? Last blood, last breath, they are both
lifeless words

don't you know promises are feathers to soothe us into
accepting our fate?
don't you know change is a spirit that lies
at the bottom of a bottle?
and when it descends, you prophesy
vain declarations from an empty head wrapped in layers of agbada.

they fight, they scream, they throw tantrums under the influence
and when they finally make it to the chair,
they become lifeless
isn't life in the chair one big vacation?
London today, India tomorrow
uncle Ajala the traveler...

Tonight, the spirit of change is upon me and I prophesy yet again
we the people shall rise and reclaim our land
we will fulfil the ancient prophecy of change;
birthed in the womb of truth.
the chosen one shall come, burning with passion
against the enemy of the people
and we shall march in victory against the cabal
yes! I see her. sorry, him. no, I mean them.

what does it matter?
These words are lifeless.

WANDERING HOMES
Sipho Mthabisi Ndebele

Tell them
Your bloodlines are not in vain
You are from men who crossed a continent
Feet accustomed to their mother's terrain
That marched to keep blood in their veins
Long before borders tattooed her flesh

Break the silence
You are a people of song and dance
Who know God by name
Tell them
They too come from northern lands
In search of a place to lay their heads
To plant roots
To raise crops and children
Tell them to check their pulse
To see if it sings of blood baths
Teach them their pupils are more educated than this

Tell them
These are our sisters and children
Our mothers
They suckled our minds and fed our thoughts
While our struggle was young they nurtured it
Sung our fathers to sleep
They too are in search of a place to lay their heads
They come from northern lands
Marching to keep blood in their veins
Their bloodlines are not in vain

Do not stop until they listen

Intersectional Superman
Zahraa' Raadhiya Khaki

He was shrouded in the regalia
Of comic book prose
Red hope slashed over a yellow
Pentagon
Blue shirt clinging to the sharper angles
Of his Vulturic shoulders
Curved inward, forward
Protecting
His Warmth as the wind buffeted
His hunger stained suit
Into a cape-ricature.
The locks in the cars beat
Heraldic
As they snapped down together
To usher in
His arrival
-the sanguine glow
Of the New Free Africa Sun
Trapped
At the bottom of the amber and green medals
Of a Chaos guard
Standing sentinel at the intersection
Drew his features
Into a desperate
Hollow-
His hand reached out

A not so closed fist
A cup
A claw
A hole
Absence awaiting absent altruism
As his flight matched the speed
Of the cars flying around Him.

THE YESTERDAY OF TODAY
Adatsi Brownson

In the dark-less dark room of trees
Our minds saw and look,
But little did we say with our ears
that we saw today in their yesterday.

The smoke was our daily salute
A shadowless date tree in a desert
We shed our leaves and yet we shed our tears
The only beauty we held was our gift of gab.

These palms are reflection of cracked history,
where rights and norms were nurtured as mystery
The result where guilt dances on the orbit of our
skull.

An invisible epoch, where vernacular was ostracized
We were left with no today
Like we were born with mental impairment on our eyes
Forgetting that our yesterday and today are two peas in a pod.

We tried making a mountain out of the molehill,

Just the same time, our day rulers paid the bill
Of who and how the who made it how.
There, we lost our resemblance to pretence

Our today was buried with greed a day before
in an open and naked catacomb with loaded rags
We waited for eternity with hope
of resurrection of light

We were branded to take in the quinine
with the inscription "we are making you better"
But they were just gilding the Lilly with refined dust.
They spoke plain but it was Greek to me.

I await the moment
Where we will hear the blended voice of a fontonfrom
revealing
through it's narrow voice a tone of FREEDOM.

How we betrayed our Brother
Beaton Galafa

It is sad I will stammer before my kids
Because the day you left
I was still in the womb of the night
Tended to by the warmth of my mother
Shielding me from witches of our fatherland
Amidst growls from screeching owls.
But I saw you in mystic visions
Your dreadlocks swam in blood
Trying to escape bruises from death's strikes
Repression hanging still in your head
Thinking – what were we, your kinsmen, doing?
Nothing.
Even after tears crept into the streets at dawn
We remained numb and scared.
We just stayed calm listening to the news
Folding our arms and bending forth
Not even on the marble you had promised to bring.
We just sat by the coffin's side shaking heads.

STREET NAMES
Blessing Turvey Damasiki Chimunyapule

Walking through the streets,
I wandered, drawn by street lights.
In their splendor, they remain,
A colonial spectre of pain.
Strange names etched in our pavements.

Remnants of an oppressive system,
The last enduring vestiges of colonialism.
Names engraved by the oppressors,
To celebrate these our usurpers;
Who are the embodiments of racism.

Their names etched on our roads,
A heroic recognition for evil deeds,
Perpetrated against the natives.
Who they reduced to base slaves.
Dehumanising them like animals without needs.

These anti-heroes heroes,
Reduced our people to zeroes.
Yet their names are so enduring.
Despite their hideous erring.
Which brought innumerable sorrows.

We drive through Louis Botha,
Curious, why that doesn't bother,
Us at all, our ignorance so epic.
Or we see their deeds as classic.
Who raped our ancestor's daughter.

They were the force behind slavery,
Acts of subversion and chicanery,
Yet we still have Von Brandis.
Celebrating our rape and dragger.

Our grandchildren will see Joubert,
As a role model to emulate.
And yet our own heroes are uncelebrated.
Robert Sobukwe in our memory obliterated.
His deeds we systematically incinerate.

We failed to extirpate as the names stand.
Posterity will see their deeds as grand.
Ignorance of our violation,
At the hands of these actors of our subjugation.
Remains a three coded stand.

War
Hlengiwe Bila

My uncle speaks of war in Syria
Riches and righteousness are upon us for life
But that's all a lie
He speaks of war around us
But my uncle has given up on pen and paper
On the mind of thoughts
He has lost his will to deliver
He hasn't any desire to please anymore or anyone
My uncle speaks of war in Pakistan
You see guns and knives were never his thing
Fear and pressure were only just a myth
He is no man for wars
He is a faithful man
But five times can conjure even the most righteous
Five times can change a grown man completely insane
My uncle has given up on poetry
Says he wishes to see no more rhythms and rhymes
The tone of the ink is a membrane of deliverance only to those
who are just
Vastness comes at a price
It's not pride we lack as humans but the capability of asking
another in a violent way for his belongings is
a piece of the puzzle
My uncle speaks of war in Mali
Telling me how a woman was stabbed a thousand times and her 6
year old boy's tongue cut
So he could not say a word of what he saw that night
He speaks no more of the living
The fact of death clasp his breath
And others,

Others like you and I cannot understand
That's why most of us choose to apprehend not by a fair fact
But my uncle sees no more of humanity
Says screw scrutiny
Surveillance cannot cure such empathy
My uncle speaks no more of love
Gun powder and fleshy wounds can break any human emotions

Questioning the questioner
Joy Odifemenuwe

The senate:
*Gengen!
What's up?
What do you mean; what's up?
I mean; what's up?
Yes, what's up?
What do you mean?
*Ehen! What do you mean?
I mean what is wrong?
Yes! What do you think is wrong?
I mean all this,
Ehen! What's all this?
Sir! What's going on?
Ehen! Mr. Journalist what do you think is going on?
Sir, I mean we heard a rumour that…
Ehen! That what?
Sir, Ehen!
Ehen! what?
Question jam question,
That is *katakata don jam *wahala,
Which way Nigeria?

Note:
*Ehen- A Nigerian exclamation
*KataKata- Pidgin English for confusion
*Wahala – Pidgin English for trouble

Assembly
Kgomotso Ledwaba

Assemble yourself
Towards yourself

Take the instruction manual
And all the nuts and bolts that
Give it authority
Out of the placenta

The first instruction is more of an
Affirmation
It reads

" You are deliberately melanated "

Seems my body is dislocated
Within this Africa

When did Africa become Africa?

Apparently there was a meeting in Europe, apparently there are still meetings in Europe
We know you use black to sell African,
And because you blurred the lines it works so well
For you.

Therapy is a dynamic of
Regaining control
of yourself
An act of love and kindness
A sign of respect

Self respect

Nigeria! One week, one trouble
Joy Odifemenuwe

*Gbosa!
200 Dapchi girls kidnapped,
How? When? Where?
Don't know how,
Don't know when,
Don't know where,
Debates here and there,
The girls are released but one.

Gbosa! The following week,
Offa robbery,
Dozens killed.
How? When? Where?
Don't know how,
Don't know when,
Don't know where.

Gbosa! The following week,
Herdsmen killed tons and occupying their lands.
How? When? Where?
Don't know how,
Don't know when,
Don't know where,
Few scapegoat caught,
We are still looking for the herdsmen.
Gbosa! The following week,

Senate president is cleared,
How? When? Where?
Don't know how,
Don't know when,
Don't know where,
Debates here and there.

Gbosa! The following week,
World cup tournament starts,
How? When? Where?
Don't know how,
Don't know when,
Don't know where,
The boys crash out,
Cynic insinuate it serves,
The head well, to get,
A taste of his medicine,
Promise and fail.

Gbosa! The following week,
Adam becomes the new chief,
He spits fire,
I will fire anyone who does not respect me.
I am not for everybody and I am for nobody,

Gbosa! The following week,
National assembly members defect
To where? How? Where?
Adam will lose no sleep
Yet he is always slipping to the villa,
How? When? Where?
Don't know how,
Don't know when,

Don't know where,
Gbosa! All I know is that,
There will be new trouble.
How? When? Where?
How? Politics,
When? Next week,
 Where? Nigeria.

My mother is a country
Xolile Mabuza

She's done packing
Her suitcase is full of sorrow, pain and shame
Her suitcase is full of questions:
What have I done that no man has ever done in this world?
Where did I go wrong?
She's looking around her house,
    Searching her room carefully
         to make sure she hasn't left anything she might need
No, it is clear that she packed everything,
Even those pearls her grandma left her
That brown small suitcase her first husband left behind,
While chasing skirts
Yes, she packed that too.

She forgot the broken pieces
That our father buried in her throat
To choke her every time she remembers him
She would cry when she picks up those pieces
And drown when she thinks of him
Tears would flood her broken face

Wash away all the pieces and bury them in her smile
So every time she smiles, she hurts and hurts and continues breaking

My mother packed everything, all her things but herself
My mother left herself behind

With her suitcase in her hand, she's ready to travel from country to country
She's crossing boarders without a passport
My mother is a country
without a national anthem but a cry
My mother is a forgotten country and we are her forgotten cities
Hiroshima and Nagasaki become real when you look at me.
My mother is a broken country with one school,
One syllabus that teaches you to say "Sorry"

Our mother left us behind
Travelled to the unknown world,
Where man never return
Our mother is a country that left all her provinces and cities behind
She sweat in the absence of the Sun,
Suffocate in the presence of Air
My mother was a neglected country
Left to take care of her provinces and cities on her own
And she worked with no hands but her soul,
Until we fed from the soil that ate up her body
Because my mother, our mother decomposed in this soil
So we won't go to bed with an empty stomach

Black don't crack
Ynarus

The secret of the blacks not to crack is the mindset. We had to get used to pain, violations, abuses, you name it... That we created a strong and powerful mind that protect us from all the bullshit people trying to put in our names. Through the centuries, we have been the most underrated, disrespected and ashamed race, that today, we don't even care about what they say about us. We once were a joke, now you are the joke because you call yourself "the most intelligent and advanced human being", that you somehow managed to have the same mindset that your colonizing ancestors had. What an advance...
In the other hand, we, the blacks have evolved, we broke the chains and we made you treat us as who we are - humans like you (unfortunately). Mind your own business so that your skin may glow like ours or keep your essence and let your rotten soul come out...

Part 6: Migrants, Assimilations, Irritants

Between Places
(A poetic novel extract)
Tendai Rinos Mwanaka

2 February 2018
Inner-city, in set squares of noise
Bubbling drones of noise, honking cars
Loud voices, hawkers, pedestrians, buildings
Inner-city buildings of a noisy language
Hot-speaks, hot-structures, hot-forms
And hot-holds the city in squares
Right across Lillian Ngoyi's four ways
Plodding traffics deeps into the heart of the city
Residential flats, some old, scaling pains, some new
Dominate his eastern view, like those pillars
Huge prehistoric pillars of brown rocks
He is cooped in the fifth floor of a flat, across are
Browns, shades of brown, off-white, white, greens
Flat on his butt, flat on his stomach,
Flat in a flat, he observes
Park Gardens is the name of his flat
To the other side, in Jeff Masemola street
Is Burgers Park, verdant beautiful lawns?
Trees, flowers, structures; it forms a green machine
That circles back into Lillian Ngoyi street
Tall jacarandas, an acacia, provide a canopy shade
To those walking in the sidewalks, adds to
And contrast the tall residential structures across
It is a "worked beauty" landscape

And in idolizing these green souls
He has mind to sketch a drawing of, paint it
But it is daylight, no moon lights his mind
He is hot in words, the room faces the sun
The east gapes large on top of the flats
With cotton white soapy clouds foaming
Sprinkled with faint fluffs of white dust flour
Bored in blue, are lakes laked in between
And in the flat gravity wills you down
You want to look down to the street
Down to the home for humans
To live in a flat is to be a wingless bird
To share the atmospherics of city birds
To drink into dreams that flies high
To live in a flat is to live
In a home away from the home you hate
Or a home away from the home you love
He is beat! Maybe a home in a home
That is almost home, but not quite so
Rights across he sees people walking in
The corridors, the walkways, rooms, on top of the flats
Are assortments of satellite dishes like ears
Of owls that hears the voices in the winds
In Jeff Masemola street, a flat, two flats off
The corner of Lillian Ngoyi, it has two
Human like figures that seems sited
On chairs, drinking tea, as they discus elevation
To stay in elevation is to stay close to dreams
And a guy in blue shirt and a red b/cap
Steals his attention, right across
The guy watches the south, he watches the guy
The guy shifts to the north, he follows the guy
Bores deep into the heart of the city

And then the guy climbs steps into
A small hut on top of the flat
This hut always seduces his eyes
He has seen people coming out smitten
And people going in, like termites
Into a hole within, in this flat
And then his eyes scan again, sees sameness,
Looks inside the room, sees sameness,
Decides into the insides, sees nothingness

My country
Zongezile Matshoba

I wish I could love my country,
known for its Ubuntu,
South Africa,
The land where we fought and died for in Soweto and Sharpeville,
The land we were imprisoned for in Robben Island young as we were,
The land we went to exile for in Angola, Tanzania, Soviet Union,
The land that we remain uneducated in, unskilled and unemployable.

Oh, I love my country
named a rainbow nation,
South Africa,
The land we toyi-toyed for with stones, burning and looting,
The land where we boycotted with buses riding empty and shops empty,
The land where we stayed-away with schools empty and workplaces padlocked,
The land of unionisation where we ensured go-slows in production.

Oh, many love to hate my country,
South Africa,
The land intolerant of xenophobia, beating others for their language and looks,
The land intolerant of homophobia, hating men and women of the same sex,
The land intolerant of immorality, judging how people conduct themselves,
The land intolerant of crime and corruption for everyone except itself.

Many wish they could love my country
full of possibilities, South of Africa,
The united states of Africa
where everyone from Ghana, Nigeria and Congo wants to come
The Canaan of Africa
where everyone starts informal businesses with little harassment,
The Babylon of Africa
where almost everyone cries in vain for the loss of soul or
belongings,
The Mecca of African glamour
in Sun City, Table Mountain, malls and national parks.

On being a refugee in South Africa
Christopher Kudyahakudadirwe

On becoming a refuge in South Africa
You become the scapegoat for all ills:

you're the reason why there's a drought;
a witch that must be necklaced;
a cockroach that must be fumigated;
a wife snatcher and a job taker.

On becoming a refugee in SA,
commit a crime, you're the first to be arrested;
Have a crime committed against you,
no one is arrested;
for you justice is just snail slow.

On being a refugee in SA
you're that dirty door mat
on which locals brush their shoes.
You're be-mocked on becoming,
reduced to a second-class human being,
one to whom society's anger is directed;
the one whose possessions must be looted
when government has failed with services.
So, to be a refugee in SA is a curse
that society has failed to exorcise

Asylum Song
Valentine Okolo

"Some are here as refugees, some are here as citizens, some are here without papers, but they are all my people."

—Gene Wu, member, Texas House of Representatives, USA.

Spirit of nomads,
escorts of wandering caravans
through time,
guide us as we commence our
journey to strange lands.
We have waved our farewells to the wind,
with our feet imprinted in river beds.
We have grasped a handful of soil
and poured it out to the four corners
of the earth:
to the East we said "go"
to the West we said "go"
to the North we said "go"
to the South we said "go"
with the wish whispered by parents
as their children set out on a journey
of unlikely outcome.

Go before us,
and may our progenies
always remember
the place of our origin.

Our children would grow up here
on foreign soil,

seeing the old land as a mystic place,
only spoken about in noon day tales
and viewed
as National Geographic episodes,
and the old tongue a riddle
that needs to be solved,
an arithmetical equation
in a notebook without pages.

For them, this is where they belong
this is where their memories reside,
this is where they have their friends,
their schools, jobs, and shopping malls.

We on the other hand
will make new ones
as we are caressed by nostalgia
of the memories we left behind,
and make up for it by trading tastes
with new ingredients for old delicacies.

displaced humans
Adorn Keketso Mashigo

do not ask broken birds about their mother. those whose fragile chests were ripped open with the sword of anger and the secrets of their people spilled out forcefully with blood tainting
the conscience of their children. don't ask them for a passport because their identity is a woman with blistered feet and bleeding lips a woman running away from the screams of bullets with her son strapped on her back, lips dripping with pus and wounds drowning in sepsis. don't ask them about their true history that's not skewed, because from their eyes salty-water is a map to their raped past. don't ask them their true origin like a mole does to light, because from their hearts love is a home filled with darkness, all the hearts of the strangers and immigrants are their nationality. they pack blood-polluted sand in their bags as their passports to show as evidence the blood-stained soil to all at the borders, that they too also once had a place they called home, that they also once sat under the sun and laughed as ordinary folks with no worry that their houses will be burnt behind them,
that their grandchildren will one day become the enemy, today they are the landless in the land of their maimed forefathers.
today they bow their heads to the god of fear. like broken birds they
have abandoned their music in the shame of their broken wings. only their home is their hearts. only their pride is thin memories. everywhere they go they are broken into pieces of shame.
theirs are scars and wounds of xenophobia. their homes are shame. they have lost their countries to men who claim to be priests,
they have amateurishly handed over power to dictators
who speak in tongues.
they have abandoned the innocence of their children to horny men, some have even forgotten the name of suffering

because they have nothing to lose.
they call themselves afrikans because the language
in which they were born became scrapes in which ancestors
converse with their children in vain.

Part 7: Portuguese Poets

Palestina
Ismael Farinha

Terra das terras que pecado cometeste que não conheces a paz,
Não me digas que não conheces esta palavra,
Palestina...
Pais dos profetas e mensageiros,
Nobre e o seu povo,
Que não tem nada de novo,
Morrem velhos, mulheres e crianças inocentes,
Indefesos e ninguém diz nada.
Palestina...
O que será das viúvas com bebes no colo?
Me enrolo de lágrimas gotejando sobre a terra em guerra.
Palestina....
Onde esta?
Oh humanos,
Saibas que o sangue do branco ou preto é sempre vermelho.
Queremos a paz, amor e carinho, como qualquer povo que merece,
Chega de guerra de luta e luto, o pais precisa de alcançar os seus planos e objectivos traçados.
Sucessos,
Sucessivos,
Sem cessar e o que desejamos
Palestina.

Zimbabwe
Ismael Farinha

Oiço a melodia de Robert Mugabe, gabo me por viver numa África de poetas,
Miro a lupa do orgulho sem escrúpulo no vai e vem do vento,
Real man teach how things goin on, today, tomorrow and for ever,
Apalpo no escuro, deparo me com o nada, manco na cadeia do tempo,
Fadiga relaciona se com orgulho e escurece o coração,
O vermelho do sangue ja não diz nada, nada é a palavra chave,
Soltam se gargalhadas altas para atrapalhar o Inglês,
Enxotados da quinta do senhor que come tudo não deixa nada no parto do Zimbabwe é bwe

África
Fernando Paciência Luteiro Palaia

Nem com correntes e chicotes conseguiram párar o teu progresso...

E agora que te vejo catapultar para desenvolvimento já imagino a tamanha sangue dos heróis em troca de uma liberdade e pagando-nos o preço.

Oh África
Oh gênesis do universo...
Que se façam negros e brancos e em ti nasceu o berço....

Oh África minha
África de Mandela, De Mandume e Nzinga...
Oh tu que arrancaram-te os filhos dos seios para libertar um mundo em troca os recebeste sem vida...

E cada vez apalpo as tuas mãos enrugadas vislumbro as cicatrizes daquela escravatura cruel e amarga.

Oh África minha
Oh mãe querida

Permita-me contemplar a brisa e o sol que germinam do deserto do Sarah
Ir as ilhas de Cabo Verbo e ver como Deus exagerou nas metáforas das tuas praias.

Oh!
Minha terra minha mãe
Da humildade que carregam os teus pés descalços aprendi que África no fundo somos todos nós...

África sou, eu és tu clamando por liberdade em uma só voz...

No ventre do Silencio
Fernando Paciência Luteiro Palaia

Diz-me

Diz-me como retribuir a força das falsas palavras que germinam de um "TE AMO" cuja a musica entoa espinhos?

Diz-me como atravessar as ruas deste silêncio que deixaste em mim e ainda assim me pedes para caminhar sozinho?

(...). Diz-me

O que farei com tanto perfume da presença desta ausência que me ofereces no cair das madrugadas?

O que hei de responder às estrelas quando me perguntarem as cores dos caminhos em que agora andas?

Diz-me como voltar a pintar o retrato da nossa felicidade que havia na parede da sala, se tu levaste o pincel?

Diz-me com que palavras hei de responder as perguntas retóricas que deixaste na banca se tu levaste o papel?

Diz-me como hei de esconder-me de ti se ainda te sinto nos choros deste soluço amargo
Diz-me como hei de abraçar-te novamente se o vácuo da tua presença é tudo que apalpo?

Diz-me...

Como voltar a ser eu mesmo se em cada passo que marcavas ao despedir-te de mim levavas tudo que SOU?
Com que água hei de regar novamente cada pétala desta flor que tu dizes que secou?

Mesmo sabendo que tu não vens eu ainda te espero
Pois acredito na esperança de reencontrar-te no ventre deste silencio.

Cansei de mim!
Fernando Paciência Luteiro Palaia

Entre estar comigo mesmo e estar sozinho as vezes prefiro estar sozinho
Pois o maior retrato que tenho sobre mim é de um cachorro molhado ao pé de um rio.

Ao som de um batuque cuja a música entoa notas amargas untada de espinhos
Apalpo as feridas que germinam das zonas mais profundas da alma

Encontro-me no fundo túnel e ao invés de luz observo a sombra de um soldado apontando-me sobre a cabeça uma arma

Cansei-me

Cansei-me de ver sempre o vento bailando em sentido contrário
Cansei-me de ver sempre a tristeza escrevendo com lágrimas cada página do meu diário

Cansei-me de mim!

Cansei de ser essa ave sem patas obrigada a voar em lugares incertos cada vez que sol se divorcia do mar
Cansei de ser esse jardim repleto de insetos, brotando mal cheiro pronto a secar

Cansei de ver as cortinas se fechando e não poder ser o protagonista do meu próprio teatro

Vou levantar-me da plateia, vou despir-se de mim e revestir-me do meu outro lado

Canse-me de mim!

APOCALIPSE 1942
Kalunga

I
Em nome do Ar
dos santos
Ámen!
Ei-lo lá
A lançar lembranças
No mira mar
Um santo em seu santuário
Sem crentes nem 10contentes
II
Da pobreza veio
e nela voltará.
Eu vi
Era arcanjo
Servo fiel de deus
Depois rebelou-se
E santodiabo ficou

DADA
Kalunga

São vidas que se b(r)otam
Para os meus dedos
Um mundo um mudo um agudo
Silêncio de barulhos
Se me corrói
Como vendaval de rosas
Cores de rosas
Perfumam o meu imo
Não sei se creio se descreio
Ou se recrio
Luzes
Meu inconsciente é dada
Na infinitude do nada

Eu sou sol!
Ynarus

Eu sou aquela luz reluzente que, sozinha no céu, aquece toda a gente.
Sou conhecida por muitos como quente, mas só eu sei o quão amena sou e o quão gélido aqui pode ser.
Já tentei me aconchegar, mas mais cedo ou mais tarde, as nuvens se afastam.
Por momentos me ponho para não ensombrar ou afugentar ninguém. Na verdade, tudo o que eu mais quero é que as nuvens brilhem, ao meu lado. Mas a única coisa que consigo é trazer à tona o lado pérfido das nuvens.
Vexada, pergunto:
- Porquê que as nuvens têm uma imagem errada sobre mim?
-Porquê que sempre que me aproximo deixo as nuvens amedrontadas?
Lua sorrindo respondeu-me:
- "isso é porque no fundo todos sabem que você não seria capaz de atear ninguém, mas é prazeroso, nem que seja por minutos, despir-te dessa luz reluzente que você carrega. É que o sol quando se aproxima ele não ofusca, ele queima."
O problema não estava comigo, mas era eu!
O problema não está em ser quente, o problema é que eu aqueço.
O problema não está no meu brilho, o problema é que eu atordoo.
O problema é que eu deixava-me desvanecer, para que os outros também possam brilhar, na esperança de reter o maior número de nuvens ao meu lado.
Mas isso mudou! Mudou, porque eu mudei.
Hoje eu conheço o meu valor e escolho minuciosamente quais das nuvens podem acompanhar-me nessa imensidão que é o céu.

Alma zombie
Adailton Zinga

Nas plaquetas da minha cognição...
Posso vialuviar choros...
Zungados nas esquinas da cidade...
Onde a polícia faz amor com taxistas e zungueiras...
Com governantes discursando o sangue popular...
E com 14inhas namoros e orgias de dicas dos papoites...

Amando o asfalto mau estruturado...
Mesmo pagando impostos...
Com aquele salário mínimo da merda...
Chorando nos hospitais populares...
Por falta de atendimento eficiente...
Andando na calçada da morte prematura...
Na saúde sem saúde
que a população vive e sobrevive...
E em Angola faz juras de amor...

Sou eu...
O político das redes sociais...
Activista social contra as religiões escravocratas....
Queimando o imperialismo com palavras...
Recitando versículos
e capítulos da morte do pobre...
e o enriquecimento ílicito dos pastores...
O clamador de educação não endoutrinada...
Que é o caminhão reparador de almas a muito penadas...

Sou uma alma zombie...
Falando para quem não me quer ouvir...
Chorando solidariedade...
Pregando o Ubuntu e africanidade...
Numa sociedade ilusória...
Alcatroada no petróleo que nada muda

Nesta Angola do JLO... Dos Eduardos e dos Santos...
Que o pobre raramente tem uma oportunidade para dar go...

Sou sim! uma alma zombie...
Dançando na passarela da morte...
Músicas sem conteúdo...
Danças sexuais e tendenciosas...
Sou a vítima...
O vilão...
O gestor de banco ladrão...
Os governadores sem governação...
Sou a fumaça clorofilada
para transmitir esperança...
Sou Ubuntu...
Sou Muntu...

Sou o bisturi que não se ajusta...
Nesta sociedade injusta...
Que luta contando estórias e cantando o passado...
Griot de palavras mortas vivas...
No vagar de uma vida de escravo...
Com padrões visto como erróneos...
Porém, que de quando em vez se ajusta...
Sou apenas eu...
Uma Alma Zombie,
Buscando humanização.

Professores sem pedagogia afrocentrada!
Adailton Zinga

Esta vossa didática endoutrinária
Que cria ovelhas que absovem a água turva do conhecimento
Que de tão ilusório, cria autómatos.
Conhecimento concebido nos laboratórios da escravidão eterna
Onde nossas falhas são exaltadas
Nossos erros cantados
Mas o de positivo que fazemos
seca rápido.

Sim! É culpa vossa.
Que nós conhecemos somente Aquiles, Sócrates, Platão e outros europeus...
E desconhecemos Ekuikui, Kimpa Vita, Thomas Shankara e outros heróis africanos.

É sim! Culpa vossa...
Pois são vocês que manuseiam estes livros deixados pelo colono
Adoram estas músicas imediatas
Amam fornicar com mulheres ociosas e ocas
Odeiam erudição
Detestam o homoliberalismo
Repugnam a criatividade
Perseguem os insólitos
E venerasm livros que exalam o externo a nós.

Sim! Tu professor sem pedagogia afrocentrada
Que se curva como ovelha
Ante às malevozidades humanas
Consequência de uma educação paraplégicamente eurocentrada.
Professor sem pedagogia afrikana
Para dar respostas as demandas sociais afrikanas.
Sim! Tu! Que ensinas a afastar-se da política
E a ser passivos,

Quando o que é necessário,
É solidarizar-se.

Vítimas da Vaidade
Adailton Zinga

És tu...
Sou eu...
Somos nós...

Quando dançamos a música da compra
Excitados com os míseros kwanzas
Comprando de tudo e mais um pouco
Sem rumo, sem foco.

Vítimas da vaidade
No asfixiável mundo capitalista
Fazedor de ladrões que aspiram grandeza
Flagelados pela pobreza extrema
Indigentes culturais!
A Nação é a mesma,
Mas todos...
Somos rivais (tribalistas, regionalistas e outros).

Vítimas por negligência
Chorando vaidade e emoções sanguinárias
Na calçada da fama suja
Matrimoniada a óbitos e paraplegia social
Nesta sociedade justa de injustiças
Com médicos sem saúde e sanidade humanista.

Vaidosos sem vaidade
Nauseando erros caligráficos e sonoros
Entre palavras de pesar
"Amém!"
"Deus seja louvado!"

Que no fim do dia,
Nada resolvem.

BORBOLETRAS
Hondina Rodrigues

Desde ovo vôo por entre linhas
Eis que me fiz nas entrelinhas
Ponta de caneta empunhada por Deus

Para lá do cinzento
Desenhei ondas chicoteando falésias

Da imortalidade
Esculpi o regenerar do tempo
Pintei coincidentes acasos e peripécias

É de mim a vida
É de mim com alguma sorte
Toda a morte em que (re)vivo

Da lavra que cultivei ainda larva
Colho letras que construíram
Meu eu alado
Eis-me palavras!

Pela borda destas asas
Respiro o belo da vida
Rabiscando na palma do supremo
Bocados da vista

Ergo-me nestas cores
Fruta amadurada
Expelindo doçura e lágrimas
Soprando dor de algum amor

E de lés a lés
Sem vez
Borboletrando.

DECLÍNIO
Hondina Rodrigues

Cada
Vez
Mais
Cá
Davas
Menos

A lua
Aqui
Gargalha
Um hades
Fétido
De um querer
Falto
De gana

Gélido
O magma
Sobre o laço
Bradeja
Em triunfo

Já não há
Nem mar
Só um banco
Solitário
De areia...

PARTIR
Hondina Rodrigues

Sejam meus passos enquanto durmo
E aprecie eu, na ida, este falho mundo
Cada ponto seja um canto meu
Cada porto, seguro como o céu...

Cale-se a voz do tempo neste ir
Em que a espera se fez moribunda
Irei carregando meus quês e porquês
Descansá-los-ei na Suprema Sofia, talvez
Não mais quererei respostas ao partir

Deixai-me, ó amores, ó desafetos
Buscar alguma vida com o trilho recto
Que se me aluviou sob pés
Forçado por aparentes dilúculos neste ser
Neste ser meu em solilóquio no ermo do ir

À borda de lugar algum, nem forte nem fraca
Eis-me disputada pelo verso e o reverso
De alguma sorte a léguas do alvorecer
Buscando, já pronta, o leito do sol-pôr
Desdenhando qual santa pecadora o negro do ébero

Oh, santa parca vida a que canto
Calhar-me-á a barca das incontáveis idas ao pranto?

Serão meus passos enquanto dormir
Contemplarei o calar do tempo ao partir
Deixai-me, amores, desamores, deixai-me ir!

TACULA
Branca Clara das Neves

- Dá licença, eu tenho documento
A poeirada turva os olhos mas não tapa a fronteira
- Mostra então sua licença!
A multidão estancada ali no sítio da árvore Tacula que tem as raízes dos dois lados

     xxx fronteira xxx

Dum lado,
pessoas-porta de um azul sem discussão
            E do outro,
       pessoas-porta de um verde sem discussão

Motores. Filas de Camiões. Kewesekis de escape podre. Sacos em pé. Cangulos. Bebés

Dum lado,
chóriço - combien? - six mil francs,
aqui terra
            E do outro,
          gimboa é quanto?
           aqui asfalto

   Chega um vento aceso de doçura
   aquele que longamente vimos chamando
    e com ele aquela senhora.
   Lhe damos nome: Bessangana.

Atravessa bidons amarelos, rinocerontes impressos em plástico, pneus, rapazes com muita carga, trouxas, carvão, as tampas brilhantes das latas de leite, bagageiros a gritar nas línguas das suas mães, as meninas a olhar de esperança e medo, a pessoa que ontem era porta sentado do outro lado, agora vincadamente nas suas calças kaki.

A Bessangana passa.
Vem de Marte mas não é verde

Os corpos amparam-se no apertão. A bacia estremece na cabeça. Nada de tocar a vedação. As farpas são lâminas.

xxx fronteira xxx

Dum lado,
vigilância audácia persistência

E do outro,
Bienvenue
No reverso
on vous dit au revoir

O rapaz da keweseki com o volante decorado às fitas de plástico rijo entrou. Por baixo da lona vai 1 passageiro com escritos numa pasta "If you come back we will kill you": Beatings Torture and Denial of Food

Ela passa, visita.
Largou quindas, quitandeiras, a sombra da Mulemba
toda a quietude suave dessas mães imaginárias
Caminha com a força de peito das zungueiras
talvez traga o tempo largo

A pessoa-boss lança os olhos cobiçosos sobre árvore Tacula: x quantos metros de madeira x quantas mesas x quantos quilos de prensado.

Ela passa, visita, transmigra.
A Bessangana não é pós-nada é o que sempre foi
o vento futuro que deixámos de muximar
e chamámos

Atravessa aquele fuka fuka como se não fosse undocumented. Se calhar também vai só ver o tio.

A Bessangana passa, visita, transmigra, encontra.
Seu pano tem a macieza da folha
Flui como o ar a água o sangue e a vida
que nem sempre é verde.

MARCHAS
Ozias Cambanje

As marchas despertaram-me aos cercos
Reconduzidas aos calabouços cerebrais
Enfurecidas com pesares do Palma-tória
Da Macomia e Ulumbi das noites insólitas
Estorvadas do meu Cabo Delgado.

NADA É LIBERDADE
Ozias Cambanje

Brota na minha vista
Uma gota de lágrimas,
Conquistando a minha testa
De inapagáveis flamas.

Nasce forte a liberdade
Prendendo-se na minha virgem alma.
Nela espalha-se a singela flama
Onde tenho a liberdade de deter a liberdade.

Nasça a liberdade
Nasça da gota de lágrimas
Nasça estendida em chamas
Nasça. Em mim nada é liberdade…

A PAZ NO POMBO PRETO
Ozias Cambanje

O eterno susto da paz
Provém da morte
Do afecto de cada preto.
Catapultado pelo pombo branco
Que unicamente sobrevoa no seu espírito
A única e incombatível cor da paz.
Num ego que só faz desmerecer
Soltando as mãos e acorrentando as mentes
Sepultando o chilrear do preto e a sua arte de ser.

Renasce a paz…
Do renegado pombo preto
Das batalhas freadas,
Escoltadas de rosto preto e,
Maquilhado de preto
E o seu troféu de preto
Reaparece acasalado de branco.

Beleza feminina
Morais José Manuel

Toda mulher é linda
Linda é
Até que corte o cabelo

O seu cabelo desce
Sobre as golas
da sua beleza

Transmite o oásis natural
A exposição dos 100 brilhos
Seus cabelos são as folhas das árvores
da admiração

Mulher é...
Um anjo demónio
Um demónio anjo
Tudo depende do seu cabelo.

10.08.2018

ESTAREI LÁ
Morais José Manuel

Quando o sol tentar queimar a tua pele
E não tiveres o protetor solar dele
Eu ai estarei lá.

Quando o mundo te desprezar
E a vida te rejeitar
Eu estarei lá

Quando as tuas forças terminarem
As esperanças esgotarem
Não se preocupe eu estarei lá

Quando pensares em desistir
A tua vida destruir
Mesmo de madrugada, estarei lá

Quando pensares enterrar os teus sonhos
E dizeres " força já não tenho "
Ai! Estarei lá.

Quando os teus sonhos parecerem distante
E tudo que fizeres parecer irritante.
Mesmo assim estarei lá

Quando não quiseres falar com as pessoas
Não importa quem, ou coisa.
Não respeitarei essa atitude, estarei lá.

Quando eu errar com você

E decidires que não quiséreis-me ver
Isso não importará, eu estarei lá.

Quando ficares velha
E a bengala almejares tê-la
Aí também estarei lá.

 Sempre e sempre estarei lá

Quem sabe?
Morais José Manuel

Foi-se o império odiado,
Aplaudido por ironia ou por glória?
Também procuro saber

Os poetas escrevem e declamam as vitórias das vozes cortadas
Dizem: - uma nova era
Um lobo-ovelha,
Quem sabe seja uma ovelha-lobo?
Mas o que todos sabem é que se foi.

OH ÁFRICA LEVANTA-TE!
Roque Jose Pascoal de Oliveira

Mãe África
Olha só como estás fraca
Olhos lacrimejantes
Bloqueio na mente

Não mãe África, mãezinha
Livra-te das más companhias
E desligue a campanhia da frente
Que ninguém mais te destrua o presente

Não te deixes enganar beleza
És linda de natureza
Uma alimentação sem rediações
Nem intoxicações

Olha só para a Europa pobre
A pobreza deles a gerar riquezas
Olha para ti África das purezas
A tua riqueza torna-te mais pobre

Oh, miúda acorda
E vai ocupar o teu lugar
Aquele que ao longo da jornada
Vens lutando para reconquistar

Oh, África
Acolheste o pai da medicina,
Mas não tens amplicilina
Para curar os infermos e as crónicas

Ninguém diz ó África
Que o Pitágoras estudou aqui,
Mas todos dizem por aí
Que ele é o pai da matemática

Os gregos minha querida
Usavam e abusavam dos
Teus conhecimentos
Faziam deles a sua comida...

E já ouviste alguém ó Africa
A falar da sabedoria áfrico-grega?
Só te querem inibir ó Africa
E exaltar os teus discípulos gregos!

Ó Africa
Já é hora
Levanta-te agora
Deixa de ser fraca

Tantos conflitos armados
Numa terra em que a maior riqueza
É a palavra? Estás a perder a pureza
E viverás como um condenado!

Quando penso nos nossos sábios
Ampate Ba, Kofilobengá, Abobacari II
Abla Pokou, Sundiatá, NeneliqueII,
Mas poucos os reconhecem como sábios!

Oh África, você ensinou
Tanta coisa ao mundo
Até banhos quentes ensinou,
Mas hoje dizem que és imunda!

Quando reflito sobre as tuas virtudes
Que beleza
Parecem mesmo a pirâmides
De Kiops, que beleza!

Oh África,

Já é hora
Levanta-te agora
Deixa de ser fraca!

Roque D'Oliveira

30. 09. 98
Às 08: 23

(Do livro "Loucamente apaixonado por ti, lançado em Fevereiro, 2015)

TODOS PODEMOS FAZER A PAZ E CONSTRUIR A FELICIDADE
Roque Jose Pascoal de Oliveira

Hoje eu parei
E pensei
Agora eu sei
Este mundo
Está mesmo imundo
O que será amanhã dos nossos miúdos?

Os males desta terra
Desesperam qualquer conterra
Enchotam qualquer visitante
A não ser os sem mente

É demais!
Não aguento mais!
Quanto teremos que sofrer mais?

Se ao menos
Eu pudesse fazer alguma coisa
Nem que fosse de menos
A vida seria um pouco maravilhosa

Olha só os meus irmãos
São deslocados,
Mas são mesmo desta nação
Então porque são abandonados?

Não. Já chega!
Vamos parar com isso!
Vamos falar de paz e isso
É que nos fará chegar
Ao paraíso

Se ao menos eu pudesse ser

A guerra
Talvez eu fosse a nova maneira
De fezer a paz nesta era
Para Angola ter
A flutuar a branca bandeira

Eu queria
Eu até gostaria
De poder fazer alguma coisa,
Mas... que coisa?

Eu também sofro, mas
O que é o meu sofrimento
Comparado ao daqueles
Que vivem numa casa de capim
Usam o fogo das lenhas
E toda a fumanceira
Que vem junto
Para se defenderem do frio?

O que é o meu sofrimento
Comparado ao daqueles
Que de manhã comem pirão
À tarde bocejam
E à noitinha
Distraem a fome
Contando estorinhas?

Porquê existe
Tantas categorias sociais?
Porquê umas
Valem mais que as outras?
Porquê que o meu diploma
Dá-me uma
E eu vivo outra categoria social?

Quem invetou isso,

De uns serem
Mais importantes que os outros?
Afinal, não somos todos
Da mesma natureza humana?

Não dá!
A ser assim
É melhor isso ter um fim!

Mas eu vou persistir
Se eu morrer o meu filho
Vai me substituir
E um dia o sofrimento
Passará para os finados!

Todos podemos fazer a paz
E construir a felicidade!

A prostituta pode vender
Seu corpo à castidade

O assassino
Pode matar o ódio

O político pode
Governar o povo com justiça

O poeta pode escrever
Sobre amor e hamonia

O padre pode
Pregar a reconciliação

O jovem pode
Ajudar o idoso a atravessar

O professor

Também pode educar

O ladrão pode roubar um pouco
Dos seus bens para dar ao irmão

A justiça pode
Servir o médico e o camponês

E o amor pode ser
Dividido por todos!

É verdade irmãos...

Todos podemos fazer a paz
E construir a feliciade!

Um dia Angola
Ainda será
Como esse dia que eu vivo...

O sol reflectido na água
Desfilando todo seu encanto
Deixando-a mais linda
Mais convidativa

Eu tenho fé
Numa Angola melhor!

Roque D'Oliveira

11. 981.
Às 16: 00
Praia de S. Tiago

(Do livro "Loucamente apaixonado por ti, lançado em Fevereiro, 2015)

POETA FARRAPO
Canhanga Soberano

Um poema, uma distração
Um trago, uma ilusão
O sono, um apagão
Depois, nova realidade, o cantar do pavão,
O pão por comprar,
Os filhos por gerar,
As doenças por tratar
As contas por pagar
Os patrões por aturar
Amores por reconquistar
.?!
Mais um trago
Já sem troco
Sou um farrapo!

À PEDRA
Canhanga Soberano

Cantam alegres
Sempre em grupo
Jovens casadas
Senhoras já preparadas
Moças cobiçadas
Todas prendadas
Viúvas e sengadas

Cantam e contam
Malambas de vidas
Estórias passadas
Problemas solucionados
Assuntos almofadados
Outros tantos exorcizados

E o martelo-pau
Curvo e afável
Contra o milho um lacrau
Tuc, tuc, tuc
"Quando fui moer o milho,
Julgava ser para consumo e negócio...
Serviu para outro casamento!"

Lições passadas sobre a pedra
Onde o milho não resiste ao pau e pedra
E elas cantam o que pensam
Fazendo farinha com destreza!

Part 8: Poetry, Art and Writing

The Novelist
Aremu Adams Adebisi

The novelist writes a story,
my eyes stalk words, he bleeds.
The novelist paints realities,
says all characters are fictional,
semblance to none, living or dead.
But he shares same outlines,
same framework with the act
that ran in circles till the end.
The media confirms it when
he dies: overdosed on drugs.
The novelist says I read
Girl Nolita today and at first
my inner self could not agree
Nabokov was to be isolated
from the act. The novelist
cuts bits of himself into tiny
words. I have once devoured
the heart of a novelist, I have
eaten another's flesh. I read the
words like an offal, like burnt
offerings wrapped in a confetti.
This novelist writes about her
thirsty flesh, pelvic exoneration,
& chemo life. Each fictive letter
is pantomimic that even in silence,

I know how my mother sounds.

A BLANK PIECE OF PAPER
Tendai Rinos Mwanaka

A blank piece of paper is torture
When the mind is untorched by the touches
Of a writer welding a pen, lighting
This pen becomes a sword of pain
Piercing to blankness the writer's mind
Burning it blue flames of the mire

A blank piece of paper burns
It burns like white tree hunger
A blank piece of paper invites
The pen to start dancing rhythmically
To the sounds in the mind mimic-ally
Wielding the pen like swordstick tines
Of a sword dulled and flattened by time

A blank piece of paper seizures
The mind into small paper pieces
Shredded, scissor-ed, razor-ed, tiny tinybits
Haphazard twits of an inchoate spirit
Who throws the pieces into the blue

A blank piece of paper tells
Tall tales better than a pen tells
In its vast, silent white space untold
Are tales waiting to be detailed?
By the blueshifts of the tolling pens

A blank piece of paper is
A blank piece of mind to
A blank piece of paper
Ay man, I give up!
This blank piece of paper beats me!

BROWN COLLAR JOB
Joseph Olamide Babalola

earth is the paper so brown, so thick
   our pen, the hoe, writes unhindered
     green is what we live to see and seek
      beneath whatever blue sky overhead
   under whatever scorching, orange sun
below whatever silvery, chilled drops

the barbers of the earth we proudly are
   the engineer of whatever fructuous green
     we impregnate the loamy, fecund surface
      we are also castrators of the unwanted
     the murderers of unyielding growths
   we are the martial artists of our world
whose cutlass skills bewilders the grasses

on our backs we do sit; not a chair at work
   bending low, attending to seasonal leafages
     the salty sweat we shed, tastes in your food
     your store operates on our persevered pains
   though your market can't survive in our absence
yet we never go on strike actions; how great

our skins may not be fresh like our produce
     yet it is as smooth as a yam tuber's; rustic
       our bodies may not be apple-like in flesh
         yet it is of a sweet, scarified pineapple's
       our A/C is of the under-the-mango-shed type
     our tattered work cloth is habitually ill-ironed
for fashion, we rock clothes of hundreds creases

we're not the rags of the earth; forget it!
   we give meaning to continuous existence
     we're not poverty-ridden; get it right!
       we are extremely rich, by nature's standard
     we're equally proud of keeping you fed
without us, just consider yourself gone

The poet's sweat
Munyaradzi Gibson Bopoto

The intercourse of our erotic verbs
Oh! and my lyrically coated semen
Impregnates thee with a poetic seed
But thy soul be aligned to discern ?
Islaam,Christianity,Hinduism and so forth
Inks disclosing a world still to come forth
And how does the writer sleep ?
When puns and alliterations weep
And screech,birthing such a creep
Viola!
the blood of a dinosaur`s clock
the Tick Tock! and Tick Tock
the opportune finger of hasty time
The fabled once upon a rhyme
Quivering pens screaming a disdained truth
That of no bliss future under the above clouds
The supreme deity`s mysterious works illustrated
As water burns crumbling to ashes.

In concert
Adré Marshall

The news lay for months
as still as a white stone
sunk in an unruffled pool,

but now, at this concert,
as the notes dance, they stir eddies
and ripples from our dormant past.

Years ago, walking past that music store
in Long Street, you heard this music,
rushed inside, and clutching

a box of long-playing vinyl records
said, this music is so beautiful,
I had to get it, for you.

And now, as Bach's Goldberg Variations
swell, and sink again into silence,
the notes spill over into sorrow,

the surface of the pool heaves in seismic
waves as the white stone
rises, and rends the quiet surface

of the water's skin; it strikes
me in the throat, and
hammers in at last the loss

of you, your well-tempered
love of music, and that far-off

harmonious world.

finger painting
Aaliyah Cassim

they say that finger painting
is for children

i sit in front of my easel
remembering a time
when i gave
pieces of myself
to my art
so freely

An Elegy to Kofi Annan
Odhiambo Kaumah

Is it thunder I have heard?
Fallen, is the old baobab tree
whose seeds of peace generations have walked

Is it lightening I have seen?
Eternally blinded, are the shining black eyes
whose lights have fallen upon us with compassion

The dark sun has looked down upon us
Wilting the very center branch of our cocoa
The roaring river has come out of itself
Flooding a prime field of our yams

Yesterday the drums of war beat
Tum tu tum shut! Tum tu tum shut!
Our spears hanged on our hands ready to strike
Yesterday the flute ringed in our ears and the night was dark
And our men's muscles filled their flesh in readiness for the battle
But when his voice came singing in the Harmattan wind,
Not a spear nor a muscles was broken
It is his voice that fought for us
It is Kofi's voice we knew!

He is not meek like the one who hides his fear in violence
No!
He is not weak like the one who verbalize his strength in threats
No!
It was his voice that climbed the hills into the caves of the enemies
It was his voice that knocked down adamant hearts of tyrants

It was his voice that detonated the tanks of piece when war came
home

Today, the drums beat with a different sound
We are gathered in the field for panafest
And now his name we call to say,
Go join the council of Nsamanfo
Go son of our land
Go Kofi
For the drums of war are torn and tired.

Take it from my hand
Fethi Sassi

I listen to you with the passion of a child
I wander like a possessed soul
Despite the fact that I'm not fond of contemporary poetry
I still love poems that rhyme
And all what is said in old poetry like Hatia and Mutanabbi
But between your words I discovered
A stop in every letter
And an angle to lubricate the words
Or to learn how to write all over again
I felt like I was walking an entire town
But is a distance enough for the nearest star
To reach the sky and light a cloud in the whiteness
Just take it from my hand, it is no big deal

lying is an artform
Goodenough Mashego

they asked him
how he'll like to be remembered
a thief who emptied public's purse & enriched his friends
added twenty kids on the bill & ballooned the invoice
plenty people fell off the deck while his hand steadied the ship
for tarshish felt like the destination as nineveh was bleak
they asked him
if he'll write a memoir or let history absolve him
he couldn't write so he let history do it
like a hero he wasn't a thief he was
unlike the thief he was but the hero he wasn't

we asked her
how she'll like to be remembered
mother teresa florence nightingale ceceilia makiwane
charlotte magxeke ruth first ellen joseph sirleaf
benazir bhutto joyce mujuru or assanta shakur
margaret thatcher mary robinson madeline albright
oluchi alek wek iman naomi campbell
oprah winfrey maya angelou toni morrison afeni shakur
condoleeza rice golda meir susan rice tzipi livni
or be remembered for an ex who shared a bed with her
who used to whisper sweet lies & swore to god they were true

she asked me
how I'll like to be remembered
sixteen holes puncturing slug exposing society's dirty linen
scalpel sharp forked tongue prophecy i spit like spittle
you ain't never met no warrior like me – believe me
sword wielding human guillotine i leave your body dead walking

got you drowning on my coffee on weedsmoke you choking
lyrical verses I'm throwing
rattlesnake plus black mamba I'm twice the threat you facing
& my rhymes *galephirimi*I'm toxic
remember me not a blunt poet I'm razor gut slicing

i asked him
how he'll like to be remembered
a rhetoric spitting bigot spiritual paraplegic
vampire sipping orphan's blood in an orgy of hate
ya thirst not my lilac wine
crave not tequila shots
in own power you trusting your prayers come abridged
every animal bribes noah's bouncers when the bar has been lowered
everything means something when we define meaning, round figures
he didn't lie he was misled
i remember you on a bed of roses you deny you slept

he asked me
how I'll like to be remembered
as that pain in your ass that left your doctor puzzled
that psalmist who wrote more songs than david I'm the 13th disciple
judas iscariot substitute a gentile searching for black jesus
circumcised like a jew barmitzva'ed with tequila & pork stew
I'm that bard that weaves words make persian rugs off my lyrics
remember me as one man who split his life into two
who lived a calvinist life afore damascus happened
damascus happened & peeled the veil off my eyes
remember me like everyone else though i tried to pretend

the poet's shadows
Adorn Keketso Mashigo

i sit—three o'clock in the morning—
in the dead of night and write about
the girls i have never got to date,
the past i can never revisit and re-live;
the day i lost myself to some stupid girl
the dreams i failed to achieve
the youthful days i miss and the lies i
told to get laid, the women i screwed
with the darkness of my evil tongue
the promises i made that never materialised.
i sit, on my parent's broken chairs
write about how the darkness of silence
filled the womb of my protest when my father
dug my mother's cunt like a dog scouring the surface
for a meaty bone, i write about the days i am left on earth,
of the raw sex i had before and still enjoy,
the things i failed to represent,
it could be time i stood for something
if not standing on my feet and proclaim my stand on this cemetery.
i sit, at home with no electricity, yet broken hopes
like the darkness of me and my brothers' room
write about the realities of our fake freedom
our democracy
the rights of abortion and all the women i have manipulated
to destroy the beginning of my unplanned seeds
the silence that fills my heart when i am alone
fearing i am fast becoming a drunkard
the friends i have lost to money and paralyzed fame
tonight i sit, all alone, in a graveyard full of broken roses
and write about chego and all the shame i have for the father

i have become. for all the wrongs i have done his mom
the route i took plotting to make money so that
he can have a better life. i never knew being a poet meant to
be a broke ass father haunted by the silence of untold stories.

Editor
Awuah Mainoo Gabriel

Ingressing a Goldyn shade
Where this Sole wishes to be
you pierce me from Bird
Marring whatever I longed for
Entangling me with Derty things Lyke these
Ah!

Could you not be all right?
Or yet never write...

Becoz you Waist Mi Tyme
You Waist Mi Tyme,
You Juxt Waist Mi Tyme
With such Derty beauties
I am Juxt an infallible god of your creations
No, not the infallible God; for I too flaw.

Part 9: Love and Relationships

DISEMBODIED MATES
Andrew Nyongesa

My husband is stolen,
Elders, please help;
I am a wife spinster,
In lonely company;
Wekesa huddles on his laptop,
Grinning at disembodied company!

My handsome man is a corpse,
My kinsmen, do help;
I am a wife husband,
Presiding over the bedroom;
Wekesa ogles at his smart phone,
 Intimate with mental mates

My husband is misanthrope,
My kinsfolk please help;
I am a married spinster
In lonely company,
Wekesa coos and caresses
Compaq in a far corner,
All the days of our marriage!

My children are gone,
Our God, please help;
I am a childless parent
Of seven children
That plop in sofas

Fondling gadgets in the dark,
Without affection for humanity.

My sons are dead,
I am a bereaved mother
Of three boys
that huddle on beds
To ogle at disembodied girls;
With negation for real ladies!

My daughters are toys
My kinsfolk;
I am a childless parent
Of four daughters
who huddle in bedrooms
Fondling small gadgets
With no moment for real men.

You, abstract companions;
Like ghosts of the other world
Have destroyed our posterity
Whatever App they call you,
Loosen your grip on our heritage.

SLEEPING WITH THE MOON
Chibueze Obunadike

the night is a silent stranger beckoning to me
through quiet eyes

I stretch myself out on the grass and
allow its silky gaze to permeate me;
to wrap itself around my aching body

in this moment, I am happy

in another dream, I am a townscrier,
always wandering the empty fields at dawn
playing the music of my wooden flute to the moon,

in this dream, we are lovers
and she is dancing, dancing, dancing.

she comes close and makes loves to me
in a language so soft it breaks my body into whispers

we are a picture of smiles and laughter
& in this moment, I am happy.

by the time she will leave me at daybreak,
melting away with the night sky
we will have made memories of each other

memories I will capture in the music of my flute
to sing to my children,
who will sing to their own children,
gathered at night by the light of a smoky fire,

somewhere under the moon

& she will dance, dance, dance

but tonight, she is not yet a memory.

we are still two lovers dancing to the
music of each other
and her body is a song I know all the
words to.

tonight, we are happy

253
Clesirdia Nzorozwa

This is Doctor Broken stein experiment number 250!

Grey hair, shaky legs, left foot facing backwards.
Disjointed I have been dancing with my shadow.
Waltz or waltz?
We don't need anyone!
Seven steps more.

This is experiment number 251!
White hair, broken legs, broken arms.
I have been crawl dancing with my shadow.
Broken records, broken seven steps on repeat.
Waltz or waltz?
Penny takes my hand,
Give Alone a chance.

We don't need anyone!
Seven steps more.

This is experiment number 252!
Falling white hair.
Decayed teeth, cracked lips, broken nails.
Broken folks, stinky wine, fragmented glasses.
Rusty sweet melodies,
Press play on the stereo.

I dine with my shadow!
More in your broken plate dear,
Delicious empty soup!
More in your plate sweet heart,
Delicious lonely peas cooked with pain!

This is experiment 253!
Shaved head, torn blankets,
Broken windows, cold winters,
Broken base, cracked back.
I sleep embracing my shadow.
More torn blankets!
Less shivering!
We don't need anyone.
Come into my broken arms.
Cuddle, rock yourself to sleep.

Experiments failed!
Men die alone!
Designed to never breathe alone!

Seasons
Gamuchirai Susan Muchirahondo

I remember a time when autumn leaves fell in autumn,
Skylight seeping through the naked branches, touching nothing but the wind's little gushes of air.

Naked, you are beautiful like bark clinging onto trunk for the sake of humanity's sanity.
A hint of dread but pouring your skin onto every ounce of me, to shield my fragile form.
Naked, you tremble like the leaves as they fall onto the earth,
 gravity having her way with your tender touch.
Naked, you reek of heaviness in your breath.
 Complete parallel to the feel of your touch on my existence.

I remember you dancing in the summer, as the breeze carried your scent of vanilla and
 sweat to my nostrils.
Your breath, hot like the atmosphere, engulfed in second hand moisture and heat.

Fallen you reflect the raindrops as they fight gravity till they die on the sand.
Fallen, you light up the day like the sunrise that soon scorches its pleasure away as it can't help but burn with all it has.
Fallen, you tremble like the puddle by the nursery school,
 a single kinetic move and you lose your composure.
 Complete parallel to your steadiness with your aching hands.

Oh I remember winter, your face cold as you perused through the neighbourhood,
seeking warmth for the killing.

Taking in all the heat but giving none, in your quest to chill the universe,
 a dark light gleaming not too far from the darkness in death, behind your glassy eyes.

Shaken you run to the north in search of the warmth you drank dry, winter.
Shaken, you look both ways before crossing the street,
 but no traffic has crossed your path for centuries.
Shaken, you look lonely and cold, or maybe it's just you.
Shaken you steal hearts, because hearts desire to give warmth.
Contrary to what I felt when you held mine.

I remember spring, young and naïve like ice-cream in warm weather.
Carrying such a glow in your trail, they drank it all and left you for dead.
Your glee consumed by them who knew how to take all and never give any.

Bold, you are fierce as the rays of warmth on tender skin.
Bold, you shed leaves to bring forth young ones.
Bold, they saw your light and wanted it for their own.
Bold, they stole from your heart what mattered most to you,
 and see you roam the streets in search of dead winter to mend yourself again.
Bold, they will find your grave embedded in sweet roses,
 a chalet of flowers protecting what's left of your broken heart.
Bold, you light fires even in your death because passion was never a flame that
 they could put out. Contrary to the love you were robbed of.

Sun Glow
(Dedication to Samatimba)
John J.J Dongo

The sun has set and as it sets
The moon shimmers and reminds us
Though you may not be in vision
You are not out of mind
You are only but over yonder
In the darkest of darks
And the brightest of brights you still glow
The rays of your love that touched us
Made us believers in the power of being,
Embracing uniqueness,
Not flawed impositions of who we should be
The sun has set but the moon reminds us
Of your love that shone once so bright.
Our hearts break,
Streaming endless tears joining to form seas of sorrow
Yet I believe, a heart that is broken is a heart that has been loved
As we look at the shattered pieces of our hearts, they resonate with your love.
You may be gone
But our hearts carry in them your story
So forever you will be engraved in immortality
Rest In Peace Samatimba

MY HEART'S EARTH
Joseph Olamide Babalola

Oh speak sweet one, let love hit again
my lust is lost, my heart is warm

she opens her mouth
I see steam gush out like a stream
her inwards must be hot, I think
but when her steamy stream enters me
and journeys all the way down my heart
her words blows off my stronghold
as if it is a chaff for her warm wind
it's indeed a flood; a deluge of love
then my heart's thick earth ceases to be

Oh speak sweet one, let love hit again
my lust is lost, my heart is warm

she opens her mouth again
I feel the breeze in her whispers
she's giving her breath away, I think
but when her breezy breath reaches me
and couples itself with my dormant spirit
her words forms in me a new heart
as if I'm a paint for her creative brush
it is indeed a rebirth; an upsurge of love
then my heart's pure earth starts to be

Oh speak sweet one, let love hit again
my lust is lost, my heart is warm

Fences
John J.J Dongo

Sometimes when you touched you bruised.
Other times when you took me into your arms you cut.
And that was my first mistake.
Not to make you leave a little room for me.
A space I could sing in. A space to call home.
So to keep up your strength,
I had to give up little pieces of mine.
Mixed up pieces of me with yours and I ceased to exist.
No longer could I trace my existence without tracing you.
And all I ever wanted was to give you the best of what was in me.
But parallel lines draw mixed emotions
And like crooked teeth they don't stand straight
Neither do they stand in faith
Mixed ways and mixed mannerism leaning on the fence.

TWO SPERMS
Kofi Acquah

Whispers have wings
They fly into ears
like a mad housefly.

They are whispers.
They are words from voices,
Told in chambers at night.
For he was a man
And I was a boy.

Words,
build manhood for the wise
the lantern,
winks on talks and times
To grow womanhood.

His shadow strikes his whispers
On my ear drum
When the skin
turns a goat.

But her palace,
wets in raining season
before talks and times
Are remembered.

Beyond reach
Revash Kun Kanjiri

I wake up looking for the warm wings I am used to
The chill weather promises to crack my chicks,
So I dared not step out.

Patiently I wait for her melodic voice to call me
I peer through the cracking window thinking I would get a glimpse
Of her.
Slowly the glow on my face fades away.
Suspicion takes a coup in my mind.

Minutes of waiting turn into days
Days into years.
The hope of her return vanishes.
In my dreams I can see her
but only in a distant horizon were the sun rests.

Bare
Anesu Nyakubaya

when your hand reached out towards me
yearning
i didn't realize it was a facade, an illusion
my mind - playing tricks on me
mistaking your intentions for my heart's pleas
desires I probably will never see fulfilled
this hand used to come bearing gifts
it used to pull me close
it used to caress me with such tenderness
it used to make me forget my cares
When it reached i thought it was reaching out for my heart
to love and to hold
in sickness and in health
not once did i think it was enticing me
that like a python it would mesmerise me
and draw me close
not to feast alongside you
but to be devoured at your table
all you wanted was fulfillment of your fantasies
I gave all
poured my whole being into your hands
for your pleasure I forgot my moral campass
for your gratification I became a slave
delved into submission
by manipulation
isolation is my new normal
you secluded me and let me drive myself insane
the little voices in my head arent so little anymore, you see
they have grown

bigger and louder
with bulging tummies and protruding horns on their foreheads
with horrible rotten teeth, and breath so foul
i weep for my innocence
lost to the shimmer of this materialistic world
that hand is reaching further than I thought it would go
past my heart
going for my most priced possession
my treasured soul
your hand reached, took it and sold it to the underworld
I woke up too late
I made my bed I guess I should lay in it

Learning to Drive
Christine Coates

I steer down my mind's road
not knowing how to brake, I dead-eye
the destination I cannot reach.

I wear my grandmother's bones,
cutlery on a silver tray,
cruise past a photograph –
an infant in a wicker chair
chewing the end of a loaf.

I colour outside the lines,
a joyride, round and round the circle.
My mother's hair feathers of the lyre bird.

I wish I could stay like this
forever, never arriving. There are
gifts in anything that will hurt us.
Oupa wears his face behind his eyes,
shadow puppets on a screen.

I swerve past a rock fall,
my father is all over the road.
I gather his pieces, put them in a basket.

We stopped saying his name –
that's how one disappears.

JUST US
Monicah Lubanga Kuta

    a)
But you and I,
We do not want to be like them
We can make it till the end
We are just two lone stars,
In a really big galaxy,
We burn brightest when together
And they think it is a shame
That the world will never know our names
But that is okay
Cause love gets ruined by money
And we are just poor kids,
In a really rich city.
Oh my, what a pity!
But we've got a love story,
Unlike the rest,
No fancy pants,
No fancy dresses,
Just us, Just love, Just love!
        Daniel Munyasia

    b)
Then,
The world will stare
Then,
The world will smile
And congratulate us
'Cause of the effort we put in so as to,
Make to the end.

The big world will be our haven.
No more lone stars
But a big joined heart
The world will scream our names
And our love won't be ruined by money,
Nor by bad hearts.
The mountains will tell the cities around
Of the happiness we have
We will be rich with love,
Trust, happen and change,
As we dance to serenades.
Just us, Just love, Just love!

Chalice of Choice
Oyoo Mboya

(... for Dorothy)
I want to do with you,
That which the moon does,
With twilight flowers,
Splitting petals to spill fragrances,
Fair fragrances of forever -

Tonight, we can cage darkness,
Behind a thousand candlesticks,
But how -
How do we stop the fireflies,
From birthing?
From bathing?
In the splendours of the lunar light -

I have drunk from you,
A concoction of confusion,
Sipped from broken brims,
Of a blood stained chalice,
Pricked lips and fractured smiles -

I love(d) you --
Maybe I still do -
Loved you short enough,
Like the full life of a butterfly,
Love is short...
Memories are long -
Of the flowers you perched upon,
Of the drizzles that washed your rainbowed wings -

Amidst this crowd,
We - my heart and I,
Stand aloof, lonely and alone,
Like crosses whose arms are weighed,
Broken with hurt,
Bent on unattended graves!

I love you,
My broken Chalice;
You -
Chalice of Choice.

Both Together And Each Alone
(after Yehuda Amichai)
Ismail Bala

Dearest, the day's gone to set
And nobody came to the festival.
The carousels keep carousing in the dark.
Both of us together and each one alone.

The stars are lost on the sky's face—
It's hard to keep tab on anything now.
The guards waited behind the hall
How much we all long for the past still.
Both of us together and each one alone.

The dawn is slicing the night in half above—
Come, and we will set out for halfway love.
Just the two of us will camp, before the park is opened.
Certainly everything can still be changed.
Both of us together and each one alone.

My love, it appears, has changed me
To sweet crumbs of cookies that was sour dung
I come to you gingerly, and I stumble.
Accept me. No dark angels fall.
For we are both together. Each is alone.

Pearls of Pain
Martin Chrispine Juwa

Drums torn by oiled palms.
Rivers flowing from wearied eyes,
Souls beckoned by some wind,
Smiling. As hope whizzes in air
Past a torn heart in hand.
But in me i thrust between bars of love like gorillas in zoos.
To love. And be loved.
A rabid hound howling in a pack,
I want to lean on walls without cracks and wash my tears away,
To be noble and gallant.
So here I sit in the middle of nowhere, writing.
Like you will not fold the paper and throw it away into rivers
Unaware of yawns and coughs I drag in pain-love.
This treasure.
This pain.

When we're together
Modest Dhlakama

When we're together: you and me,

Feeling you touching me here and there
Never thought your touch would moan me.
Never knew I would be craving for you
And I don't want that to waste away.
Baby, you're all that I need.
Baby, you're all that I dream of.
Baby, I want you badly.

Every night and every day
I know I need you more.
All those little things you say
Blow me away into nothingness.
Take me away to that island
In the middle of the boiling ocean
And like children let's play.

When we're together: you and me
The mercury is rising always
And the volcano is violently erupting.
Temperatures are messing with our tempers.
Kindling a fierce fire inside us.
Soon we'll melt and fuse into each other.
Baby, you're all that I need.
Baby, you're all that I dream of.
Baby, I want you badly.

Lightning Bolt
Martin Chrispine Juwa

Her eyes told stories I couldn't discern.
In a flash,
We grew wings and waved them in winds,
As we flew below the summer skies
We blinked as her eyes kissed the sun,
Like a sea lost in times of storms
Like a sea wandering away from land
Sometimes I think,
Falling in love,
We ride a lightning bolt.

Touch of an angel
Modest Dhlakama

I'm rusty and dusty
I need to be greased
By that touch of an angel
That ignites all the senses in me
Making me feel like a woman again.
Let me drown not but,
Part my lips and
Give me the breadth of love.

Why should I stay starved?
I need to quench that thirst.
Unwind the twine
That binds my body
Set it free from this cage
Where it's trapped in.

Let me live like tomorrow
Is never again to come
And learn to love again.

that moment I left
Nkwana Joshua Serutle

that moment I left you
to another city
I kept looking back hoping
my eyes will pull you closer
to my arms
again

I smelled your fragrance
on my T-shirt
to feel your presence next to my seat
I undressed every building past the road
hoping to find you inside
waiting for me to open the door

every pedestrian cross
was you passing
wearing your favourite dress
your smile trimmed between your cheeks
and your dazzling walk hypnotizing the robots
to close
so I can see you passing through

I kept searching for you
in every taxi we overtakes
and the one overtaking

us
hoping that maybe
you might've followed me

I might've left you
to another city
but you
never left
in me,
I keep seeing you
coded inside my skin
and
every time
my eyes
blink
you're here
and never left

Peas
Ntseka Masoabi

Sharing;
a verb,
or rather a word that carries
a heavy vibration of memories that capture
indulging smiles
and good times
preserved in the caves of our hearts.

For instance,
after long mournful days of lost homes and
short stories of fathers betraying their families,
my close friends, Tello and Khauhelo, and I
sit across each other on light-brown chairs of an old
rectangular wooden table
to share a delicious meal
of hot green peas soup mixed with onions and carrots.

Ironically,
Our kitchen is always short of something – this time,
salt.
Like always,
we somehow allow
our laughter and silly jokes to season the meal
so that while we eat,
we get to busk in the warmth of our long conversations.

AN ENCOUNTER WITH GRANDMA.
Paradzai Givemore Macheka.

In my grandma's hut we sat
On a reed mat so innocent
Rain outside was heavily pounding
Some naughty rain drops were sneaking
Through grass thatch that was worn out
Falling onto almost everything in the hut.

My beautiful white lover
Clung to me like glue on leather
Disillusioned by the smoke
Emanating from the fireplace
Where the firewood was wet.

I had just introduced
Sarah as my to be wife.
After hearing this news
Grandma stared at the rain
Through the open door
And from her wearied eyes
I could clearly discern
Her deep routed concerns.

Vividly I pictured Grandma visualising
This delicate white innocent girl
Balancing a water bucket on her head
Washing clothes on a rock in the river
Sweeping the whole big dusty yard daily
Preparing pap in a pot on a wooden fire
Holding the ox-drawn plough in the fields
Kneeling down when greeting elders

Then the type of grandsons from her.

I looked at my aged grandma
Then at my white girl
Then at my black skin
Then at my rural village
Then tears of joy effortlessly
Fell down my fluffy cheeks
Grandma curved a toothless smile
My girl exhibited a snow-white smile
We all smiled and warmly hugged
Our eyes painting a new picture
Of course times are changing.

Last time
Pelonomi Itumeleng

The last time
You left me
with orgasms
Left my feet vibrating to a tune in sync with your being.
That night
You held me like
I was home
You spoke to me a language
I understood.

You moved me from the kitchen counter
to the floor
to the wall
you whispered
"I want you to know my dimensions"

and then one after the other, orgasms followed.

Last night
It had been months
of trying, to convince myself to get over you.
and there you were
As you turned
i remembered the transitions from the back, sideways and from the top.

but damn these artists.
rocking up in spaces to disrupt my peace.
How dare you?
Hug and hold me like i am still home?

I am trying to forget the memory, Sthandwa sam
and I hope to have you faded
that when you rock up again
My heart does not follow you.

Blood
Sibulelo Manamatela

I am woman   I am no stranger to blood
not all blood is re(a)d   red the colour or
read the verb but   all bleeding is loss
not all loss is re(a)d   red the colour or
read the verb   once a man came to bleed
between my legs   blood is rust
men have come to rust   between my legs
men decay easily   in moist vaginas
they always find   a reason to stay
even when   its bleeding even when
they're the blood   rust is loss
I am woman   I am no stranger to loss
loss has come   to materialize   between my legs
ejaculation miscarriage   discharge period infertility
wanted babies   that do not   come are a loss
loss is absence   when I think of absence
I think of fathers   there are fathers
who have   an absent presence
there are fathers   who are runners
at least the dead ones   have an excuse
when I was in school   blood was said to be an excuse
for lazy girls to   not swim during P.E
when I grew older   blood was said to be an excuse
for all the failures   of lazy blacks
but blood is   not an excuse
blood is the event   blood is its extent
black people are   its largest measure
I am black   and woman
I am no stranger   to blood and loss

and loss of blood
our elders tell us not to
speak of blood
bleed quietly
only means a length of
stay indoors when
do not let your blood seep
clothes sheets
bleed quietly
to wipe blood
a hospital I am
I am hospital
every month
makes my vagina
men still come to
men have come to
but
a mortuary some men
between my legs stiff
they found a reason to
I let them
I let them die
I am good at
I am hospital
moaning
are a taboo
I am black
my blood

blood is code word
tell the men that we bleed
discreetly
period
time
you're bleeding
through
moods smiles
but be prepared
bleeding men need
black woman
bleeding
between my legs
a place of healing
bleed between my legs
heal between my legs
all hospitals have
became cold
inconsiderate dead
stay
stay
I am blood
mourning
I miss pleasure
all my moans
urgh and uhm
and woman
is taboo.

TO THINK THAT WOMEN ARE DEMISEXUALS
Amani Nsemwa

For my love to consummate
Is like the love of a kitten to the threads,
Like Toupees to the balded Rockefeller;
I forever wonder, how do I choose
Hairy bonny chest
Over the soft,
Tender breasts.
How do I choose the bearded chin
Over an ample smile, residing in a well crafted curves.

My pap was a Con man,
Saying all the people are equal-righted,
But me,
The beast parodies my visions,
Like I were a creep,
An aspired creep.
I were here, under the sky
Chasing wind and counting the stars,
Not knowing you can't trust the ocean,
The desire,
For as how they carry you to satisfaction,
So do they
Towards demise.
To think that women are demisexuals.

Hands.
Fikile C. Makhubo

Hands,
are like a set of two colours.
Black and white.
Fists or open hands.
There is no in-between, no grey areas, and no rainbows.
You are either playing the music or punching bags.

Now listen to the poetry of it all.
Cupid shooting arrows.
Brothers in arms.
Mothers tying nooses in their bellies.
Monsters under the beds.
Uncles in the bed.
Monsters in the bed?
Shhh…
Little girls can keep a secret, right?

Hands have no memories.
Fingers are clueless about previous lives.
Three weeks ago, two worlds shook hands over a new friendship
found exchanging guns and
nuclear weapons.
Who again, is responsible for dishing hope?
Some promises were never planned,
who knew, the children would be raised by pictures of their hero
fathers?

Ha o tshaba,
o tshaba seipoine hoba nthwe motho ke moipone empa,

o etsa eka ha a ipone.
(If you should be afraid, be afraid of the mirror, because a person sees themselves and still pretends not to see.)

Black men,
they drew a circle around another black man because he was a black man,
put a circle around him and lit a match...
As bon fires are always so warmer when someone is screaming in a horror story.
Young men,
they tore her to shreds, tore her rags to shreds and left a stick inside her...
Because they had to prove she was missing something in men by finding gentleness in women.
Old man,
saw a child, saw a woman in a child and a child needed to be a woman because
at least some man was blessing her with his attention.
One man,
he forgot to be her lover, forgot to be her protector
and became a scream to her beauty.
A punch to her beauty. Another explanation why she fell and hit the cupboard.
Broken mirrors or broken niggers?
Hell is a home we all go back to,
to make sure the windows are not open and the floors are clean.
To feed the dogs and remind dad that should he need anything...
We are just a pair of hands away.

NIGHTSKIES
Dennis Omolo

The skies at night remind me of you
Like birds in flight you were graceful and true
Memories etched on my mind like a tribal tattoo
This journey is getting harder because it's meant for two
But the hourglass is flipping and I don't know what to do
Life has no rewind button so my chances I rue.

I remember the first days when you I did woo
Your face had more detail than a portrait Picasso drew
Those eyes of blue, surely the best I ever knew
Fair hair glinting even as the Harmattan blew
If you were a dangerous island I'd risk my leaking canoe
To anchor at your shores is a feat for only a few
About this rare conquest I'd run and tell my crew.

Shall I compare you to the famous landscapes of Peru?
Or a thousand fiery sunsets viewed from Malibu?
You know you're fine wine, not some illicit brew
This painful incurable longing must be West African voodoo.

So I hope you come back before the melting dew
For the future can be bleak with its ever changing hue
Will you retrace your steps and walk these paths anew?
Our flight could last longer than that spear Yego threw
The gilded celestial carpet has been laid out for you
The moon and the stars hope you say, "I do!"

A traveller's note
Fikile C. Makhubo

I have learned the art of packing.

It is laying your rags on their back inside your suitcase
instead of on their knees like lumps of disappointment.
You can never fold emotion enough to fool reality:
God does not hear prayers.

I have learned to leave friendships behind unfinished
and create new ones as I go.
That human beings are imperfect and it is important to know that early
least you expect heroes from civilians.

I understand now,
needing help can be helpless yet
expect very little from people who are a cry for help in helping you.
Desperation exists but always remember to keep a toothbrush in
your side pocket
for every time you'll need change.
Trust is not that fragile, it was always broken.

I have learned the art of moving.
Like magic doesn't exist or memories weren't created to last.
My feet have learned how to tiptoe around wounds and closed
doors.
To intrude without shifting the natural order of things.
I have learned how to be a guest.
For children to be asked to show me their dancing moves
and sit down when the news are airing.
Foreign lands tend to refuse with their sons and daughters.

I have learned to light fires with my fingers.
To pick love off the side walk and dust off its rust.
To live like promises are roasted on a twig.
I have come to fight cupid arrow to arrow siyofa silahlane. (Till death)

Somewhere between all these lessons,
I was searching for the little me that promised me a better life.
And all my dreams that asked me to follow them.

I never know where I'm going but as soon as I leave,
you'll always wish you could have done more for me.
Do not worry old friend,
I saw you trying…
Le jwale ke lebohile. (And I'm grateful.)

Part 10: Trauma, Sexual Assualty and Gender Issues

SPARK TO FIRE
Nnane Ntube

Songs sung in remnant notes
Cacophonic voices raining stones
On complaints that harnessed pleasure in lecherous gunshots
Complaints left lying low under fascist boots
If I were a woman, I would have let their toes
Penetrate the core of my roots with snootiness,
Infuse not in my mind scribbled fragments of hope!
My songs, snowballs to the flame that mirrors your face
Did you think I'll embrace your gaolers?
Sing your songs again!
Hang Xylophones on snippy lips!
They're dirges you sing to idiotic, idle leaders
Who deposit faeces in idyllic states.

THE POND OF DEATH
Okey Ifeachor

The pond of death on the plateau
Water cemetery unknown to many
Underserved home for the brutally killed
The pond of false innocence full of human guilt
Protected by the wombs that birthed the dead
Surface serenity betrayed by underneath bestiality.
Scour the pond
Scour the pond of death
Expose the savagery of monumental proportion
Let posterity know the evil in the land
Let the guilty pay the price
To assuage the blood of the innocent
That our land may be healed
Let the pond not eat our people again.

The African Girl Child Shall Rise Again!
Nnane Ntube

Sour cup of life, stuffed into my unguarded mouth
Thick lips that enveloped my voice
Choking my rights with a tongue of insults
Silent blows I received on this frail body
Where he forcefully made his refugee camp
A camp he spat on, destroyed its tents and unruly forced himself in
A camp he spread shingled body on
Buried stubby legs on, planted rough chest on
After which he poured leftover insults
Upon this bleeding reception
I was his free space in this dark corner of the earth
I was the African girl child, neglected by tradition
Where is the town-crier to alert the neighbours of my suffering?
Where are the ngongs to echo my shivering voice?
Unfazed by my strength and unflinching determination to rise again
He looked at me in dismay and hidden admiration
As I strut in a dishy package,
The African girl child shall rise again!

LIKONI FERRY
Kariuki wa Nyamu

sundown
stranded
following whole day ferries
break down
at Likoni
crossing channel.
rush hour
dog-tired wananchi,
goats, chicken,
beba beba and mkokoteni guys,
market women,
ladies and
gentlemen
scramble for space
in MV Likoni
blocking cars,
tuk tuks,
boda bodas
causing panic
and near stampede
but anyway, I must not whine
for Likoni ferry isn't mother's!

there we are
  inside MV Likoni
a brew of
sour sweat
and bad breath
hit my nostrils
as ghastly faces

stare at me
I sneeze, blow my nose
but anyway, I must not whine
for Likoni ferry isn't mother's!

then, a kinky-haired man
presses my bottom
good heavens!
I feel (it)
and gape at him,
my heart throbbing
he presses, again
I feel (it)
bulging
   "Jamani, what is he up to?"
Anyway! Since this is a city
I've to hold my purse firmer
   my thoughts screaming
"Please, please don't!"
I turn, he looks on
sweating, his eyes very red
I jump a little in panic
as I remember the ghostly Coastal cat
and as we wildly alight MV Likoni
               the man vanishes
into the crowd
                    then, I hear an elderly woman whisper
   "Ewe mwanangu, what's on your back?"
I turn and touch my bottom
Ugh! My hands just touched something thick and
slippery, on my dress?
What the hell men?
   I curse

but anyway, I must not whine
for Likoni ferry isn't mother's!

THE FIRE IN YOUR BELLY
Ojonugwa John Attah

The fire in your belly was lit on that cold night
You only wanted to warm yourselves
It was too cold that night
Just from warming your hands, you began to warm your legs
You went on to warm your bodies
That was where he went in
The entire region was covered in darkness
'Let us light this up,' he said.
At first, you said no
In your mind, you had looked on him as your knight, your saviour
You let him use the stick of matches to light up the dark fireplace
You really warmed yourselves that cold night
A few moons later, the light in your fireplace had moved to your belly
It had become a wildfire that could not be quenched
'I can't let it consume both of us,' he said
'Do you want it to consume me alone?,' you asked him
'I don't know but you have to put out the fire yourself.
I cannot burn with you. Afterall, the heat is more than I can withstand.
Now, the narrative has changed
But it was on that cold night that the fire was lit.
You now have two choices, to let the fire consume you and produce gold

Or to quench it and stop good fortune from getting to you.

mirror
Aaliyah Cassim

you show me
the surfaces of things
inverted
hoping that i
will like what i see

because if i don't
i will shatter you
pick up
the pieces
realise
that there is nothing
beneath the glass

Dark Nights
Aubrey Sandile

Mucky rivulets of our sewer beauty parlour
Two daughters of the seed of carnality play in remorse
Bar graphs of decline, corrupt officials ravish these innocent faces with their
devilish appetites
Daughters of Africa forage the wallets of sickly perverts and sadistic
paedophiles.
The black mamba has not shade its skin
The wolf is looking dapper in a sheep's skin and the daughters are under the
bridge alone
Vermin copulate in ecstasy next to their cardboard.
Body welts and stinging belts her national anthem
But the nightmare has just begun.

Help
Ayomide Odewumi Mitchelle

I pop my pills,
Even though it kills,
Me from the inside,
I still abide,
To the medication,
To the endless recitation,
Of how I must be free,
From the devils inside me,
You cannot correct my imagination,
With therapeutic sessions,
You can sure try,
But I may cut till I die.

And then they begin,
Who did this to you?
Tell me who was this fool?
That so rubbished your life,
That so destroyed your might,
That so killed your smile,
That made you want to die,
Please tell me once,
Once, just once, just once,
So I may try to relate,
So we may postpone your expiry date,
At least a whisper in the day,
So that we may find a way.

And so I reply,
You really want to know,
You really want to figure out, how so?

You want to know the person or beast,
That makes living like misery,
I do hope you can make it pay,
"Cause its depression" I say.

A Falling Bitterness.
Aubrey Sandile

To you it's just an observation.
But through me, it is wisdom missing.
Why is failure a friend and a foe?
To lose these wars before these battles.
You are alive and proud.
Your theories are damned theories.
A mere talk of a man.
Defeated,, conceited by carnality.
Screams of the abyss.
Leave it, for it is not yours.
Oh God! I fear your love than life.
I would rather die
Than live in this lie.

You take my breath away
Bilton Boka

You take my breath away.
Like literally when I'm close to you I can't breathe.
You leave me in a state of confusion-
Where my mind and heart are two separate beings chorded by a thought.
You leave me in a state that my lungs beat and heart breathes.
You leave me in a state that my tongue walks and my feet talks.
I think I don't need any mathematical equation to realise that you got me flap gusted.
Like literally gravity is the only thing that is keeping my heard to my toes.
Hope the words that I want to say will show in my eyes.
Because I doubt I have the physical capability to breathe when you are two inches in front of me.

You take my breath away.
You take the air inside of me.
You suffocate my very existence in those couple of moments.
You ignite my pulse to such a speed that I can blow up.
You paralyze my whole body like a stroke.
You leave me in state of being dumb.

It's amazing how you got me twisted by the tip of your fingers.
You got me under your strings just as a puppet.
It's amazing how you got me obeying you like a servant without doing anything.
It's a real work of art on how you stole my heart.
And made me like a statue.
Breathless and Life less.

A Feminist Letter
Kelvin J. Shachile

Dear Ebuka,
I choose to sit in the office and work, I know it hurts you.
Ebuka I wash, clean and cook, but I need to shine too.
My hair is still long without a head wrap, not that I'm headstrong.
My nails are still soft like hibiscus petals and fragile like frangipanis.
I am like a queen on a throne.

Ebuka, I choose to wear my skirts and pink heels,
At first trembled like an African chameleon on a feeble twig,
The thing is, they listened.
Is that what made e'm say I should leave and you agreed?
Ebuka I will stay!
I am not furious, just curious, why do you fear my presence
In the home today?

Ebuka, the bible might have said the man is the head
And a woman is like a flower that decorates the home,
That is a lie.
I am beautiful and lovely but not for eyes but for mind and ears too.
Marriage and Family are animals with two heads without a tail,
What a powerful monster!

It roars with power and makes greater influence that shapes
Without guilt.
It makes love sheer and fulfilling.

Ebuka, I am stopping here,
When you get home return my things in the house.

Not that I'm afraid to leave but I'm choosing to stay
Away from being considered weak.
Which for truth I'm not.

Ebuka, I'm not furious but curious,
who said being under a man's head is African?

The World Was Silent When We Died
Nosakhare Collins

The sea is bloody & deadly silent

How many times have you seen a photo
Of boys at fifty, becoming joyful to stare at;
Stinky patches with bullets and sticky stains:
When we stared at it on our secret box.

Imagine how the world would look like
If a boy is paralyzed like a broken needle,
And dump in the gutter to rot;
Or find him dead by mysterious weather.

You need not imagine the photo you see
Of a boy laid dead by lethal weapons;
Sprawled on the scarlet bed of a free life,
And holding hands with the sound of silence.

Their skins can turn senescent thoughts
fading away like a floating sea;
Show you how to nail sadness into a wanderer's wall,

Just to forget the photo and remember a boy who wanted to turn war at peace.

But remember the naked children laughing
as if there were men,
Who shall turn this naked photo of dead bodies,
And grow to remove the rotten leaves of dust.

The supernatural tricksters mutual admiration jazz club
(for the poet Diana Ferrus)
Abigail George

I cannot predict the future.
I would watch films until
they began to feel like blue
pills to me. They make me
feel fine. Sublime. Nostalgia.
The characters filled me up
like sparkling wine, the bubbles
of champagne with lack.
With hope, their stories. America and Paris,
outer space ghost nations.
I was marked from the beginning.
There was, is still a part of
me that is intrigued by her.
When I was a child I played the games
of a child in the dirt with paper
dolls and had high tea parties.
Picked up shells on the beach.
Made garlands with seaweed.
Nabokov reminded me that
children died of broken dreams
every day in this world and that
they were to be found like the
dancing bones and heartbeats
of con artists, disaster artists, tricksters,
hustlers, bone-thugs-and-harmony-
everywhere across cities in Africa.

She.
Kennedy Chege

She's wired to a circuit of electric desire,
She belongs to a circle for the weird and queer-
It's been long since she tasted a man.
She believes she's living a different life,
For she lives to love a different love,
And yearns for a crave she should fear.
Silently starving for the taste of girls like her,
She is crazy for the feel of another girl inside her.
She spends cold nights hiding her hot embers,
She spins her laughs to sad sniffles each time she remembers...
But her twin soul still sings her nightmares,
With a voice filled with self-seduction.
Temptation barks behind her back everywhere she hides,
Like a hungry hound, it bails for her blood,
Daring her to look back at where she's come from,
Tearing her apart into pieces of her other persona.
While wishing she does not remember what made her;
She slowly gets into character,
Until she becomes another Her.

Father, listen to the silence
Lwanda Sindaphi

Father, these feet are conflicted.
Sometimes they crawl,
a reminder that I am still a toddler.
Sometimes they stand rigid
a reminder that I am still man.
I love my daughter with a limping heart
with a crippled spirit
with a constantly drowning love.
For long, father, I have been gathering fragments to build my masculinity.
Still now, I have not built anything,
I am scared of building things from a gaping wound
festering silence
paralyzed intelligence.
These bricks and blocks keep imploding.
This perennial wound pre-figures the next smile.
There are days when I smile just to make my pain orthodox
but the presence of my daughter always molds the silence.
Her shimmering pigmentation engenders your unknown face,
my mother says that she has borrowed your architecture.
Her existence unearths the dormant wound of growing up with you
every time I am with her.
I drape her presence in euphoria to conceal my ungovernable transparency.
My love for her is deeply rooted in the wound of being fatherless
for years.
Father, I am nostalgically feasting on your absence
and your absence feasts on me, too.
There is too much unhealthy feasting
this void weighs

too much weight
This silence is pregnant with my mother's wail.
Her soliloquy perforates through the abdomen
I cannot breathe.
Tell me
how does a father become absent in his presence?
Perhaps, my love for my daughter is the past.
It is nostalgic,
my love for her is my wound
I am not yet father
but a father in the making.
Remember, I am still gathering fragments to build my masculinity.
How do I build her femininity, when I am still uncertain with my own architecture?
How does one love from a gaping wound?
How does one give something he never had?
Did you feel the same when you decided to walk away from my mother?
Did you feel like a toddler?
Did her pregnancy paralyze you?
But you didn't have to collect pieces to build yourself like me.
Father, this silence weighs
too much weight.
This distance reeks of a carcass
with maggots intruding.

Regression / Recession
Kgomotso Ledwaba

I know it's strange;

But I think I need the space to be depressed
I think the archaic model of African masculinity
Has me suffocating in my bedroom, because "God" forbid I reveal myself
To myself

Who stylishly wears the World's expectations on their shoulders?
Barely any of us

I don't know which version of me will show up,
I hear it's poor form to submit to confusion.

So half the time I refine pretence, and the other half is spent rebuilding myself.
I am learning to keep parts whole,
And to keep my penis wholesome.

The world is damaged by the phallic fallacy of identity
Fear is a governing policy, all men exercise
Privilege is not power itself, rather the balance of power
So it seems some have to lessen, as others gain
Who lessens? For whose gains?

I share the failure of capitalism with my fellow Africans
One percent of one percent, what does that give you?

Africanus

How do we make it to Ethiopia?
When African Unity is fractured into a hundred tribes
A hundred identities
A billion times we restructure consciousness

Grief
Lwanda Sindaphi

When I saw her,
my squishy, mooshy cheek daughter,
after a series of disconnected sunsets
and sunrises,
my fleeting delirium faded away immediately.
My heart fidgeted to the right,
turning frail,
giddy,
seeking to be centered.
Deformed, but moving.
Displaced by memories.
I, then, remembered
segmented sensations.
How I held her as an infant.
How she melted my masculinity.
Hastily, I fled the discomfort of revealing my vulnerability.
Refrained from unveiling my emotional stature,
prudent that I might be judged.
My bravery persuaded my grief to slumber in dormancy.
Gradually it erupted,
Surfaced inevitably. As a
father, I discovered that

feelings are obstinate.
You command them to hide
but they always reveal.

Under My Sister's Shadow
Xolile Mabuza

My sister and I aren't best friends, we fight a lot and some days we go to bed not talking to each other. We always find something to disagree about. One of our big disagreements is the color of the sun. I say it is orange but Temakhetselo says the sun is red so we don't always see eye to eye. We do agree on one thing though, that the sun is beautiful when rising and hot during the day. Temakhetselo is the first born and the most beautiful one in the family. She has big eyes and light skin and I, the last born, have small eyes and dark skin so I only exist at home. Our parents told us we were beautiful especially Mama. Tearswould roll out of her eyes when she said, "You're both beautiful." From the look on her face you could tell that she was proud to be our mother, well every mother would be. Life was easy when Temakhetselo and I were home because there we were both beautiful but as soon as we left the house things changed. The kids we went to school with didn't know my name and only referred to me as Temakhetselo's younger sister. Even though Temakhetselo was two grades ahead of me my class mates remembered her name instead of mine. She was popular because of her beauty.

Often times a part of me wanted to be popular like her but the children in school taught me that black is ugly and that black will never be enough, so every school day was hard but Wednesdays were the worst. On Wednesdays we had sports and since Temakhetselo wasn't good at sport I tried so hard to at least do every sports hoping that people would remember my name but still no one had interest in remembering a black ugly girl like me. The only thing everyone wanted to remember was how beautiful my sister was, I spent my entire life in high school under my sister's shadow. I couldn't wait for school to be out so that I could be at home where someone remembered me and called me by my name. Every Wednesday evening Daddy would buy us ribs & chips. We'd sit at the table to eat, Mama would look at me and say, "Today was hard wasn't it?" Temakhetselo would answer first to say, "She's just tired from her sports." A part of me would start screaming, telling Mama that, 'Yes, it was a hard day and I am tired of living under her daughter's shadow. I am tired of being told I'm ugly. That I lose my name every morning when I leave our house.' But the words never left my mouth, I wouldn't say all those things, especially not to Mama who tells me that I'm beautiful every morning so I'd just nod my head to agree that indeed today was hard.

Part 11: Translational

ÌWÀ

Luqman Maryam

Ìwàlewà
Ìwàlèsìn
Eni tí ó bá níwà, O n gbogbo lóní
Ìwà máa ń gbéni débi gíga
Ósi tún máa ń so ènìyàn di eni ilè
Ìwà ni èsó ènìyàn
Ìwà a maa gbé ni níyì
Ósì tún máa ń bu èté lu eńiyàn

Ìwà la fi ń lo ilé ayé
Ìwà la fi ń gbé ilé oko
Obìrin so ìwà nù
Ó lóhun kó lórí oko
Ìwà ni eye kòní,
Tí ó jékí igi dá tí ó sì fòlo

Ìwà gbéni pàdé aláànú
Ó sì tún gbé aláànú jìnà sìni
Ìwà ní ń sí lèkùn olá
Ótún sí lèkùn olá

Ìwà ló ń so eru domo
Ó sì tún so omo deru
Èéfí ní wà kò sé pamó
Kò sì sè daso bò
Aso ńlà kóni èèyàn ńlà
Sùgbón ìwà lafí ń mo ènìyàn gidi

Tónjú ìwà re ìwo omo ìyá mi
Torí ìwà rere lèsó omo ènìyàn
Ìwà ni a fí ń mo omolúàbí láwújo
Ìwà lóbí ewà
Eni tóní ewà tí kò ní ìwà, asán ni

Tí a kò bá ní owó, kò kí se èsè
Tí a kò bá ni àlááfia kîise àdánù
Tí a kò bá ni ipo, kîise àbùkù
Sùgbón eni tí kò níwá, ohun gbogbo ló sonù fun

Olá tí ò sí ìwà, olá kó rárá
Èsìn laí sí ìwà, asán lójé
Eni to ni ipo lai sîiwà, asán lójé
Eni to ni ipo lai sîiwà yio si pada parun

Ìwàlewà òhun sinì kókóró olà
Nítorí náà iwa lójù.

CHARACTER
Luqman Maryam
Translated from Yoruba by *Luqman Maryam*

Character is the best beauty
Character is the best religion
One with character has it all
Character elevates one state
Character can also bring one down
Character is a person's ornament
Character breeds prestige
Character also breeds contempt

Character is a key to living
A woman is married for her character
A woman without manner will not find a good suitor
The death of character makes the bird flew from the tree when the branch breaks

A good character attracts helper
It also deprives one of helper
Character is the key to riches
It is also the key to wealth

Character can set a slave free
It can also enslave a freeborn
Character is a smoke, you can't hide it
Neither can it be covered with cloak or silk
A mammoth regalia might not symbolise royalty
But a noble man is known by his character

Take watch of your character
As your character is your adornment

Character distinguished the noble man from the gathering of hoi polloi
Character begets beauty
Beauty without character is vanity

Being ripped off is no sin
Lacking good health is not a total loss
Being without a post is not farcical
But when character is lacking, everything is lost

Wealth without character is no wealth
Religion devoid of character is in vain
Being in position without a good character might ruin you
Your character is your beauty and key to wealth
Thus, character is the greatest virtue.

Kgatelelo ya monagano
Mosima Kagiso Phakane

Ke a fokola
Ke fetša botšhi bja matšatši
Letšatši le ntlhanametše
Ke aparetšwe ke a maso
Efela ga a tshephiši medupi
A ntlišetša fela madimu le magadima
Ke fela ke gadimela morago
Ke nyakana le mo ke ilego ka relela gona
Mo ke ileng ka senya gona
Gore ke tsebe go go lokiša
Dintho tšaka di a šiiša
Di gana le go fola
Ke fela ke khunama ka pelohlomogi
Ke re Ramasedi a nhlabišetša la selemo le seruthwana
Go fediša marega ao a kgatlhišitšego tša pelo yaka

Ke a fokola
Ke phelela bohloko ge le hlaba le ge le dikela
Ke ngadilwe ke nkadingala
A re ke boloi a ba a felelwa
Ka emaema ka ba ka tenwa
Ke nwele, ke komile, ke sohlile meriana ka go fapafapana ga yona
Ke khupile dipilisi ka go fapafapana ga tšona
Ke a fokola gomme ke hloka thušo
Kgopolo yaka ke maphotho a lewatle
Pelo yaka ke hlaga ge e kopana le bjang bjo bo omilego
Ke kgamathetše madi a dintho tšeo di sa bonwego ke batho
Ke ikwa nke ke letlakala la go oma ge le tšeatšea ke moya
Go thuša eng go fihla bohloko ka ditshego le myemyelo
Ke tla bolela le mang re rata go ahlolana ga kalo

Ke tla thoma ka go reng bohloko bo raragantšhitše leleme laka

Ke a fokola gomme ke hloka thušo
Lebitla le iphetošitše motswalle waka
Le iphile kgopolo yaka
Le ngokara bošego le mosegare
Le tshephiša go fodiša dintho tšaka
Le ntshephiša legae le leswa
Le ntshephiša khutšo le lethabo
Ke a fokola, ke hloka thušo

Depression
Mosima Kagiso Phakane
Translation from Sepedi by *Mosima Kagiso Phakane*

I am struggling
I spend most of my days
Without sunshine
Covered by dark clouds
But they don't promise rain
They bring only storms and thunder
At times I look back
To try figure out times where I slipped
Times where I went wrong
So that I can fix my wrongs
My wounds are scary
They don't want to heal
At times I kneel-down with my sorrowful heart
I plead to the Lord to let the summer and spring sun shine upon me
To end this winter that froze those of my own heart

I'm struggling
I live for pain when it rises and when it sets
The traditional healer gave up on me
I went up and down but eventually had enough of it
He said it's witchcraft but eventually run out of reasons
I've drank, swallowed, chewed different types of medicine
I've taken different types of pills
I'm struggling and I need help
My mind is ocean waves
My heart is wild fire when it meets dry grass
There's blood all over me from wounds no-one can see
I feel like a dry leave in the wind

What does it help to hide pain with laughter and smiles
Who can I talk to when we all judge each other so much
How do I talk when this pain tied my tongue in knots

I'm struggling and I need help
The grave pretends to be my friend
It took over my brain
It cuddles me day and night
It promises to heal my brain
It promises a new home
It promises peace and joy
I'm struggling, I need help

O bolaile ngwana
Mosima Kagiso Phakane

Ke kwele gabotse
Gore go boletšwe
Gore e latswa ya yona fela
Efela ga se ka tseba gore go ka senyega
Go fihla ka tsela ye
Ye yona taba ke hlobaboroko, dipšhišamare
Mmele wa leseanyana o fetošitšwe lefifi la bošegogare
Gare ga gagwe go kitima madimu le tšhišinyego ya lefase
Lefase le metše a ka godimo meno
Aowaaowa hle malome a bana
Bana ba tla rarelela ke bomang
O iphetošitše sebata seja-batho
O iphile le digotlane tša maabane ruri
O kgathola a mokgako ka kgang
O reng o fula le mašemo ao a sego a gago
O reng o fula dipeu di sa tšwa go bjalwa

Malome, o bolaile ngwana
Lefu la go feta la thipa le sethunya
Tšeo, di bolaya nama fela
Wena malome o mmolaile moya
O mo hloletše lebadi
La go ya go ile
Ga a sa tseba molalatladi
Go na fela tša matlakadibe gare ga kgopolo ya gage
Ka magadima le meoya ya go šiiša
Le a hlaba letšatši efela mahlasedi ga a mo fihlelele
O bolaile ngwana hle
Hleng o mo dirile sehlabelo
Go hola pelo ya gago ya maboya

Nnete ga o motho
Ga o na botho
O mmolaile a sa ithuta bophelo
O mmolaile a se a go dira selo
O mo thubetše ngoako o se wa feleletša go agwa
O bolaile ngwana

You killed a child
Mosima Kagiso Phakane
Translation from Sepedi by *Mosima Kagiso Phakane*

I heard very well
That it was said
That all are only fond of those they gave birth to
But I never thought that the damage
Would get to this extend
This is really disturbing, very devastating
The body of a child has been turned into darkness at midnight
Storms and earthquakes haunts her whole internal being
The world has turned against her
No, no uncle to the children
Who will protect the children
Now that you've turned into a people eating monster
You gave yourself even children born yesterday
You force yourself onto them
Why do you harvest where you never planted
Why do you harvest even the unripe fruits

Uncle, you killed a child
Death worse than that of a knife or a gunshot
Those ones kill the flesh

You uncle killed her spirit
You caused her a scar
That will never fade
The rainbow is foreign to her sight now
It only rains heavily and with storms inside her mind
Its only lightnings and very bad winds
The sun rises but its rays don't reach her
You really killed a child
Why did you make her a sacrifice
To please your horrible heart
Honestly, you are not a human being
You are not humane
You killed her when she was still learning life
You killed her and she never did anything to you
You crashed her shelter before it would stand
You killed a child

Ke leeto
Mosima Kagiso Phakane

Ke kwešiša gabotsebotse
Gore go boima kudu
Go kodumela ge le tlhaba
Le ge le dikela
Le hlabe le be le dikele
Go se nko yeo e tšwago lemina
Go bohloko go bona nke bja gago bophelo
Bo eme nke kutu ya morula
Mola dithaka di tšwela pele
Go emaema purabura le lešira
Wena o sa ikaparetše makgeretla
Tša maotwana a mane di thuntšha lerole
Wena o hloka le kiribane ya lešidi
Dikanapa di imelwa ke tša Madiba
Tša gago nke di sohlasohlilwe ke magotlo
Mengwako ke ya kgoparara
Wena o sa bolawa ke thibangthibang
Gare ga dipula le madimu
Kgothala hle kgaetšedi yaka
Bophelo ke leeto
Re swere la go fapana
O tla kgopša wa betha fase ka sekgothi
Ge o ka dulela go itshwantšha le ba bangwe
O ka se fihle felo
Ge o felelela bophelo pelo
Sepela ka go iketla
Sa gago sebaka se sa etla
Se iše pelo mafiša, kgothala
Kodumela moepathutse
Lehumo lona, ga le humanege kgauswi

It's a journey
Mosima Kagiso Phakane
Translation from Sepedi by *Mosima Kagiso Phakane*

I understand very well
That it is too hard
To sweat when it rises
And when it sets
Yet it rises and sets
Without progress in your life
Its hard when it feels like your life's progress
Is as still as a Marula tree trunk
When your agemates are progressing in life
They are in graduation gowns and wedding dresses
You are still in torn clothes
Their cars are blowing dust
You don't even have a wheelbarrow
Their pockets are being weighed down by Madiba notes
Yours seem to have been chewed by rats
They live in mansions
You still go up and down trying to block holes in your own shelter
Through rainfall and storms
Let go of your worries my mother's child
Life is a journey
Each of us on a different adventure
You will trip and fall head-first
If you keep comparing yourself to others
You won't get anywhere
If you keep rushing life
Don't rush anything
Your time will come

Don't be so sad, let your worries go
Work harder hard-worker
Success doesn't come easily

Shungu dzangu Mhai!
Johannes Mike Mupisa

Ko zvadiniko nhai mai?
Baba ndizvo zvamafunga here?
Chokwadi kumbunyikidza dzangu kodzero here nhai,
Chikoro handiti makandiregesa?
Mukandisairira kumafuro kumbudzi,
VanaGamuchirai vakapembera nemufaro,
Vachiti tawana manyoro mafuro,
Nhasi ndosvimha misodzi,
Shungu dzangu mhai!

Vakandiita suku nasai kumafuro,
Dzokonoke kumba mandigarirazve,
Makati VaMuchineripi vauye,
Vachisunda rino zidumbu,
Mhazha ichihwinya sehuyo,
Musoro wakati mbu sehumbukumbu yenhedzi,
Chamakakoshesa ihomwe yairira masenzi,
Hezvo paguru tsve-e,
Chokwadi here kundiita chimushini chekugadzira vana?
Shungu dzangu mhai!

Handichina changu,
VaMuchineripi vakati danga nderavo,
Musha ndewavo,

Mbudzi ndedzavo,
Ini wacho vakati ndiri wavo,
Saka changu ndechipi?
Ndadzungaira mhai,
Shungu dzangu mhai!

Zvakona izvi mhai,
Musha wakadai kwete,
Kodzero dzangu ndadzidza,
Ndapinda muzvirongwa zvemadzimai,
Ndorarama upenyu hwandaishuva,
Ndavhunurawo,
Mudzimai wanhasi ngaapepuke,
Ndidzo shungu dzangu mhai,
Handizorori kusvika mudzimai wese asumuka.

Cry of the girl child
Johannes Mike Mupisa

Why beloved mother why?
Father is this what you have decided?
Disrespecting my rights,
You denied me right to education,
And sent me to the pastures to look after the goats,
Upon my arrival Garikai and his friends celebrated,
In me they saw greener pastures,
They fondled and abused me in all ways,
Mother, you destroyed me.

I refused to continue going to the pastures,
And you were waiting for me at home again,
You invited Mr Muchineripi,
His bald head shining in the scorching sun,
The white strands resembling a mushroom,
You put importance on his fat pockets,
And forced me into a polygamous marriage,
Where I was turned into a child bearing machine,
Mother and father you killed me.

I have nothing,
Muchineripi owns everything,
The cattle and cows are his,
The homestead is also his,
What then is mine?
Mother, I have literally nothing.

Mother I am done with this life,
Can't continue in this marriage,

Mother, you destroyed me.
I am now a champion of women empowerment,
I now live life I have always dreamt of,
I have sloughed,
I am a new being,
Let every woman open their eyes,
That is my wish mother,
I will not rest till women find their rightful place.

Afurika Chidadiso
Johannes Mike Mupisa

Gonamombe risidi nongoro,
Hwitakwi pamajaha,
Muhwisazvose,
Mufanegungwa chita chine nyota,
Chodokwaira nerute chichiyeva,
Dunhu remitunhu Africa.

Muwanazvese mupakatiri,
Vuyavaya hwenzizi hwunoyevedza,
Limpopo, Zambezi naNile,
Nyanza hatirevi vuteputepu,
Muchiviwa semhongora,
Chiri chii chisimo?
Zviwanikwa chaizvo isharaude,
Nzou idzamatsama,
Zvipembere idutu.
Africa chidadiso!

Minda chaiyo ziendanakuenda,
Masango idzikatiri,
Zvicherwa ungaingai,
Isaruraude zvese ideteranwa,
Africa! Africa, uri chidadiso,
Ruvheneko rwepasi rose.
Guvhu renyika yose.

Africa hauna ngava nechita,
Vazhinji vanotodavo chimedu,
Vagokun'en'ena zvishoma nezvishoma,
Vachitotsa rifa remwana weAfrica,
Zvino zvinoda undyire here?
Undyire hwomunya Africa,
Pasi nahwo hwavuraya chidadiso,
Africa uri chidadiso!

Africa
Johannes Mike Mupisa

Beautiful Africa,
The king cock,
Beast of beasts,
The beauty of the earth,
The continent of continents,
Beautiful Africa.

The harbour of all,
Envied by all,
What can't you find in it?
Rhinoceros are plenty,
There are vast tracts of land,
The forests are indeed a marvel,
Rivers flow everywhere,
Limpopo, Zambezi and the Nile,
Oceans, I won't mention,
They make the marvel complete,
Minerals are everywhere,
You suffer from indecision due to their variety.
Africa our marvel.

The land which of no worries,
Everyone wants a piece of it,
Corruption is now the disease eating up the marvel,
A share of the legacy of Africa,
Taking a share through illegitimate ways is unacceptable,
Africa is our marvel.

Zimbe mujombo
Johannes Mike Mupisa

Kwaradada pagwenzi,
Mbikiti seuto ramambo,
Banga richichema nenhomba,
Dikita richisinira sechitubu,
Ziso rakati udzvu sembovora,
Tsinga tare tare seshizha remubovora,
Zvigunwe zvichifanya pasi sebugwa,
Hana ichikindidza sengoma.
Mbovora muzarima.

Bhodhoro dzvi kuruboshwe,
Nhare ngai ngai kurudyi,
Ichizeya muruvoko sechitaitai,
Shereni dzichitamba muhombodo,
Yemashizha ichichokoteka muchikwama,
Fambe fambe ze-e ze-e pi-i,
Pote padombo remasare, dhuma.

Nyahwa nyahwa ndiye mone,
Roseva seva banga riya,
Muchidya, muruvoko, muchidya,
Huro nzve-e nzve-e,
Mba mba mba,
Dombo dzvi,
Go go go dzoro,
Mushiya nevhu mbunde,
Bidiribidiri pfau pfau zi-i,
Forototo muviri favava,
Sumu ndiye ze-e ze-e pi-i,
Dzadzara dzadzara kunanga kumusha,

Ruzha gwemasirivha hakuchina,
Yasara yemashizha,
Murukukwe pfe-e,
Shozhonoke shozhonoke hwe-e,
Svatu waru jombo rorira pazhe,
Dzachenera kuzvivhikira,
Haiwawo!
Pasi iri izimbe mujombo.

Hornets' Nest
Johannes Mike Mupisa

Hiding behind the bush,
Attentively like the king's guard,
The knife thirsty for human blood,
Sweat gushing out like a fountain,
Eyes terrifyingly out like a chameleon,
Veins and arteries visible like a pumpkin plant leaf,
Toes embracing the earth like the nails of a monitor lizard,
The heart throbbing like a drum,
Murderer in the thick darkness.

Clutching the beer bottle in the left hand,
The right hand gripping the mobile,
Providing the light to illuminate the darkness,
Flickering in the darkness like a firefly,
Coins jingling in his pockets,
While the notes breathed in his fat wallet,
Staggering here and there,
Falling here and there,
Owing to the drunkenness,
As he made it near the big rock he met the man in the thick bush.

He tiptoed towards the drunk,
Grabbed him with deadly intent,
His knife went through the lap,
Went for the neck but missed,
The drunk's hands fortunately grab a rock,
Made it for the head,
Blood bathed the earth,
Soul and flesh separated,
The drunk staggers here and there,
Heading towards his home,
The jingling coins now silent,
Emptied in his pockets by the struggle with the man behind the bush,
Enters his hut and goes for the bed,
The noise of the man in boots awakens him in the morning,
Handcuffed for self defence,
What a world it is,
It's a hornets' nest indeed.

RUFU
Prosper Kavunika

Rufu uri mudadi asina nyadzi
Rufu uri munzwa usina tsitsi
Rufu uri mutambudzi asina mupomhodzi
............Haunyare..................
Unobvutira vasisina chavainacho
Unonyebudza vasati vane chavanacho
Hwema hwako basi unosiya mazera ose achiungudza
Mumvuri wako hauna chipenyu chinobuda pauri
Pawapfuura napo rutsoka rwako rwunosiya rwanyora pahana dzedu
Pawabata chanza chako chosiya chabvarura panyama nhete
Izwi rako haruna kana mumwe zvake anoda kuri teerera
Chimiro chako hachina akachitaura akachipedza
Uri mupangara unobaya muchanza cherusvava runokambaira
Unombandidzira kukwana chete nepausingadiwe
Unonyangira vazhinji vakarivara.
...............Wakaipa chose.....................
Chidembo chikange nani , chikapfuura munokanganwa nezvacho
Imbwa ikange nani, ikanetsa munosungirira
Mbavha ikange nani, inotendeuka wani
Inga zino rikabviswa vende racho rinopora wani
Ko yako mbeu yaunodyara mundangariro dzedu sei usingaikohwe
Ko rako ganwa risingaguti rakakurei
Mavanga ako kubva zvawatimaranzura haasati apora.
...............Rufu wakaipa chose........

Death
Prosper Kavunika

Death you are mocker with no shame
You are a thorn with no mercy
Death you are a tormentor with no restrain

You have no shame
You take even from those without anything
You deceive even those who have nothing yet
Your scent alone leaves many garnishing
Your shadow do not possess life in it
Where ever you pass, your feet leave footprints on our hearts
The touch of your hand tears our flesh
No one wishes to listen to your voice
No one has ever dared to look at your image

A thorn that pierce inside the soft palm of a toddler
You push for space even where you are not welcome
You pounce on many unannounced

You are so evil....
A skunk us better, if it passes we soon forget about it
A dog is better, if it misbehave you put it on a leash
A thief is better , he can repent
Even if the tooth is removed, the wound will soon heal

What then is your seed that you plant in our memory that you never harvest
How big is your mouth that you are never satisfied
Your scars that you gave us have not healed since

Death you are horrible

Albino
Adjei Agyei-Baah

yours is a hard tale to tell
one already known in every household –
chewed like granny stick,
tossed from one corner of the mouth
to the other

you who hardly see the shadow of your own
a cold fate of indoor life
to avoid the full bite of the sun

which eye passes you by
without taking a second look
at your oddity?
which pew contains you
without keeping others at bay?

a white scar on the face
of a black continent?
the remaining remnant of the rabid raiders?

a tale is told of your crooked destiny –
the sapien who took an early exit
when God's hands
were still wet with clay

you, the ruiner of marriages –
the child who brought no honor

to the midnight sweat of his father

the stigma of mother's dishonor –
the midwife's regret
of not buying a mother's conspiracy –
a gentle squeeze was all that it takes

but at your doorstep
I lay my wreath of sympathy –
the child who never smiled at the sun

for so close you must stay
around your father's hut
for in the witchdoctor's eyes,
you are a pot of gold!

First Published in GRAINS-A Journal of the Association of Nigerian Authors-Ebonyi State Chapter, 2018

Ofiri
Adjei Agyei-Baah
Translated into Asante Twi by *Adjei Agyei-Baah*

w'akosɛm ka yɛ kana
nea yɛdi ho nkɔmɔ wɔ afie afie mu
na ɔwe ne sɛ tweapea ɛda abrewa anum
na ɔdi no atotoatoto wɔ n'ano kaam

wo a w'ani ntwa wo sunsum soɔ
hyɛbrɛ a ɛde faakotena na ɛnam
senea ɛbɛyɛ a owia renhye wo

ani bɛn na ɛtwa wo so a
ɛnhwɛ wo ahwɛ prɛnu?
asɔre akunwa bɛn na wotena so a
afoforɔ ntwe wɔn ho?

kotwa fufuo a
ɛda abibiman moma so?
nkaedum bi a ɔbofoɔ bi gyaa no akyire?

ɔka awerɛhosɛm bi fa wo ti bonee ho
onipa a wodwane firi Onyame anim
berɛ a na ɔde dɔteɛ rema wo honam

wo a wogu awareɛ
abofra a woammfa animuonyamhyɛ
amma n'agya wɔ n'anadwo mpaso agodie mu

ɛna aniwuo ba
nea ɔgyee wo awoɔ nuu ne ho sɛ
wɔantie wo na suu antwa wo nkwa tia

nea na ɛsɛsɛɔyɛ ne sɛ wobetua wo home kwan

na wo pono ano
na mede mawerɛkyekyerɛ nhweren regu
abɔfra a wonsere nkyerɛ owia

na wo agya sese ho
na wɔɛsɛsɛ wotwe bata bre biara
ɛfirisɛ, wɔ dusinii anisoɔ no
wo yɛ sikakɔkɔɔ puduo

In The Grey Hair of Soyinka
Adjei Agyei-Baah

There's something mystical
About your gray hair, Baba
Not in its seductive whiteness
Your flowers that continue
To bloom on high
Even in its twilight years

Your hair is much more of a spectacle—
Rising embers that end as fireflies
Fire flights that radiate a dream fulfilled
A dream fulfilled which remains our haven
The expansive shade of the baobab tree
For generations to savor our ageless tales

This hair indeed envisioned a path
This hair, the stepping stones of African literature
This hair whitens the dark corridors for humanity

Indeed, this hair caused a stir
Perhaps the reason it knows not a fall

Soyinka Tirim Dwene
Adjei Agyei-Baah
Translated into Asante Twi by *Adjei Agyei-Baah*

biribi nwanwasoɔ bi
wɔ wo tirinwii fitaa yi mu, Baba
nnɛ ne fufuo a ɛtwe aniwa
wo nhweren a ɛkɔ so yɛ brom
wɔ ne nyini awieɛ

wo tirinwii yɛ krabɛhwɛ
gyafruma a etutu sɛ anadwo bogya
gyafruma a ɛkyerɛ daeɛ awieɛ pa
daeɛ awieɛ pa a ɛhyɛ nkuran
onwunu a yɛ nya firi ɔdadeɛ dua ase
ma nkyirimma bɛtie anansesɛm

wo tirinwii twaa sa pa
wo tirinwii yi yɛ Abibiman atwerɛ sibrɛ
wo tirinwii yɛɛ kanea wɔ sum mu de maa adasa
Ampa, wo tirinwii yi de ahokeka bae
sɛsɛɛɛno nti na antɔ baha

CAIO E LEVANTO
Maria Manuel Godinho Azancot de Menezes

Morro e renasço, caio e levanto,
quantas décadas houver.
Morro e renasço, seco lágrimas do pranto,
as que me são permitidas ter.

Prossigo, meu corpo a doer,
enfrento a mesquinhice sentada,
a ociosidade que nega fazer,
quantas idas e processos fachada!

Quando o monstro ignorância inveja,
tenta ofertar humilhação.
Enquanto a corrupção vergar almeja,
eu clamo justiça de coração.

Eu clamo o que é meu de direito,
e no mar revolto sem fim,
busco nos antepassados do peito,
Tsunamis que guardei em mim!

Erguem-se em espuma no ar,
respiro, e clamo um direito que é meu.
Volto e regresso, mesmo a arfar,
reclamo um direito que é meu.

Orgulho na honra herdada,
enfrento o escárnio encaro a ironia,
a maldade pura lá nucleada,
só Deus sabe, se irão mudar um dia.

FALL AND RAISE
Maria Manuel Godinho Azancot de Menezes
Translation into English by *Maria da Conceição Saraiva*

Die and rebirth, fall and raise,
so many decades exist.
Die and rebirth, tears dried,
simply the ones that I am allowed to have.

Proceeding with my body aching,
i bear the spitefulness sitting,
the idleness that refuse to do,
so many journeys and guised processes!

When the monster of envy ignorance,
tries to offer humiliation.
while the corruption seeks to break,
i claim justice in my heart.

I claim what is mine by right,
and in the sea insurgency without end,
I trace my dearest ancestors,
Tsunamis kept within me!

Rise froth in the air,
I breathe, and claim what is mine by right.
I go back, return even gasping,
I reclaim what is mine by right.

Pride in the honour inherited,
i confront the mockery and face the irony,
the pure evil fissionable there,

only God knows, if they will change one day.

JE TOMBE ET JE ME LÈVE
Maria Manuel Godinho Azancot de Menezes
Taduction un French de *Anabela Pezarat Correia*

Je meurs et je renais, je tombe et je me lève,
combien de décennies sont là.
Je meurs et je renais, je sèche les larmes des pleurs,
ceux que l'on me permet d'avoir.

Je continue, mon corps à faire mal,
je fais face à la méchanceté assise,
l'oisiveté qui refuse faire,
combien de trajets et processus de façade!

Quand le monstre de l'ignorance envie,
il essaie d'offrir l'humiliation.
Tandis que la corruption veut se plier,
je pleure justice de coeur.

Je crie ce qui me revient de droit
et dans la mer turbulente infinie,
je cherche dans les ancêtres de la poitrine,
des tsunamis que j'ai gardé dans moi!

Ils montent en mousse dans l'air,
je respire et je revendique un droit qui est le mien.
Je vais et retour, même haletant,
je revendique un droit qui est le mien.
Fierté d'honneur hérité,
je fais face au mépris je fais face à l'ironie,

la cruauté pure y centré,
seulement Dieu sait, s'ils changeront un jour.

MIGRANTES
Maria Manuel Godinho Azancot de Menezes

No dia -a- dia dormem leve sono.
Leve porque a alma pesada mói,
no tempo longo de mau Outono,
a terra sofre e o corpo dói.
Nós dormimos bem, abençoado abono!
Mas alerta porque um irmão se destrói!

Atirados no mato, mar ou rio,
 vão a pé, no bote ou falua.
Lançados vagueando no corredio,
da madrugada ao morrer a lua.
Com a esperança só por um fio,
fugindo dum país que já só tem rua.

Lá na terra não há labor nem lençol,
os homens se surpreendem a chorar.
A terra de impiedosas armas e sol,
obriga crianças inocentes a mirrar.
Há mau trato há miséria em rol,
sucumbem pessoas com dor sem par.

Vale a dúvida e sonhar com a sorte,
crentes na paz e noutra terra o destino.
Melhor que certeza na morte,
é enfrentar oportunista sem tino.

Vale procurar no Sul ou no Norte,
um cantinho de paz um alegre sino.

MIGRANTS
Maria Manuel Godinho Azancot de Menezes
Translation into English by *Nuri de Menezes Torres*

Day by day they doze light sleep.
    Light because the heavy soul grinds,
through the long and hard Autumn's time,
the earth suffers and the body hurts.
We sleep well, blessed praise!
Then alert because a brother is destroying himself!

Thrown into the bush, sea or river,
they walk on foot, in the dinghy or by canoeing.
Launched drifting in the flowing,
since dawn until the moon vanishes.
With hope hanging by a thread,
fleeing from a country which has just a street.

There is no labor or bedsheet in their lands,
men surprise themselves crying.
The land of merciless arms and sun,
compels innocent children to wither.
There is maltreatment there is unbounded misery,
people succumb with unparalleled pain.

It is worth doubting and dreaming with good fortune,
believing in peace and destiny of another land.
Better than certainty in death,
It is an opportunistic challenge without vision,

It is worth looking for a safe place, a joyful bell,
in the South or in the North.

MIGRANTS
Maria Manuel Godinho Azancot de Menezes
Taduction un French de *Anabela Pezarat Correia*

Ils dorment un sommeil léger chaque jour.
Léger parce que l'âme lourde broie,
pendant le long temps de mauvais Automne,
la terre souffre et le corps a de la douleur .
Nous dormons bien, cadeau béni!
Mais sois alerte car un frère est détruit!

Jeté dans le fourré, la mer ou la rivière,
ils vont à pied, dans le bateau ou barque.
Lancé errant dans la course de la vie,
de l'aube jusqu'à la mort de la lune.
Avec de l'espoir seulement par un fil,
fuyant d´un pays qui n'a que de la rue.

Là-bas, sur la terre il n'as pas de travail ni de drap,
les hommes s' étonnent à pleurer.
La terre d´armes impitoyables et du soleil,
il oblige des enfants innocents à se dessécher.
Il y a de mauvais traitement il y a la misère dans le rôle,
il y a des gens qui succombent avec la douleur sans pareil.

Il vaut la doute et rêver avec la chance,
croyants en paix et destin dans un autre pays.
Mieux que la certitude de la mort,
c´est faire face à l'opportuniste sans jugement.

Il vaut la peine de regarder dans le sud ou le nord,
un petit coin de paix et une cloche joyeuse.

POR ÁFRICA
Maria Manuel Godinho Azancot de Menezes

Procuro nos montes, nos desertos, nos mares.
Procuro o quê? Não sei, apenas sei que procuro!
Talvez um grito que ecoe pelos ares,
um socorro com letras ainda no escuro.

Procuro nas casas, nas ruas, nos media.
O eco do grito de luta sem armas dos avós e dos pais,
o eco do grito de água fértil dos olhos da mãe misericórdia,
o eco do grito dos sonhos de amores nas catedrais.

Um grito, um lápis eficaz para os filhos de Adão e Eva.
Procuro uma febre que sacuda a terra silenciosa de África
violentada,
um clamor que pare quem cria a treva,
uma visão de uma onda de força convulsiva que já tarda!

Procuro sem me cansar, até um gigantesco alarme soar em cada
ser que pensa,
estrondoso rugir de montanhas enfurecidas de verdades,
um pesar de consciência dorido como cabeças presas à prensa,
procuro um grito fértil que germine em todos sensibilidades!

Dentro e fora de África, para África.
Onde procuro? Como se procura?
Em mim, em ti, um qualquer primeiro que exemplifica,

caminhos humanos e certos para a cura.

Não finjas cegueira!
Hei! A catástrofe é tão visível á nossa beira...
Hei! Homem Íntegro! Não queiras sonambular...
Não finjas que não vês,
inicia por ti um acordar!
Não vires a cara desta vez.

Corta pacto vaidoso, fútil,
recua nas barbáries em nome de Deus,
repugna saques e sangue de mina e fúsil ,
foge de desonras pelos teus !

Olha a gente de olhar sonolento e enevoado,
sem o brilho alegre do verde esperança.
A que lhes resta é porque te vê humanizado,
aguardam impotentes justa aliança.

Olha a pele baça! doente! suja ! a mão não é mais côncava a pedir...
Mal anda e de corpo rendido, tenta erguer a alma !
Na sua mente se mantem um sonho no porvir,
 "Que tu o vejas, e da vontade, tudo imana".

Ele vê-te, irmão.
Ah, o segredo é esse sim!
"Se tu também o vires, dar-lhe-ás a mão! "
Com constituição, com instituição, com o coração por fim!

FOR ÁFRICA
Maria Manuel Godinho Azancot de Menezes
Translation into English by *Licínio Assis*

I look upon the mountains, the deserts, the seas!
What do I look upon? I don´t know, I just know that I look upon!
Maybe a scream that echoes through the air,
a rescue with letters still in the dark.

I look upon the houses, the streets, the media.
The echo of the unarmed scream of struggle of the grandparents and parents,
the echo of the scream of fertile water from the eyes of mother mercy,
the echo of the scream of love's dreams in the cathedrals.

A scream, an effective pencil for the children of Adam and Eve.
I look upon for a fever that shakes the silent land of raped Africa,
a scream that stops those who create the darkness,
a vision of a wave of convulsive force that takes long enough!

I look upon without getting tired, until a gigantic warning sounds in every thinking being,
a roaring roar of mountains enraged with truths,
a sorrowful thoughtlessness of sorrow as heads locked to the press,
I look upon a fertile scream that germinates in all sensitiveness'!

In and out of Africa, for Africa.
Where do I look upon? How to look upon?
In me, in you, any first one that exemplifies,

human and right paths to cure.

May you not pretend blindness!
Hey! The catastrophe is so visible on our side ...
Hey! Right Man! May you not dare to sleep ...
May you not pretend you don't see,
you start a wake up!
May you not turn your face away this time.

Cut vain pact, futile,
go back in the barbarities in the name of God,
repel loot and blood of mine and fuss,
run away from dishonour for the ones of you!

Look at the ones of drowsy and foggy looks,
without the cheerful glow of the green hope.
What's left to them is because they see you humanized,
Awaiting powerlessly for fair alliance.

Look at the pale skin! sick! dirty ! the hand is no longer cupped to beg ...
It hardly walks and with a surrendered body, it tries to lift the soul!
In its mind it keeps a dream in the future,
 "May you see it, and from the will, everything spreads up".

He sees you, my brother.
Ah, that is the secret, yes!
"If you also see him, you'll give him your hand!"
With a constitution, with an institution, with the heart at last!

POUR L'AFRIQUE
Maria Manuel Godinho Azancot de Menezes
Traduction un French de *Sami Marcelino Benzaza*

Je cherche dans les montagnes, les déserts, les mers.
Je cherche quoi ? Je ne sais pas, je sais à peine ce que je cherche !
Peut-être l'écho d'un cri dans les airs,
un sauvetage en lettres encore dans le noir.
Je cherche dans les maisons, les rues, les médias.
L'écho du cri de la lutte sens armes des grands-parents et des parents,
L'écho du cri de l'eau fertile des yeux de la mère miséricorde,
L'écho du cri des rêves de l'amour dans des cathédrales.

Un cri, un crayon efficace pour les enfants d'Adam et Eve.
Je cherche une fièvre qui secoue la terre silencieuse que l'Afrique violée,
Un cri qui arrête ceux qui créent les ténèbres,
Une vision d'une vague de force convulsive qui tarde déjà !

Je cherche sans me fatiguer, jusqu'à ce qu'une alarme gigantesque retentisse dans la tête de chaque être pensant,
Brouillant rugissement des montagnes enragées de vérités,
Une triste conscience de la douleur tel des têtes pressées à la presse,
Je cherche un cri fertile qui germe dans toutes les sensibilités !

En et hors de l'Afrique, pour l'Afrique.
Où est-ce que je cherche? Comment chercher ?
En moi, en toi, un quelque un premier qui exemplifie,
Chemins humains et droit vers la guérison.

Ne prétends pas d'être aveugle !

Hey! La catastrophe est si visible de notre côté ...
Hey! Homme intègre! Ne pense pas à dormir ...
Ne prétends pas que tu ne vois pas,
Commence pour toi-même un réveille!
Ne tourne pas le visage cette fois ci.

Coupe le vain pacte, futile,
recule dans les barbaries au nom de Dieu,
répugnance au pillage et le sang de mine et fusil
fuis toi le déshonneur par les tiens!

Regardez-nous aux gens de regard somnolent et brumeux
sans la lueur joyeuse du vert de l'espoir.
Ce qui les reste est parce qu'ils te voient humanisé,
Ils attendant impuissant une juste alliance.

Regardez la peau humide ! malade, sale, la main qui n'est plus
concave pour demander ...
Mal marchant et avec un corps rendu, tout en essayant d'élever
l'âme!
Dans son esprit, se crée un rêve du futur,
« Que tu le vois, et de l'envie, tout émane ».

Il te voit, mon frère.
Ah, le secret c'est celui-là!
"Si tu le voie aussi, tu le donneras ta main ! «
Avec la constitution, avec l'institution, avec le cœur, enfim!

Part 12: Poetics

An Interview with Beaton Galafa
September 24, 2018

We engage Malawian poet in a conversation about his writing and life in China where he is currently based doing graduate studies

Tell us about yourself

I always want to be known as a friend to friends, an enemy to enemies, a brother to my siblings, a son to my mother and father, and Malawian. It makes me feel more human. I've had so much interest in writing from a very young age, but it is at Chancellor College that I consider as having finally taken this path: still budding, with works appearing in various literary magazines, journals and anthologies around the world. In addition to the rejection and acceptance mails, there have been two other situations that have kept me going. In 2014, I participated in the Commonwealth Creative Nonfiction Writers Workshop in Uganda – the first of its kind for East African writers. I met literary gems whose ideas about writing I even understand much better now. The second was the Writivism Literary Initiative 2017 Online Mentorship Programme. I submitted a story in the nonfiction category, and I was selected as a mentee. This, and several other literary engagements with friends, continues shaping my writing. It's also a learning process that will never stop.

Tell us about the poetry scene in your country

Poetry in Malawi has always been at the centre of life for many people. It has served as both social and political activism as well as a form of entertainment since independence. There are names that cannot be divorced from discourses on poetry in the country. Names like Jack Mapanje, Frank Chipasula, Wokomaatani Malunga, David Rubadiri and Steve Chimombo. However, currently, it is vernacular poetry that is dominating the local scene – which is even more pleasing. But this poetry is more of recordings and performances – with the need to satisfy audiences at times compromising literary quality. This is a debate that appears to stay forever, on whether this contemporary poetry is 'really' poetry – which is even (again) more satisfying, that people in various platforms are continuously engaging on poetry(or stuff that resembles it). There are also some names that are doing well in contemporary poetry written in English.Just this year, a Malawian poet I had never heard of before, Grace Sharra, became second in the Babishai Poetry Prize 2018 – a continental poetry writing contest for African writers.

You are a student in China, what migrant or exilic issues have informed your poetry?
There is a lot. The good and the bad. As you would predict. The ambiguity of curiosity and naivety – or in forms worse than the two – from prejudice against Africa in my daily experiences. And, the pain of dealing with friends who don't give a damn about it – whose lives appear to revolve around other things immaterial to our own space as Africans. I have also met a lot of new people with new experiences – and have been to new places both through Chinese poetry (in English) and travels that have inspired my own writing.

What do you think is lacking in writing, or poetry-making on the continent and how do you think we can solve this?
Reading contemporary literary works by established and emerging African writers, you would think there isn't much to worry about.

But when I narrow it down to my own country, challenges are still there. Our governments haven't taken the arts that seriously. For example, there are no known fixed literary workshops or contests funded by government in my country. The writers are trying their best – but you should know the importance of government interventionist programmes in an economy like ours. There aren't any literary journals affiliated to arts universities where literary enthusiasts would place their work too. I mean, these are universities where literature– and creative writing, is taught. I don't want to touch on the art of writing itself, and the quality of works we (especially emerging writers like me – desperate for literary acclaim) are producing because I don't think I am experienced enough for that. I might shoot myself in the foot. But, I'm looking forward to such a time when I will be able to discuss this – having accepted all my writing mistakes of the past which the pomp in my tenderness refuses to acknowledge now. And this, I think is the mistake of most of my peers, and those younger. We might learn much later in our literary graves.

Tell us of new African writers you have recently read their work who are not from your country
Recently, my focus has been on contemporary short fiction and poetry anthologies. I've also been reading some nonfiction, but in anthologies too. So, the response would be a bit complicated. I've read most of these works because of an ongoing project – I had to submit a chapter to a book that talks about addiction in Africa, and I chose the literary side of it. I'm not sure whether what I sent will be accepted, but it still led me to a discovery of some fine works by emerging and established African writers in the anthologies I've read, with stories anthologized by Writivism, Jalada, African Writers' Trust and Emma Shercliff and Bibi Bakare-Yusuf. In these anthologies, I've read works from Binyavanga Wainaina, Alexander

Ikawah, Richard Oduor and many others from across the continent.

Do you have any upcoming projects ready for publication, tell us about them

When a question like this comes, I always say yes, though it might not really mean yes. I have poetry that I think is ready for publication. I have sent my manuscript to a number of publishers before – but that I'm mentioning it now should already give you a hint on the responses I've gotten. So, I keep adding and removing some poems from it, and re-reading and revising some, until it will be accepted for publication – or until I will venture into self-publication (the latter might not be soon, it might as well be, depending on the odds).

Tell us about your work in BNAP

The Humming Bird. This is a poem that left me the moment I wrote it down. I can't talk about what inspired me to write it, to avoid ruining the inspiration behind readers' own interpretation of the poem. It's good for both me and those who will happen to read the BNAP 2017 Anthology. It saves me from spoiling their fun – and the labour of having to explain every poem of mine that has been published.

An Interview with Archie Swanson
September 03, 2018

Tell us about yourself

I'm a South African that grew up in the midst of the apartheid era South Africa. My political awareness was shaped by my Grandfather and both parents who were liberal-minded as well as the school I attended (Diocesan College). I studied economics and have been involved in fruit exports which has taken me to many countries as has my love for surfing. I am published in various anthologies and magazines. Last year I was shortlisted for the Sol Plaatje award as well as the UK Bridport Poetry Prize. My poetry collection *the stretching of my sky* was published this year. I serve on the Board of the South African Literary Journal that published the longest standing poetry magazine in South Africa called *New Contrast*.

Tell us about the poetry scene in your country

As we all know, there really isn't money in poetry (except for the famous few!) so we do this for the love of it. South Africa has a very vibrant and active poetry tradition and what's really great is the explosion of poetry among the school-going generation and college and university students and school leavers. We have regular poetry readings around the country. In Cape Town there are the weekly Off the Wall Poetry Performing and Grounding Sessions open mic and guest poet gigs in Observatory. The Poetry Circle in the Central Library meets once a month and there's also a guest poet once a month at Kamili Coffee Shop. I think the University of Western Cape also have readings in the University Library from time to time.

Archie, 3 years ago when I interviewed you, you said you, "started writing when I was 13 and had poems published in our school magazine" what were the issues at the heart of a 13 year old Archie versus the issues at the heart of the 62 year old Archie.

The first poem I ever had published nationally appeared in *English Alive* in 1973 (English Alive is an anthology of South African High School creative writing that is still going strong). This is the poem:

mapolisa - the police

in the still night
        as a cat whines in the darkness
a shadow lurks
        mapolisa
and the people crouch
        in clenched fists
                of black terror

That's fairly radical for a school kid I guess, but that's the way I felt then and that's the way I feel now.

Here is a poem about Sharpeville I wrote just two years ago. It's the same eye and the same voice:

tell me i lived

robert sobukwe
our holes are dug
our coffins neatly aligned
our faces - masks

robert sobukwe

speak for us
write in our books
gather the dust of our blood

robert sobukwe
speak to me
tell me i lived
tell me i mattered
tell me i count

robert sobukwe
sing to me
sing a deep song
sing a lullaby
sing a methodist hymn

robert sobukwe
hold me
hold my warm hand growing cold

robert sobukwe
gather my soul

Having said this one learns the craft – there is the truth that it takes 10,000 hours – actually it takes more. You learn to understand your voice and your craft as time goes by and you do this by publishing and reading your poems as well as listening to the voices of other poets. I write on a variety of subjects. I write about what catches my eye. I always write for myself first – often trying to explain something to myself or capture my thoughts about something I'm experiencing. I try to write in a straight-forward way so others can understand what I'm saying.

How do you get around life and your creativity, how do you achieve balance between these, living and creativity.
For me there has never been any separation between life and poetry. I really don't sit down to write - rather I find myself grabbing a pen and paper anywhere and everywhere to get things down that have caught my eye and inspired me.

If you were a poem, what type or form will you be in, and why?
I would just be free verse – unpredictable – free – not constrained by norms – experimental – pushing boundaries.

"Most of our indigenous history in South Africa, and I guess the rest of Africa, has been handed down from one generation to another through story telling", What stories do you feel you have handed down to your children
I spend a lot of time with my daughters. They are wonderful free-spirited generous people who laugh easily. I don't think I've ever sort-of sat any of them down and said "Now hear this!" but we are a family of story-tellers and I think everyone is good at it. Usually they are hilarious stories. I do tell them some of their family history, but it bores them I think!

What type of sports are you into.
I love most sports but surfing has always been my first love. The ocean is a great tutor. A tutor that never speaks yet speaks volumes – teaches how insignificant we are – how nature is to be respected and loved.

Tell us about your recently published poetry collection, what is it about, what do you want to achieve, and where it can be bought by those interested in procuring a copy

the stretching of my sky really has no theme. It is a gathering of poems about places, people, politics, tragedy, happiness, travel, loss and love. The 49 poems are accompanied by over 60 colour images – the paintings and drawings of friends as well as numerous photographs. Its available only in South Africa. In Cape Town it can be bought at The Book Lounge, Clark's Books, The Olde Book Shop, The Central Library Book Shop and elsewhere in some Wordworth Book Stores and the Temanos Book Store in McGregor. It's also available at the University of Cape Town, Stellenbosch University and University of Western Cape libraries as well as the Cape Town Central and the Jacob Gitlin Libraries.

You have been with the BNAP family from the beginning, give us a perspective opinion of the project
It is the little flame that has become a wild fire. Obviously this was your vision, Tendai and what a vision it has turned out to be! There cannot be another joining of so many poets from our great African continent that comes close to this – so many countries and so many voices. Not just that, we communicate with one another through the groups regularly – we support, challenge and grow. Here you are about to start on the 4th BNAP anthology – it's amazing, not even to mention the Africa versus Latin American, Asia, North America collaborations that have been a spin off. It's been a privilege to be a part of this. May BNAP go from strength to strength and receive the recognition it deserves!

An interview with Oscar Gwiriri
September 13, 2018

Tell us about yourself.

I am Oscar Gwiriri born on 15 June 1975 at Honde Valley, Eastern Highlands, Zimbabwe. I am a published writer featured in 4 anthologies; Shaurai Nduri Dzazuro Nedzanhasi, Gwatakwata reNhetembo, Hodzeko Yenduri, Mupakwa werwendo, and three English anthologies; A tribute to Penny; Africa, UK, and Ireland: Writing Politics and Knowledge Production Vol 1; and Best "New" African Poets 2017 Anthology (BNAP). I have also published nine vernacular Children readers, and co-authored A Practical Approach to Agriculture Form 1 book. Three (03) of my short stories were published in magazines too.
Professionally, I am a Certified Forensic Investigation Professional, who holds a Master of Science in Strategic Management Degree, Bachelor of Business Administration, Associate Bachelor of Business Administration Degree, Diploma in Logistics and Transport, Diploma in Workplace Safety and Health, and eleven (11) United Nations Peacekeeping Certificates. I prefer writing much more in the vernacular (Shona) language to promote the Zimbabwean indigenous heritage.

Tell us about the poetry scene in your country.
The majority of Zimbabweans are writers by nature, and poetry seems to be the genre which dominates the writing scene. There are both established and upcoming poets who mingle and exchange ideas on poetry writing. Taking advantage of the social media frenzy, most writers have formed up online groups strictly for writers. I belong to various Whatsapp groups such as the Writing

Issues Only group formulated by a well celebrated writer, Memory Chirere; Writing for Children group, WinZim SuperClass group which won a NAMA award in 2016, Indigenous African Languages group, Writepreneurs group, ZimWriters & Poets group, Writing Short Stories group, and the Poetry, Writers & Critics group. The poetry scene is very active, with performance poets also dishing out their talent at various functions and social clubs. Of late, I have witnessed much poetry, motivational books, and novels book launches in Harare. Whilst many poets bemoan lack of swift publishing, there is entrepreneurial book publishing mushrooming throughout the country, and some writers have successfully taken the self-publishing route.

You have described yourself as a new generation writer, what do you think sets you most apart from the old generation?
This question is a little bit tricky to me in that I still do not understand when a writer should be considered new or old. Is it old by virtue of age or having written a long time ago, or old by a number of publications? If it is by a number of publications, then I am amongst the elders, but if it is by generation, I can say the old generation is our mentors and we must give due respect to them for having set a foundation for us. I have heard new writers crying foul over the elders' dominance in the publishing sector. I consider that as mere ignorance of what publishers look for. Publishers are business minded, and they go for an already marketed brand name. It is upon the new generation to compete actively by presenting deep thought manuscripts which are worthy publishing, than to be jealousy of the established (old) writers. A good writer should come up with something new in the market, something that fills up a literal gap.

How do you get around with life and your creativity, how do you achieve a balance between these, living and creativity?

Time is never on my side. There are too many things to write about, and I am afraid of dying before I complete my draft short stories and novels. I am always short of time to read both the old and new books, since I can never be a good writer without being a wide reader. I spend a third of my day at work, and allocate the remaining two thirds to the family, reading and writing. Most of the times, I sleep for less than six hours, due to night time reading and writing. There is a time when I was captivated in writing a novel throughout the night to an extend that I was shocked to hear the cock roosting. I try to balance between work, family time and creative writing. Sometimes I wish I could hold the clock.

What do you think is lacking in writing, or poetry making in the continent and how do you think we can solve this?
I think writers are writing as much as they can, but without feedback from readers, a writer may get discouraged. I had been off creative writing for almost a decade, and I was motivated to write again when our house-maid stated that she did a literature set book by someone with the same surname as ours, not knowing that I was the actual author. Knowing that when you write, someone is going to read motivates the writer. I give thanks to Tendai. R. Mwanaka for linking the world writers through his witful publishing projects and social media initiatives. There should be online co-ordination which cuts off the distance barriers amongst us, and bring up inter-continental writers together. Marketing initiatives and publishing seem to be minimal across continents, and more effort is required from every book stakeholder. Writers should preserve the dynamic indigenous writing styles or capture indigenous activities such as songs in their stories as a marketing and preservative measure of their heritage. All my novels have poetry and songs incorporated, just to reflect the nature of my people in a happy or somberly mood. I appeal to those who have a translating talent to assist in converting good books into other languages.

What type of sports are you in.
During my spare time, I watch WWE (Wrestling). My time is too limited to concentrate on outdoor sports. I usually go out when I need to research or observe something to write about. However, I grew up practicing the Bruce Lee Martial Arts style, Jeet Kune Do. I believe Martial Arts somehow correlate with writing.

Tell us about your recently published book, what it is about; what do you want to achieve, and where those interested in buying a copy can do so.
My most recently published book is an indigenous old world novel called Hatiponi. The main character, Hatiponi discovered infidelity between his mother and nephew (cum-father) in a bush. Hatiponi force marched the two to the village, but mysteriously disappeared to another village before they arrived at the Chief's court. Whilst he was at another village, he competed for a princess in a wrestling match whereby the wrestling ring was suspended above a crocodile infested pool. The starved crocodiles mauled all fighters who fell in the pool. Hatiponi won the match against his rival nephew who fell in the pool, and everybody believed the alligators mauled him. Hatiponi then married the princess. Back home, his mother later died of hypertension, and her aggrieved spirit tormented him to go back home. A witch doctor was consulted, and it was advised that Hatiponi should go begging for corn for an appeasement ceremony (Kutanda botso). The condition of the ritual was that he should never engage with a woman, but a poverty-stricken granny who needed some grains unfortunately lured him. The ceremony was abandoned when the witch doctor's spirit picked it up. Hatiponi went back to his throng, but only discovered that his rival nephew had impregnated his wife. The nephew captured him as a prisoner. All the sufferings Hatiponi went through were because of aggrieving his mother.

The novel is in the Shona language, and may be translated into other languages as time goes by. It is available at Progressive Publishers (email: progressivepublishers@gmail.com). My intention is to keep the old world literature alive and preserving the ways of our ancestors through incorporating their indigenous knowledge systems in my creative writing. However, my latest English short story (translated) is in a Zimbolicious 3 anthology published by Mwanaka Media and Publishing Pvt Ltd.

Do you have any upcoming projects ready for publication? Tell us about them?
I have a children reader Chitima nditakure going for printing, and have been recently commissioned for a secondary textbook, A Practical Approach to Commerce Book 4. I have shelved a Shona novel manuscript entitled Chenzira. It is my wish to have it published posthumously, unless if I change my mind.

If you have read the BNAP 2017 book already (or part of it), which pieces stuck out of you and why?
I enjoyed African Haiku (pg 391) by Babajide Michael Olusegun. The first poem reminds me of the unique South Sudanese tribal marks, "shorthand of our ancestors." I see brilliant thoughts in this Haiku. Tumelo Mogotsi's poem Women like me (pg 47) reflects the real African girls' upbringing. Daisy May's Bleed (pg 300) mesmerises me, as well as Raoul Djimeli's Poem 111 (pg 302) which takes me right to the seashore. What a reality written by Amara Sesay, Farting (pg 388). I am still reading, though randomly.

An Interview With Anton Krueger
September 19, 2018

As we head towards the Launch Of Best "New" African Poets 2017 Anthology at National English Literary Museum (NELM), we decided to engage one of the poets who will be gracing the occasion and reading his poems in the anthology at the event, Anton Krueger

Tell us about yourself
I haven't shaved in about two weeks and I'm at that sort of inbetween stage where I have to decide whether to commit to a beard or let it go.

Tell us about the poetry scene in your country
There seem to be a lot of readings around, and I would guess maybe ten or so publications a year in English, possibly more in Afrikaans and maybe less in other African languages, I don't know. There are a few quality magazines and journals like *New Contrast* and *New Coin*. *Prufrock* isn't bad and there are some good sites, like Aerodrome, Litnet and so on.

You are an Assistant Professor at Rhodes University in the Drama Department, how much does poetry influence your work in theatre, or how much does theatre influences your poetry. Recently a fellow poet at a reading advised us poets to act out our poems, to make theatre out of our poems so as to get them to the readers, do you feel this will help.

There seems to be a slight divide in SA between poems produced that are inherently performative, that lend themselves to vocalization and gesture and personality of the performer and so on; as compared to writers who are better at style, by which I mean the text on the page, (*stylus* – the instrument used to make an inscription) rather than vocalization. So some poems might not go over well at public readings, whereas others wilt when they're on the page and can only be appreciated as performance in front of an audience. So there are different approaches.

On 21 September you will be one of the poets reading at NELM on the Launch of Best New African Poets 2017 Anthology. What will you promise those who will attend? What does a poet reading his own poem(s) brings to the listeners of a poem that they don't get when they read the poem themselves.
I can promise that the audience will get chips and snacks and maybe some nice cheese. Nelm, usually gets in quality catering. As for your second question, well, I think there is something in the voice that conveys meaning, maybe hidden meanings that even the writer isn't aware of, that could resonate with listeners.

Tell us about your three poems in Best New African Poets 2017 Anthology.
Two of them have been published before, they're part of a series of family poems. *My Sister Sonia* and *Uncle Noodle*. So those are personal poems about family members and my relationship with them. The third one *Seraphine* hasn't been published yet, it's about the great French Outsider artist Seraphine Louis, who I got to know about via this Belgian film: https://en.wikipedia.org/wiki/S%C3%A9raphine_(film)

Give us an overview of your published books so far.
I've done two academic books, a collection of poetry, and co-written a book of comedy monologues / stories. Then I also have a

bunch of plays available at publish on demand type sites like Playscripts.com and Stagescripts in the UK.

Your debut novel was recently shortlisted for a prize, tell us about this novel and what it means to you to be shortlisted.
The manuscript has been longlisted, the short list isn't out yet. (It might be by the time you put this up, but I'm not sure if I'm on there or not). It's a story that takes place during the Fees Must Fall protest of 2016 which involves real incidents, such as the police firing on students and so on. I interviewed people involved in the situation from different points of view; but the characters are all fictional. The story is told from seven very different points of view and my hope was that even though they might not agree on how and why things happened the way they did, different people in the conflict might still at least feel that their view has been somewhat represented. Okay, that might sound like a heavy book, but actually it's quite fast paced and also has a lightness to it and hopefully some humour as it moves rapidly between multiple intersections in the lives of diverse people from different generations.

What type of sports are you into.
Not any, really. I used to play a bit of squash with my dad. He's very much the scientist and always looked down on sports as a bit silly. I did try to educate myself later and to get into the sporting meme but its tough. I can watch an important game if it's like the final of something or other. It's better to watch it with other people who are into it; so I guess that can be fun. The only Rugby game I've ever watched was the World Cup final in 1995, when I was in Japan. And I did see a cricket game once as well, and also the last World Cup soccer final. That's pretty much the sum total of all the matches of things I've seen.

If you were a poem, what type or form will you be in, and why?
Blank verse.